Lethal Friendship

D1059149

Lethal Friendship

✦

A Mother's Battle to Put—and Keep—a Serial Killer Behind Bars

Sue Young

iUniverse, Inc.

New York Lincoln Shanghai

Lethal Friendship
A Mother's Battle to Put—and Keep—a Serial Killer Behind Bars

Copyright © 2005 by Sue Young

All rights reserved. No part of this book may be used or reproduced by any means, graphic, electronic, or mechanical, including photocopying, recording, taping or by any information storage retrieval system without the written permission of the publisher except in the case of brief quotations embodied in critical articles and reviews.

iUniverse books may be ordered through booksellers or by contacting:

iUniverse
2021 Pine Lake Road, Suite 100
Lincoln, NE 68512
www.iuniverse.com
1-800-Authors (1-800-288-4677)

ISBN-13: 978-0-595-34422-2 (pbk)
ISBN-13: 978-0-595-79182-8 (ebk)
ISBN-10: 0-595-34422-4 (pbk)
ISBN-10: 0-595-79182-4 (ebk)

Printed in the United States of America

To my beloved daughter
Kathryn Ann Young.

Without her God-given faith at a time when I had none,
I would not have lived to write this book. Through the
years, her kindness, love, and ongoing encouragement
have been and are a constant source of strength.

and

In memory of my greatly loved elder daughter,
Martha Sue Young.

I am deeply grateful that Martha's faith in God translated
into a life of
integrity and a deep caring for people.

I am so proud
of both of my daughters.

Contents

Acknowledgments

There will always be a special place in my heart for Lt. Dean Tucker (deceased) and the East Lansing Police Department, and later the Michigan State Police and the Meridian Police Department. I will be eternally grateful to my friends in C-CAP for their friendships and their incredible work in battling a serial killer, especially Dr. Frank Ochberg; prosecutors Jeffery Sauter, Stuart Dunnings, and Patrick Shannon; Donna Irish; and Senator William Van Regenmorter. The journalists who covered the case in the early years are also special to me.

My gratitude goes to my parents, Susie and Roland Box (deceased), and my friends, whose prayers, presence, calls, letters, and sometimes money enabled me to keep going—in particular, Laurie Downes and Gerry Shaver, Jan Williams, Margaret Timnick, and Judy and Bob Fazesske. Thanks to friends from out of my home state of Michigan, Dr. and Mrs. Don Bowes, Dr. and Mrs. Bob Dunlap, Jo Nell and Robert Bailey, Myrtie Matthews, Betty Collins, Idell and Herschel Moffett, Flo Allen, Doris Gessner, and Mary Kay Ash (deceased).

My thanks go to my longtime friend and prayer partner Ann Johnson, who rescued my original manuscript, notes, recordings, and newspaper clippings from permanent storage in my basement and started me writing. My thanks go to my good friend and fellow C-CAP member, Bonnie Bucqueroux, for connecting me to Michigan State University's School of Journalism as a guest speaker, for believing that I had a story to tell and that I had the ability to write it, and for encouraging me to keep going when I felt like quitting.

My thanks go to Florence and Marita Littauer and Karen O'Connor for their CLASS Professional Writers' Workshops; also, my appreciation and thanks go to my lawyer, Gary Bender, my graphic artist, Shelee Bush, and my assistant, Joan Kusler. Special thanks go to Georginne Parisi; and Sue Yelvington O'Neil, Sheila Carlson, and Joyce Curtis, who helped preserve my sanity in dealing with my computer!

Foreword

I suppose there are "how-to-cope" books for families who have lost a loved one to a serial killer, but Sue Young's book, *Lethal Friendship*, goes far beyond this. It reads like a police procedural novel, a courtroom thriller, and most importantly, a wise and courageously written guide for victims of violent crime. It is rooted in the author's own experience of losing a daughter and fighting for over twenty years not only to keep her killer behind bars, but to create new victims' rights legislation.

The author catches the reader's attention in the first three sentences of the book, and she sustains the suspense chapter after chapter. Her story is a small classic in the psychology of grief. She shows how the loss of a single life has a ripple effect on hundreds of lives. Yet, the story is essentially hopeful, showing how religious faith, authentic friendships, community organizing, and political action can have a healing effect in the face of tragedy. I highly recommend this book for families and victims' rights organizations, for professionals in law enforcement and legislation, and, not least, for clergy and counseling professionals.

Leicester R. Longden, Ph.D.
Associate Professor, University of Dubuque Theological Seminary

Preface

The primary material used to create this book came from having lived it. My memory was refreshed by recordings I created in 1980 about the events surrounding the disappearance and death of my daughter. At times, Martha speaks through her own writings.

Additional information came from my constant interaction with law-enforcement personnel, prosecutors, victims, victims' advocates, forensic experts, public officials, the department of corrections, and information from *The Lansing State Journal*, used with permission.

In addition, I used Dr. Frank Ochberg's files, writings, and reflections written for an organization called Committee for Community Awareness and Protection. Also, I made extensive use of the complete court transcripts from both trials: the 1979 case, *People v. Donald Gene Miller*, held in Berrien County, Michigan, and the 1998 *People v. Donald Gene Miller* in Chippewa County, Michigan.

My work is not done. As this book goes to press, the clock is again ticking, advancing steadily toward the time when a serial killer will again be eligible for parole. As unbelievable at it seems, even a judge may find it difficult to determine the exact length of a sentence because of the ambiguity of Michigan law. Will his sentence again be shortened by automatic time reductions?

Although Michigan now has a "truth-in-sentencing" law, which offers more protection to citizens of this state in future cases, there was no such law in effect at the time of this case.

Even if we can be successful in keeping this murderer behind bars it is inevitable that there will be more cases where serial predators, killers and sadistic rapists who evolve into killers, will be plea bargained. However, today the U.S. Supreme Court has given us a remedy when it upheld the right of the State of Kansas to civilly commit a serial rapist who had said that he would rape again when he was released from prison. This is discussed in detail in Chapter Thirteen. Several states have such legislation. Michigan does not. Does Michigan need such a law?

It is my wish that this book will expand your knowledge and increase your awareness. I hope it will both inspire you and fill you with outrage so that you will mobilize to ensure that our government safeguards us from the release of serial killers. It is also my intent to call attention to the roll of judges so that you will become knowledgeable about the judges you elect. Obviously good judges are crucial in protecting us. Most importantly, I hope you will be inspired so that you realize that you, as one person, can make a difference.

1

Just Friends

It was a very ordinary scene that last evening of 1976. My older daughter, Martha, came into the kitchen to give me a quick kiss goodbye before heading out the door. I never imagined that it would be the last time I would see her.

Since she had broken her engagement to Donald Gene Miller two nights before, she had no big plans for New Year's Eve. Instead, she was going to spend a quiet evening babysitting for a couple from church while they went out to dinner and a movie. It was, however, no surprise that Don stopped by to accompany her. He had talked Martha into remaining friends and insisted she keep the ring as a gift. We never could have envisioned the consequences of this simple agreement to be "just friends." To think that this would be a dangerous decision would have seemed absurd—even paranoid.

After all, we lived in the peaceful university town of East Lansing, Michigan. Our community seemed untouched by big-city violence. This was a time when "serial killer" was not a part of society's vocabulary. Donald Miller was no stranger. The Miller family lived just down the street, and Don's older sister was Martha's friend. They had attended the same high school, and our two families worshipped at the same church. Don was a quiet boy, respectful of adults, and he took Martha to Bible study. He had never been in trouble with the police; in fact, he was a criminal justice major at Michigan State University. I had no reason to be concerned—quite the contrary.

It had been a glorious Christmas. My daughters, Martha and Kay, and I had gone to Pennsylvania to enjoy Christmas with our good friends Don and Grace Bowes and their children. We had been friends since our first meeting in West Pakistan in 1960. It was there that we spent five years together as Methodist missionaries. Don was a missionary doctor for the Methodist Board of Missions and my husband, Le, was an architect and engineer. We were sent by the mission board to build a permanent facility to house United Christian Hospital, in Lahore. This was the hospital where Don worked as a doctor. We first met when our family of four was squeezed into a three-room apartment with their family of five. In these cramped quarters, our friendship began. Our family's quarters would not be finished for a month. Over the next five years, we would often receive medical attention in the Bowes' living room. It was there, during outbreaks of epidemics such as cholera, that we gathered with the Bowes family to receive our vaccinations from "Uncle Don." Through our shared experiences, we forged a deep bond of lasting friendship.

Our Christmas celebration in 1976 had actually begun in East Lansing with the anticipated arrival of Dawn Bowes at our home. Dawnie was the second daughter of Don and Grace Bowes. Both Martha and Dawn were nineteen-year-old college students. When Dawn elected to visit us in East Lansing instead of flying directly home, we were delighted. In anticipation of the visit, Martha, who was always ready for a sewing project, went into high gear. She was in the process of making drapes for each of our bedrooms, so now she doubled her efforts. Kay had selected dark blue velvet, and those drapes were almost finished. If there would not be enough time to complete the other two bedrooms before Dawnie's visit, Martha decided her own room could wait. She was eager to see me enjoy the drapes I had selected for my bedroom, which were made from turquoise raw silk fabric. She was determined to finish them before Dawn arrived, and she did. The fun continued as Dawn rode with us to Pennsylvania to be with the rest of the Bowes family.

With all of this history, the Bowes seemed as close as family members. Martha and Kay even got into the habit of calling Mr. and Mrs. Bowes "Uncle Don" and "Auntie Grace," and I became "Auntie Sue" to the Bowes children. Some time together with them was just the refreshing break my daughters and I needed. The past four years had brought much upheaval. In 1972, a separation marked the end of my twenty-year marriage to Le Young. Like many other women, I started over, at the bottom of the economic barrel, with no money and no home. After the divorce that followed, I began picking up the pieces of our lives. Mary Kay Cosmetics provided me with the opportunity to build a business that enabled me to support us. Still, 1974 was a traumatic year: my father became quite ill, I had major surgery, Martha graduated from high school shortly after my release from the hospital, and my divorce was finalized.

Our lives became more positive with my father's recovery, and my parents helped me purchase a home in East Lansing. Now, as 1976 came to a close, my business was growing. I could afford to take a little time off. Since my mind had been occupied all year with my work, I did not spend much time in the kitchen, other than to do basic cooking. So it was a real treat to relax in Grace's kitchen. It was fun to be with her, cooking, visiting, and getting ready for Christmas. Most of the time, the girls went off on their own, leaving the kitchen to Grace and me.

The Bowes' large finished basement became our daughters' domain. This newly created space took on the atmosphere of a girl's dormitory for the three oldest Bowes' daughters, Nadine, Dawn, and Valerie, as well as for Martha and Kay. Nadine was a year older than Martha but had been in the same class during our years in Pakistan. Valerie was a year older than Kay. Often, Nadine, Dawn, and Martha hung out together during the day while Kay and Valerie teamed up. Sometimes, Brian, the younger brother, and Shereen, the youngest sister, were included in the day's activities. As a parent, it was very satisfying to see all of the children having fun together. In the Bowes household, there was always one car available for running around the small town of Danville to do Christmas shopping. At night, all of us enjoyed family dinner together. Following the evening's activities, it became "pajama party" time for the girls. After they disappeared below we could hear the sounds of their voices interspersed with giggles and laughter late into the night.

All too soon, the day of our departure, Tuesday, December 28, arrived. We were having such fun it was hard to leave. The Bowes urged us to stay until New Year's Day, but Kay had planned to fly out on Wednesday to visit her father in Texas. She wanted to be there to celebrate her dad's birthday on Thursday. Also, Martha had promised Don she would go with him to his grandparents' party on Thursday for a late celebration of his birthday, which was on December 28. She knew he would be disappointed if she was not there. Besides, she had promised she would be there, and she always kept her word. We needed to leave in order to keep these commitments.

Because it was snowing on Tuesday morning, we stretched our visit a few hours longer while we waited for the trucks to clear the main highway. We made it home by 11:00 P.M., which made it possible for Kay to leave on schedule Wednesday afternoon. The next morning, Martha and I helped Kay get ready for her trip before driving her to the airport.

During Martha's time in Pennsylvania, her engagement and history with Don had been dominant topics of conversation. Now she was eager to have some "one-on-one" time with me to discuss these matters. As the two of us drove home from the airport that afternoon, we chatted about our plans for the next few days. Soon, however, it became clear that Martha's feelings regarding her engagement were dominating her thoughts.

The talk we had centered on her reasons against marrying Don. A major concern was the model of marriage she saw in Don's parents. Martha didn't like the way his father talked about his wife. She was concerned with what she perceived as the lack of respect he showed her. Martha seemed very uncomfortable with this.

Martha expressed uneasiness about the time the Millers had asked our family to come to their house for dinner. At the time, the Millers all agreed the invitation would need to be delayed, saying it would take two weeks to clean up the kitchen and living room. They would have to throw things out in order to uncover the table.

Don said because the house was always such a mess, they never had company. Martha loved having guests for dinner, so it concerned her that Don's family spent most of their time by themselves. Martha lived to be around people, and she was afraid Don would cut her off from all her friends. She feared he would want to dominate her completely once they were married. She got an inkling of this soon after they began dating, when she began to feel deprived of time with her friends. Even though Don had not introduced Martha to any of his friends, she was shocked to realize that he had no friends to ask to be ushers at their wedding. Obviously, friends were not important to Don.

The young man Don selected to be his best man suggested nothing less. Martha described her experience of accompanying Don to ask this "friend" to be his best man. When Don asked him, she said, the fellow appeared rather shocked that he'd been chosen. Although Don had gone to high school with him, they had had no contact in the three years since graduation, yet Don described him as his "best" friend. It puzzled Martha that Don would consider himself so close to this former schoolmate.

In Don's family, the money always seemed to be spent on things the father wanted; the other family members were usually denied their requests. Martha observed that the father wore nice clothes and dressed stylishly, while Elaine and the children did not. Don's only winter coat was the one his father had worn in the navy during World War II. It also seemed strange that in a middle-class family, Elaine had no washing machine. Don said his mother did the washing by hand. Every two weeks, Don's father would take his mother to a coin-operated laundry to wash sheets. Money did not appear to be the problem here. Gene had a sports car, two motorcycles, two trail bikes, and a truck. Would Don expect to spend the family income on himself and deny Martha the basics? she wondered.

The problems Martha saw mounted. The fact that Don was twenty-two years old and had never had a job (except for the few weeks he had worked during the previous summer in a resort area) was yet another cause for concern. My daughter had worked during the school year and each summer. Don was making no money, but he wanted her to save hers for when they got married. For his own part, he had no plans to go to work so he could put aside money for the marriage. Since Don had spent all of his life at home being taken care of by his family, could he, or would he, be able to support a family? Martha wondered, "Will I end up having to work to support both of us?"

There were also differences in their views on education. Martha loved school, liked to study, and got good grades. "Don never studies, and his grades aren't good," Martha told me. She liked athletics and social interaction at the university. "Mother, I like to do things," she said. "It's not only that he doesn't, but he doesn't want me to either!"

In our discussion, we concluded that these difficulties would not disappear after the wedding ceremony but were certain to intensify. I reminded her that she had had doubts about dating Don almost from the beginning.

"Yes, that is true," she agreed. Martha had finally, on her own, come to the realization that she did not want to marry Don. With this settled in her mind, the discussion shifted to when she was going to tell him.

Martha had a date with Don that Wednesday evening and again on Thursday evening for the family celebration of his birthday. In her typical thoughtful manner, she was concerned about being as kind as possible to Don in breaking off their wedding engagement. She did not want to cause him embarrassment in front of his family on Thursday, so she planned to break the engagement following the Thursday party.

That Wednesday evening, while Martha was on the first of her two dates that week with Don, I had an enjoyable time relaxing and reading. I read an article in the book section of *Reader's Digest* entitled "Life after Life," which related accounts of near-death experiences. This subject interested me, since faith in God and the afterlife had been a very natural thing for me since childhood. I grew up in awe of the beauty and wonder of the world around me, therefore faith in an almighty God, creator of the universe, seemed a very logical proposition. The marvels of a magnificently crafted world pointed clearly to the hand of a master designer. The lavish beauty of a spring garden, the varying shades of green on a spring day, majestic mountains, glorious sunsets, the vastness of the ocean, and the beauty of a single pansy or a rose in all its rich colors touched me and announced the presence of a caring Master Artist.

By itself, an intellectual belief in a Master Designer would not have provided the kind of faith that would sustain me through the storms of life. The bedrock of my faith lies in the person and character of Jesus Christ, who came to show us the love of God and demonstrated the depth of that love by His willingness to pay the ultimate price for us. However, for me to put my faith in Jesus, I needed verification that He was who He claimed to be. I searched for facts. To me, the most conclusive historical evidence I found to verify His existence was the fact that his followers' lives had changed dramatically following His death and resurrection. In fact, they were transformed to such an extent that they would rather be eaten by lions than give up their faith in Christ. It is unbelievable to me that hundreds of his followers would enter into a conspiracy to fabricate a lie, and then be willing to die for that lie. It seems unlikely that even one person would be willing to die for a hoax he helped create. Perhaps even more astonishing is that they died without bitterness toward their persecutors. Today, men and women are still losing their lives because of their Christian faith. In fact, more Christians were martyrs in the last century than in all the previous centuries combined. I am so grateful that early in my life I found the proof that I needed to trust Jesus with my life and to develop a relationship with him. This faith became my life preserver during the dark days that would follow.

As I read the *Reader's Digest* piece, I was inspired; the author presented a very loving picture of God at the point of death. This gave me a warm, mellow sensation. I was feeling great peace when I greeted Martha upon her return. Martha's mood seemed to be good as well, even though she had gone ahead and broken the engagement.

"I didn't wait, Mother, because it just wasn't working out," she said. She was pleased, however, because everything seemed to have turned out fine. Don hadn't seemed too upset. He wanted to remain friends. Because she was relieved that he seemed to have taken it so well, and since she did not want to hurt Don's feelings, she had seen no reason why they could not be friends, so she had agreed. Because they were still friends, Don wanted her to go ahead and attend his belated birthday party the next evening, which was held at a friend of Don's grandmother. Martha kept her promise to attend with the whole Miller family.

Friday morning, New Year's Eve, I went to cash a $125 check for Martha before going to lunch with my friend Flo Allen. After shopping, Martha stopped by The Great Steak Restaurant in East Lansing to show us the new pair of shoes she'd purchased to wear to a party Saturday evening. She visited briefly and talked about our plans to spend New Year's Day together. She told Flo we planned to do some cooking the next day. She especially wanted to prepare a Southern dish, black-eyed peas, for "good luck" in the New Year. She told me not to give her the money from the check. "I don't want to lose it while I'm running around this afternoon. Just bring it with you when you come home, Mother," she said.

That evening, while Martha baby-sat, I attended a potluck supper with friends from the church. It was a midnight supper. I stayed long enough to eat and "ring in" the New Year, and then I headed home. Since the event was in the neighborhood, I got home a little after one o'clock. I expected Martha to be home. I was surprised that she wasn't. She'd planned to have Don drive her home as soon as the baby's parents returned. They had said it would not be a late evening. Even though Martha was nineteen and Kay was sixteen, I had always waited up when one of my girls was out. On that night, I remembered a discussion during Christmas at the Bowes'. Both girls had made a big deal of my waiting up for them, saying, "Mother, at least you could lie down. Don't just sit up! You know we always call if we are going to be late." I knew this was true, so I had responded, "I know, sweet, you are great about calling and being home when you say you will be. Okay, I will."

Now, because I remembered Martha saying she would be home early, I thought it strange that she was not there. This is not like her! I thought. I began to be concerned. I considered calling the Millers' house or the home where Martha had been babysitting. It occurred to me that maybe she had called and when she found out I was not home, she decided to stay out awhile longer. Then I thought, "Well, it is New Year's Eve. Maybe he took her dancing. Perhaps he did something fun for a change! Why am I worried?" I wondered. I began to rationalize. I was sure Don would protect her. After all, it isn't like she is out at night by herself; she has a man with her who cares about her. Surely I could count on a man in love to protect the girl he loved—and Don loved Martha.

I reasoned myself into taking the girls' advice. I got ready for bed, expecting each minute to hear Martha return. I knew I would be aware of it the moment the car entered the driveway. Because it was one of those frigid nights where tires make a loud crunching sound as they pass over snow, I knew I would hear them before the front door opened. The debate I was having with myself continued. It was foolish to be upset, I thought. In my mind I could hear Martha scolding me for being worried. As I sat on my bed looking at the phone and the clock, I thought, "I'll just stretch out. It's almost two. I'll give her thirty minutes, and if she isn't home by 2:30, I'll call." So I lay down, listening and waiting.

Then I did something I had never done before…

2

Portrait of Terror

...I fell asleep.

The night had passed. It was 7:00 A.M., January 1, 1977. I awakened with a start. From my first moment of consciousness, I was overwhelmed by a horrible, sickening feeling. There was no lingering sleepiness. Instantly, I was completely awake—aware that it was now morning, aware that Martha had not come in for the first time in her life. I had an indescribably dreadful sense that something was wrong. *Oh, dear God, what's happened?* Maybe, maybe, I hadn't heard her come in. *Oh, please God! Please, please, please...*

I bolted out of bed and down the hall to Martha's room. The sight of her empty bed confirmed my worst fears. The bed was made, the covers just as she had left them the day before.

Panic set in. *What do I do?* "Oh, dear God," I cried as I ran downstairs. A wishful, nonsensical thought gave me momentary hope. There are beds in the basement. Maybe, maybe she had come in and retired to the basement, not wanting to disturb me.

"Martha, Martha!" I screamed as I ran down the second flight of stairs. I was greeted by silence. One look at the beds in the basement told me no one had slept in them. "Oh my God!"

My mind started issuing commands: *Be calm. Think. Be logical.* In my panic, I ran right by the phone on the lower level and back up the stairs to my bedroom. I called the Millers. Don's mother, Elaine, answered.

"Elaine, is Don home?"

"Yes?"

"Well, is Martha there?"

"No!"

That one word had an immediate chilling effect, and a wave of horror spread over me. Inside I was reeling. For a split second, I was bewildered. *How could that*

8

be? Don is home and Martha is not! Then it hit me. That single word "no" ripped through my body producing feelings of terror that I had never felt before. The word "no" told me what had happened. In that instant, I knew what had happened. (Nevertheless, I would try to suppress that certainty in the days, weeks, months, and even years ahead.) That "sense of knowing" said to me, *Oh my God! He's killed her!* This wasn't just a thought, it was a deep-rooted certainty. Until that precise moment, I had not even the remotest fear that Don Miller could be violent. Never before had I considered such a possibility. At no time, before or since, had I had such an insight, for in that split second I knew with absolute clarity that he had killed her!

As this unspeakable horror settled upon me, my world started spinning. I couldn't speak. I was sick in the pit of my stomach. In this stunned state, I could hear a voice that seemed to be coming from a great distance. Slowly, the voice came into focus. It was Elaine's voice. She was saying, "She's got to be home, Sue. Did you look under the bed?"

Maybe Elaine couldn't think of what to say to me. The sheer absurdity of the question snapped me back to reality. *Under the bed? How stupid!* I thought. *A nineteen-year-old girl is not going to crawl under a bed! That's something a small child would do.* Yet I just sat there on the side of my bed, unable to respond. In the silence, I could hear Elaine's voice again. She was saying, "Well, go look!"

My mind was staggering with thoughts of what to do next. I knew the suggestion was ridiculous, but the easiest thing to do would be to comply with Elaine's request. I was certainly in no mood to argue, so I ran through the house again. I even looked in the bathtub, in case she'd by chance slipped and struck her head in the shower.

Once again, I was on the phone. "No, Elaine, she is not here."

"We'll be right over," she said.

I replaced the phone and walked downstairs to wait for the Millers. I could not accept that Martha was gone. I was desperate to be proven wrong, so I told no one about my gut feeling. I moved in a fog of terror. It seemed like an eternity before Don, his father, and his mother arrived. Actually, they arrived shortly after I called.

"Don, what happened?" I pleaded. In a very flat, unemotional voice, he told me he had brought Martha home at five minutes before two and that she had sat down on the front porch and waved goodbye to him. As he drove away, he said Martha was sitting there looking at the stars.

Silently, as I struggled to process what he had said, I asked myself, *How could I have not heard her? I was awake at that time.* I was also wondering, *why on earth would she stay outside in such icy weather? This makes no sense! That does not sound like my daughter! On a summer night, yes, she might stargaze, but not on a night that was seventeen below zero! Martha is not crazy!* However, questioning Don's story was not a priority right then. Openly doubting him didn't seem a very smart thing to do either. It wouldn't be wise to alienate him.

Instead, I looked at the parents and asked, "Shall I call the police?" They nodded.

When the police dispatcher answered, I begged, "Please, help me! My daughter Martha Sue Young did not come home last night." My words tumbled out as I tried to make the officer understand that she had never stayed out all night and wouldn't do that. I needed to convince him that this was urgent; that she was not the kind of teen who would cause me to worry like that. I told him that I knew something awful had happened to her; otherwise, she would have come home or at least called me to come pick her up. I was aware that a person is not considered missing until twenty-four hours have passed, but I knew we couldn't wait that long. Every minute counted with Martha out there somewhere in this sub-zero weather. I told him, "Too much time had already passed. She's been out in this dangerously cold weather all night." I begged, "Please, please help!"

Thankfully, he said nothing about waiting. For some reason, he believed me when I said she was not a runaway, and he took her disappearance seriously. He immediately dispatched a police car.

◆   ◆   ◆

After talking to the police, I dialed another number before 8:00 A.M. on New Year's Day. My call awakened my friend Gerry Shaver. "Gerry, I need you. Martha didn't come home last night." Gerry didn't hesitate for a moment. There was no small talk. Her only reply was, "I'll call Laurie [Downes, another close friend], and we will be right over."

◆   ◆   ◆

The police log sets the time of my phone call at 7:35 A.M. Ken Ouellette was one of the officers sent to our home. He was a young man slightly older than Martha who had also graduated from East Lansing High School. From the moment he entered, he seemed to identify with Martha, acting as if his own little sister had disappeared. The presence of the police comforted me and gave me something positive to do. Later that morning, he called the detective who would be put in charge of the investigation, Sgt. Dean Tucker. This was the first time Sgt. Tucker would hear the name Martha Sue Young. Officer Ouellette's call alerted Sgt. Tucker about the disappearance, adding the comment, "Things don't look right."

From that point, the East Lansing Police force went into action. After arriving on the scene, some of the police checked the outside of the house for unusual markings in the snow. The deep snow was not fresh, so there were no tire tracks to provide any clues. Martha's car sat parked in the driveway, right where it had been before her disappearance. They looked for signs of a struggle but found none. It took me weeks to realize that what I had *not* seen was significant. There were only footprints, no other markings on the porch. There was no large, distinctive marking that would have been made by someone sitting in the snow, as Don claimed Martha had done. Here was proof that his statement, "She sat down on the door step," was a lie.

As one of them came into the house, my friends Laurie and Gerry hurried through the front door. Their presence was an enormous comfort. We had met in a Bible study and they had continued as my prayer partners. Here were two friends I could depend on completely. They also provided an extra pair of ears to listen as the investigation continued. Later, my friends and I could compare notes.

Then Officer Ouellette asked for a description of Martha. How do you put into words a description of your daughter? I told him, "She is a very pretty blonde, with a natural wave to her hair, blue eyes, very fair skin, five feet, five inches, 125 pounds. She appears smaller and more petite because of her firm muscle tone."

"Do you have a picture?"

"Yes, this is a picture of Martha here on top of the piano. Martha gave me this photo last year for Christmas." The officer asked if he could take the eight-by-ten photo to the police station. I told him, "Yes, of course, but I do want it back." Looking at the picture, I realized it had been taken while she was wearing her contacts. The previous night she had worn her glasses, so I went to look for snapshots from Christmas in which she was wearing them. When I found them, I gave him one.

"Do you remember what she was wearing?" he asked next. Yes, I remembered everything she wore, except what was under her jacket. I hadn't seen whether she'd worn a blouse or a sweater, since she had already put on her jacket before she came into the kitchen to kiss me goodbye. She had worn her blue ski jacket, which was trimmed in fake fur, over a rust-orange plaid pair of slacks. Since it was too cold to wear the lightweight jacket that matched her pants, the rust plaid jacket was hanging in Martha's closet. It was so frigid that Martha had not even wanted to go from the house to the car wearing just that light jacket. She had worn a wool scarf around her neck. Also, if she had been planning to stay outside for very long, she would have worn the wool cap that matched her scarf. She had left her boots inside and had worn her tan shoes. I remembered that she was wearing one other distinctive item of clothing. I had given both daughters identical bracelet watches as Christmas presents the year before; Martha had worn hers every day. As I was trying to describe her clothing and bracelet watch, I realized I could give the police Martha's jacket from the closet so they could have the exact material and pattern to match the pants she wore. Also, I could give them her wool cap, which matched her scarf. And they could look at and take pictures of Kay's watch and shoes, which were identical to Martha's.

The next question was, "Would your daughter choose to run away? Is she having any problems anywhere? What about at the university?"

"No, she would never run away from her family. She changed universities because she was homesick for Kay and me. We haven't had a fight; she isn't mad at either Kay or me. If she was angry with either of us, all she would do is go in her room and slam the door. She never stays angry for long. Soon she comes out of her room, ready to make up. She is basically happy with her life. She doesn't have any big problems. Her biggest problem was her relationship with Don, but she has handled that.

"Now she is excited about getting on with her life. Martha feels that her life is going very well. She enjoys school. She likes to study. She has already selected her classes for the new semester, and she is registered at Michigan State. She has even purchased her books." My mind became flooded with thoughts of Martha's plans for the year ahead. She had so many things going for her. She was really blossoming, and I thought I had never seen her look happier or more beautiful. Shaking loose from my reverie, I continued, "She is looking forward to getting into extracurricular activities this term. Martha is excited about going back to work at American Bank and Trust, where she was employed last summer. She felt complimented that Mr. McRay, her boss at the bank, was so pleased with her work there last summer that he called before Christmas and asked her to come back in January. He even scheduled her to work on Saturdays so that her job would not interfere with her classes. The job was tailor-made to fit her needs."

As I was talking, the officer made notes so he could contact every person I mentioned on the chance that someone had heard from Martha. In spite of my assurances that Martha had not run away from home, the officers had to thoroughly check out that possibility. I understood that. We were on the same side. If we found that she had run away on her own, that would be wonderful news. It would mean she was alive! All I wanted was for my daughter to be alive and well. When Officer Olluette asked if there was a suitcase or any of Martha's clothing missing, I replied, "I have not noticed anything missing, but I haven't specifically looked."

"Then can we check?" he asked.

"Of course," I replied.

We looked. Nothing was missing from her closet that I could tell. No suitcases were missing. The things that had been left behind silently argued against voluntary disappearance. All of her makeup was sitting where she had left it the night before. I pointed out the significance of this to the officer. Martha had been faithfully using Mary Kay skincare products since she was twelve, so it would have been out of character for her to leave without it. I knew that she never went anywhere without it. She even took it on camping trips. And there it was, in front of us.

As we looked around her room, the officer continued questioning. "What if something frightened her last night? Would she have enough money with her for a plane, train, or bus?"

"The only cash she had was from a $125 check I cashed for her at the bank yesterday," I remembered. "I don't think she would have taken it with her to baby-sit, but I will look," I said as I started opening her dresser drawers. In the top center drawer lay the $125, still in the bank envelop just as I had given it to her. Seeing the money reminded me that Martha had been shopping the day before, so I went to her closet. "She bought some new shoes yesterday to wear to a party she planned to attend this evening." We discovered the new shoes in her closet, still inside the box from the store.

I continued to be reminded of Martha's plans for the beginning of the year. The shoes had triggered thoughts of Martha's calendar posted on the bulletin board in the kitchen. As things I thought might be important occurred to me, I led Officer Ouellette up and down the stairs all over the house. So down the stairs we went to look at the bulletin board in the kitchen. Martha had placed a cookie recipe beside her calendar. She'd planned to make those cookies for the party that night. She was looking forward to being with her friends. She would not willingly miss it. Also, being the dependable girl she was, she would not promise cookies and then fail to deliver.

My thoughts went back to the subject of money and transportation. "As for money, she couldn't have had more than a few dollars left after buying the shoes.

She probably only had her babysitting money in her purse. But if she had wanted to go somewhere, wouldn't it have made sense to take her car? You see it sitting in the driveway; it hasn't moved from where she parked it Friday afternoon. She has her car key with her on the same ring with her house key. If she had wanted to run away in this awful cold, wouldn't it make more sense for her to drive than to walk?" The young officer seemed to agree with my assessment. After we had checked everything we could think of, we went back into the living room.

The Millers were still in the house. Don came into the living room while I was talking to the police. He offered to make me some tea. While turning down the tea, I wondered, "What is he thinking? Why is he so calm? He claimed to love her, and he does not even appear to be upset."

The officer asked me, "Is it possible that she could be staying with a friend overnight?"

"I don't think so. She would have surely called me first. If she were in trouble she would run to me, not away from me. But I'll check to see if Martha has contacted anyone."

"Would you give us a list of her friends and her address book?"

I nodded.

"We will contact these numbers. Also, does she know people anywhere across the country besides your friends in Pennsylvania and people from her school in Texas?" When I said that she did, I was told to call everyone. I later found out that between me and the police, we had contacted friends in Michigan, Pennsylvania, Colorado, Tennessee, Ohio, and Illinois. We called any place where she knew anyone she might feel she could turn to for help.

Oh dear God, help me! What could have happened? A running conversation was going on in my mind. I could not share my thoughts with my friends Laurie and Gerry in front of the Millers, so I struggled to handle the situation in silence. Mentally, I admonished myself. *Calm down. Think! Think! Oh God, I've got to think. Suppose she was frightened. Maybe a stranger attacked them, and Don was a coward and ran away instead of protecting her. Or, maybe she and Don had an argument. Maybe he got angry and hurt her. In his anger, perhaps he left her. Maybe he is too ashamed to tell us. Could she be lying somewhere, badly hurt, in this dangerously cold weather? It was well below zero last night. She has been out there so, so long. She will die out there if we can't find her soon.*

I knew my thoughts had entered a black pit and that I was in danger of a complete emotional breakdown. Thoughts of Martha being hurt and abandoned in temperatures that would not support life were more than I could stand. Silently, I began to lecture myself: *Hold on there. You have got to keep control. You are all she's got to depend on. Think. Ask Don. Give him a chance to open up,* I told myself. *Perhaps he did leave her. If he will just tell us where they separated, we can start to look in that area. He's got to help us find her!*

Out loud, I asked, "Don, what do you think happened to Martha? Maybe there was an accident. Did someone hurt her while you were out?" He shook his head no.

"Don, what do you think we should do?"

"I don't know," he said in a matter-of-fact, disinterested way. He offered no other thoughts. He was totally unengaged.

What is wrong with this boy? He doesn't seem to care. Everyone is trying to think of some way to help. He's not even trying to think. All he seems to know how to do is offer me a cup of tea, I fumed to myself.

"Martha was such a nice girl," I heard his parents, Gene and Elaine, say to the police. My heart nearly stopped. *Why are they using the past tense? Do they know what has happened?* Then, Gene Miller said to Don, "Come on. Let's check transportation—airport, busses, taxicab companies—to see if Martha could have left town." Gene checked Martha's bedroom on the way out of the house. I have no idea what he was doing there, and I never questioned him about it. With that, they departed, leaving Elaine Miller behind with my friends Laurie and Gerry.

Following up on Don's story, that he had dropped Martha off before two after which she sat on the front porch, two officers went door to door asking each neighbor along our street if they had seen a struggle take place or if they had seen any car other than Martha's parked in the driveway. Judy, our next-door neighbor, had been taking her Christmas tree out to the curb at around 1:30 A.M. She had stood in her driveway and had a conversation with the paperboy on his early morning route. She had seen nothing amiss. Across the street, an East Lansing police sergeant was having a New Year's Eve party. Policemen and their wives were leaving around two o'clock. Since there was no curbside parking allowed on our street, they walked down the block in front of our house to get to their cars (which were parked around the corner). The street was quiet as they left the party. No one had noticed any cars or anything unusual. If anything suspicious had been going on, I am sure their police training would have kicked into gear.

As the day progressed, we heard the distinctive sound of a helicopter flying low. It was an ominous sound, for I realized they were searching for Martha. On a rational level, I knew that too many hours had passed with my sweet daughter out in that bitter cold for the search to yield good news. On an emotional level, I could not accept what my mind was telling me. As evening approached, I became more and more frantic. I couldn't stand waiting any longer. A second night could not set in without our finding her! If she were still alive out there, she would not survive another night. I knew the police had been looking for her all day, but I had to look too. All I could think about was my child out there someplace, hurting, in all that heavy snow. And it was cold, so cold. I announced my intention to go look.

Our minister had arrived that afternoon. "If you want to go, I'll drive you. You are in no condition to drive," he said. I directed him to drive down by the large vacant field in the long block that separated our house from the Millers'. I got out to walk on the sidewalk along the edge of the field. The snow was so deep no one could have traveled far into the field away from the road. Even so, perhaps I couldn't see her in the uneven snowy field. There I allowed myself to do something that I had held in check all day. I started screaming her name. My eyes searched the snowdrifts for any sign of her as I screamed, "Martha! Martha!" In response, there was only the stillness of the deep snow cover as the sun slid fast from view. I gave up on that location and hurried back to the car so we could move onto another area while there was still light.

Next, we drove to an area where Martha and I had bicycled during the summer in a park near our home. We looked there, and then we looked along an undeveloped road north of town, leading to another park. We drove slowly as I watched for any sign of her. Suddenly, I saw something on the road.

"A scarf! It looks like Martha's! Stop! Stop! Let me out!" We turned around and circled back. I got out to examine the object. It was only a piece of material, not Martha's scarf. Onto the park we went, where, as night made its final approach, I walked around screaming her name into the stillness.

My heart was pleading with God: *Lord, I know you know where she is. Please help us find her!* No sense of direction came. Instead, I remember thinking about the three days Jesus was separated from Mary when He stayed at the temple at twelve years of age. It occurred to me that Mary certainly could identify with the mother of a missing child. At first, the thought was comforting, because they did find him after three days. *But, oh Lord*, I pleaded, *I won't be able to stand not finding her for three whole days!* Of course, I went on to remember that Mary's son was ultimately killed. My mind flashed back to three evenings before, the lovely peaceful evening when I had been reading about the loving presence of God meeting the person in the story at the point of death. I screamed inwardly at this new insight. *Oh, no! NO! Dear God, were you preparing me for this?* Somehow, I knew that was exactly what He had done.

When it was too dark to see, we went home. At some point late in the afternoon, one friend stayed with me while the other went home long enough to collect and pack an overnight bag from each of their homes so that I would not be left alone during the night. Finally, the Millers went home for the evening. As they left, I turned on the porch light in case Martha found her way home. I know it was silly, but somehow I felt having the light on might in some way help. Consequently, I left that porch light on all night for months. To turn it off somehow meant admitting that she was never coming home again.

Alone at last with my two friends, we shared our thoughts. I had begun to feel that if the Millers didn't leave I was going to scream! At the same time, I felt I could not antagonize Don, because he was the only hope I had of finding out about Martha. We discussed our concerns. We began with the story Don had told about Martha sitting in the snow. Since this was her first winter in Michigan after spending two years in Texas, it was even more unlikely that Martha would sit in the snow in sub-zero temperatures. My friends couldn't imagine anyone doing that. "Besides," I said, "she had on lightweight pants." The cold would penetrate those trousers immediately. She could not have sat there even a minute." Then we questioned how anyone could surprise her on an open porch when there were no high bushes around in front where someone could hide? Also, Martha would have known that I was upstairs. She could have rung the bell or screamed to get help from me if there had been any trouble.

Laurie and Gerry had also noticed that Don's parents had been referring to Martha in the past tense all day. "She was such a sweet girl."

"Yes, that bothered me too," I said. "It sounds like all of them are sure she is dead. Why?" What did Elaine and Gene know? Was Gene covering for Don? Also, we had noticed that Don and Elaine had given the same precise time when Don had returned home. Why would Don know that the time was five minutes to two when he left Martha on the porch? Both he and his mother claimed it was two when he returned home. It sounded like they had invented a story together.

We talked about how strange Don had acted. He had seemed so unconcerned, while everyone else had been actively looking for answers. Laurie noticed he had asked no questions. Gerry agreed. "He makes no suggestions, yet the woman he claims to love is missing. He remains so undisturbed." Then she added emphatically, "I have sons, and this is not normal; this is not the way a young man in love behaves!"

I voiced my fears. "Maybe there was an accident and Martha was killed and he was frightened and ashamed. If he would just tell me, I would understand. Tragic accidents do happen. While talking to him today I tried to give him an out, to make it safe for him to tell the truth and change that dumb story."

Laurie gently prodded me into a change of activity. It would be helpful if we did some work. "The Christmas tree needs to come down, so that can be our work," she suggested. The tree came down and the ornaments were packed away...and then we waited.

All day, I had put off making the phone call to Texas to tell Kay what had happened. I needed to call my parents too, but that also presented major problems. I could not tell my parents without telling Kay. I hesitated to make the call for fear of interrupting Kay and her father's plans to go to Mexico. *Besides, Martha will come in at any minute.* However, I could hesitate no longer. I had to make the call the next day. I couldn't let Kay leave the country, where I would not be able to reach her, while this was happening.

My friends suggested we at least lie down. We prepared for bed. I could not bear to be by myself, so the three of us stretched out on my king-size bed. We lay like sticks until the first sign of daylight. I don't think any of us slept. Each of us was lost in our own thoughts, waiting for the day to begin. Then, just as daylight was returning we heard a *wonderful* sound. The front storm door opened!

"Oh, thank God, Martha! She's home!" All three of us jumped out of bed with a start, ready to make a dash down the stairs to meet her. But there followed no welcoming sound of Martha's key in the lock.

Then, the truth jolted us again. The neighborhood paperboy had thoughtfully placed the newspaper just inside the storm door. That paper carried the front-page story of the disappearance of nineteen-year-old Michigan State co-ed Martha Sue Young. That article began the media coverage that persisted into the year 2000 and beyond.

3

Warning Signs

Monday morning, the police came back to perform a thorough, systematic search of Martha's room. They studied every scrap of paper. Even pillowcases were removed in an effort to find some kind of clue; the cases were shaken and even the seams along the ends of the pillows were checked to make sure nothing had been hidden inside them. Nothing was overlooked, including Martha's Raggedy Ann doll, which was also taken apart. Not even the detectives had any idea what we were looking for. As I participated in the search, the memories welled up in my mind. I thought back to the time when Martha had started dating Don.

◆　　　◆　　　◆

When Martha had graduated from high school in 1974, our search for colleges took us to Southwestern University in Georgetown, Texas, located about seventy miles north of my parents' home in Luling, Texas. This school was a favorite of my father. It was an incredible answer to our prayers when Martha received a scholarship with a ten-hour-per-week work program. Martha and I rejoiced as she accepted the offer. It was while she was home for the summer, after her freshman year at Southwestern, that Don, the brother of one of Martha's friends, asked her out. They went to the nearby Ionia County Fair and had a wonderful time riding the rides and taking in the fair's other activities. The event bustled with people, energy, and variety. It was Martha's kind of place, teeming with life. It was such fun that Martha anticipated more dates with Don much like the first one. Don continued to ask Martha out. After the initial date, however, he just wanted to "hang around" with Martha. He was not interested in taking her to parties, movies, or campus activities. He didn't want to share her with anyone or anything. He wanted to come over and just watch TV or talk. The one place he would take her was to Bible study. While that was fine with Martha, that wasn't the only thing she wanted to do. They continued to date until fall, when Martha went back to Southwestern. After that, they started a correspondence. During the fall, I began to hear Martha's first doubts about whether she wanted to continue their friendship.

◆   ◆   ◆

My thoughts shifted back to the work at hand as I searched alongside the policemen in Martha's room. As we removed the contents from her vanity, we discovered a packet of letters addressed to Martha from Don. I stood there holding on to the letters, wondering aloud what we should do. I expressed my hesitation about whether we should read them. I had never before read any of her letters. It had been only three days since Martha's disappearance, and I visualized her coming home and being enormously embarrassed to discover that the police and I had so invaded her privacy. The officers persuaded me that it was necessary, so we settled down to read them.

Each of us took several letters. As we came across something that might be significant, we focused together on one letter. When the detectives read something they didn't understand, they turned to me to see if I could provide additional background or clarification. We discovered that Don used a very limited vocabulary and that all of his letters were disjointed. He seemed to have a hard time expressing himself. He overused certain words and phrases, such as "wow" and "weird." They were full of exclamation marks. To me, it seemed Don was always struggling to convey emotion. His letters were full of sketches, extremely childish depictions of dark themes such as graves and crosses. Often the drawings didn't appear relevant to the subject matter of the letter. He used the refrain "Praise the Lord" constantly. He couldn't write more than a sentence on any subject without dragging God's name into it. One letter was particularly strange. Don had written it while working for a summer resort on Mackinaw Island, located in the Straits of Mackinaw between Michigan's lower and upper peninsulas. Besides the fact that it was dripping with religious sentiment, the letter contained a bunch of trivia about his life on the island. Then, abruptly in the middle, Don described a miracle as nonchalantly as if he had been writing about eating lunch. He wrote that he had fallen off this gigantic cliff on the island. "It was about 200 feet down, but I miraculously landed safely." Then he dropped the subject and never mentioned it again. As we discussed this letter, Detective Rick Westgate decided to check it out. He checked with scientific experts who confirmed there was no way a person could fall off that cliff and survive unscathed. At the least he would have been mangled and in a hospital intensive-care unit. If it had been a bona fide miracle, the whole island would know about it, and there would have been some verification.

Other letters spoke of how much he missed not Martha but his sisters, particularly his younger sister, Irene[1]. He described Irene's visit to Mackinaw with the kind of joy you might expect to be directed toward a girlfriend. The letter suggested that he had reversed the roles of girlfriend and sister. It was as if he was writing to Martha about Irene, the love of his life. I wondered if Martha had thought it was as strange as the police and I now did. She never mentioned the letters to me. I know that Martha could not have imagined the extent of Don's relationship with his sister.

A couple of years later, the police would tell me that Don had engaged in incestuous relations with Irene. Twenty years later, I was surprised to hear Don's father confirm on national television that Don's mother knew about this relationship. Gene stated that his wife "had told him about it only after Don had been arrested." He continued, "She didn't think it was of very big consequences, and she thought I would probably be a little more upset than she was with it." Ironically, in the same interview he had described Don as the "ideal son…he caused no problems."

Reading these letters reminded me of another one. It was such a disturbing letter that Martha had called to share it with me. She had received it during her last year at Southwestern. She called that spring from her dorm room in Texas, crying hysterically. In the letter, Don reprimanded her for not agreeing to marry him. It went on to state that it was "God's will" for Martha to marry Don. If she didn't, it continued, "her family would suffer horribly!" This threat deeply disturbed Martha.

At the time the phone rang with Martha's call, I was in the middle of preparing and serving a spaghetti dinner to a group of Kay's friends. Her guests were already seated at our dining-room table. Because of the timing, I listened with a divided mind. I must confess, in retrospect, although I was concerned that the letter had upset my daughter terribly, I did not realize the importance of what Martha was saying at the time. Instead, I concentrated on trying to calm Martha. At that moment, I couldn't understand her strong reaction. I tried to reassure her. My reasoning went something like this: "Sweetie, it is just a letter. He is in Michigan, and you are safely in your dorm in Texas. What can he do?"

I must confess, I thought she was overreacting. I urged her to cut off communication with Don, since he was upsetting her. "Just don't talk to him on the

---

1.   Denotes name change. The asterisk appears the first time the name is used.

phone. Even if he calls, you don't have to talk to him. You can hang up. Don't read his letters—throw them away unopened." Because I was in the midst of hosting Kay's party, I felt I should cut the conversation short. I learned later that Martha didn't share all the details of the letter because she did not want to upset me. Now, of course, I wish I had called her back after the dinner and really listened to Martha's fears. But at that moment, I didn't realize that conversation was of far greater consequence than a dinner party.

When Martha decided to tell Don she did not want to date him anymore and stopped writing, I thought the matter was settled. I was terribly wrong. When the author of this letter claimed to be speaking for God, I should have heard the alarm bells thundering in my ears. This letter should have frightened me as much as it did my daughter. Such a claim could indicate either insanity or a desire to exercise complete godlike dominance over another person. Either way, the wise thing to do would be to stay away from such a person. Why didn't I see this warning sign flashing right in my face? Why didn't I protect my daughter by making sure Don didn't get anywhere near her? Instead, I soon dismissed thoughts of the letter. Now I cannot understand how I could have been so stupid. Without any additional misgivings, that letter should have prompted me to see to it that Martha held fast to her fears about Don. Instead, I later welcomed him back into our home as a friend.

During the two years Martha attended Southwestern, she made the dean's list, formed a close group of friends, was very active in her church, and joined the Phi Mu Sorority, the French Honor Society, and the student math group, but simultaneously she experienced great homesickness. I never could understand that. How could she be enjoying her college experience so much while at the same time becoming more and more homesick? With each visit home, it became harder and harder for her to return to college. Finally, I asked if she would rather complete her studies in Michigan. Although it meant she would have to give up her scholarship, I did not want to insist on her doing something that was causing so much misery. I wanted what was best for Martha. So at the close of spring term in May 1976, I happily went to Texas to bring her home. She transferred to Michigan State University in East Lansing in time to begin the fall semester.

I offered Martha the opportunity to live on campus so she could be more a part of MSU; however, she was adamant that she wanted to live with her family. This was fine with me, because Kay and I were happy having Martha home again. Again, in hindsight I can only say, "If only..." If only I had insisted that she remain in Texas to go to school, rather than bring Martha home without a thought about the letter.

It was inevitable she would come into contact with Don again, living in East Lansing and attending the same church. When their paths did cross, he asked her if they could still be "just friends." He wondered if they could go places together with his sisters and Kay, like old times. Again, she didn't want to hurt him, so she said okay.

By June, Don was coming over without his sisters, until he left for a summer job at Mackinaw Island, six hours north of Lansing. During his absence, they frequently corresponded, and as the summer progressed Martha began to look forward to the fall, when Don would be back. "It might be nice, after all," she thought, "to know someone on the huge Michigan State campus." Perhaps he could introduce her to other students there (maybe even other boys—because he was, after all, only a friend.) She thought he would be someone she could go to football games with occasionally, or perhaps out dancing, since she would be new to MSU campus life. Southwestern was a small school, so she looked forward to the fun and variety of student activities to be found on a large university campus.

However, shortly after Don came home, they began to have problems once again. It became clear that he wanted to be more than a friend. Yet, there were no football dates. No dancing dates. All he wanted to do was take her to Bible studies or come over to the house and sit with his arms around her. He was smothering her efforts to develop a social life on campus. He even got a copy of her class schedule and began to "show up" on campus outside her classes. There he waited for Martha and accompanied her to her next class. She had no chance to meet and get to know her classmates, as he was constantly around. Perhaps that was his idea: to isolate her from other people. He also found out when she studied at the library and would appear there. He then sat down and stayed with her until she left. Since he didn't want to study, he interrupted and made it difficult for her to concentrate. This was frustrating for her, because Martha loved school and enjoyed studying. Don did not, and he repeatedly found ways to disrupt her studies. Even when Martha specifically told him not to come over to the house because she needed to study, he appeared uninvited.

Today, I would recognize these classic signs of stalking and think them ominous. At that time, I knew nothing about "stalking," so I just considered it frustrating. He constantly found excuses to come to our home. He started showing up with "gifts." How could she refuse to let him in when he had brought her a gift? (The "gifts" seemed strange for a twenty-two-year-old man to give to a girl he was trying to impress. They were cheap trinkets from discount stores.) Kay and I didn't share our feelings with Martha, but we wondered to each other, "How can she be pleased with such childish junk?"

Although we never discussed the gifts, Martha began to see them as a symptom of a problem. "Mother, he acts just like a little boy," she would say, adding in her characteristic way, "but I don't want to hurt him." In the midst of all these negative feelings, Don came over early one morning in late November and asked my permission to marry Martha! I was stunned. I looked at Martha in disbelief. Surely this announcement by Don must have been just as surprising to her. But she looked happy and excited about the prospect. What on earth had Don done to so dramatically change her mind? I was puzzled; this did not fit with what Martha had told me in our talks. I was speechless. While I was standing there trying to make sense out of this, Don continued, saying that they planned to get married a year later, in December of 1977. *How do I respond?* I wondered. Since they did not want to marry immediately, I thought I would have plenty of time to talk with Martha. It didn't seem wise at the moment to remind Martha in front of Don of the genuine concerns we had shared about their relationship, so I agreed to the engagement.

Kay's response was very different from mine; she did not mask her feelings. Kay was more courageous than I was. Kay had never taken a liking to Don. She considered him a jerk and a pest and was not subtle about expressing her feelings to her big sister. When Martha told Kay about the engagement, the two sisters were standing in the kitchen. Don was still in the house, within earshot. Kay didn't care that Don could hear and angrily asked her why she had accepted. "Because he asked me," Martha said. Both Don and Martha clearly understood that Kay was not happy about the engagement. Kay walked out of the room and went upstairs. In the days to come, Kay continued to express her disapproval. In spite of her sister's counsel, Martha went ahead and accepted the tiny diamond engagement ring that Don brought her.

Although I had given my approval, I continued to puzzle over Martha's acceptance of Don's proposal. There had to be some other reason that Martha was not disclosing. During the weeks immediately following the announcement, I listened intently to Kay and Martha's discussions about Don. Kay saw rage and uncontrolled behavior in Don. He would get angry and act out his rage. Kay reminded Martha of events they had both witnessed, such as the time they were all in Don's car on their way to a roller-skating rink. Don's sisters were needling him, as usual, and he got angry. He began driving recklessly, "like crazy. It seemed he was going 130 miles an hour," Kay asserted. The incident frightened Kay, and she did not want to ride with Don in the future.

To Kay, Don seemed like he was always ready to explode. In recalling Don's actions, Kay said, "He'd act so angry it seemed he had to *do something*!" Kay reminded Martha of the time they were building a snowman. In a good-natured manner, people began throwing snowballs at each other in fun, definitely not trying to hurt each other. But Don reacted violently when someone threw a snowball at him. He blew up and started yelling and hurling things that could injure people.

I thought Kay must have been overreacting. After all, he was the neighborhood boy who came over to eat, went around in your car, and stayed at your house at night until he was told, "It's time for you to go home." It couldn't be as bad as Kay claimed. He seemed so mild mannered. In my presence, Don was pleasant, accommodating, and helpful. Kay recognized a huge red flag. To my sorrow, I did not. How I wish I had really listened to and understood what Kay was trying to communicate to Martha and me. If only I had really considered the character of the person voicing these concerns. Kay had always been trustworthy and dependable. She did not lie to me. She used good judgment and common sense. She selected friends who were also trustworthy! Why didn't I listen to her? Why did I feel she was overreacting?

Although there was something about Don I, too, did not like, I couldn't exactly put my finger on it. One aspect of his character that bothered me at the time, though I scarcely would have admitted it, was his overbearing piety. I tended to blame myself for feeling that way. Maybe I was just being unkind in my opinion. I took my faith in God seriously, so why did his talk bother me so much? When I analyzed what he said, there didn't seem to be anything wrong with it. Nevertheless, it did having a jarring effect on both Kay and me. It seemed he refused to discuss anything without invoking God and Jesus and quoting scripture. *Why do I feel this way?* I wondered. *What's wrong with me?* I argued with myself that I didn't want to ascribe bad motives to his manner of speaking. I didn't want to judge him—but somehow, things just didn't add up.

This was another major warning sign, one which I would recognize today. Experts in law enforcement now tell women that we need to trust our instinct that tells us "something isn't right." Instead of recognizing it, however, I was influenced by society's conditioning. Our culture had trained women to "be nice" and to attribute good motives to other people. My top concern should have been the safety of my child rather than another person's feelings.

Much later, I would realize that on a subconscious level, my feelings marked him as a phony. I realized too late that it is essential to pay attention to uncomfortable feelings, even if they defy reason. That "still small voice within" needs to be heeded. It speaks Truth to us. Gavin DeBecker wrote a book on the subject called, *The Gift of Fear*. Fear truly can be a gift, one to which we should listen.

From time to time, Martha wrote down her prayers and expressed her feelings in poems. Among these prayers I found one that indicated she had been given that "gift of fear." It began, "Dear Jesus," and continued, "Lord, I don't know why I feel like I do—only you know. How can I tell why I don't trust people? How can I know to trust him? Thank you, Lord, that I can trust you…is he trying to stifle me? Does he even know, Lord, what he means? He seems so like a 'little bittie kid,' not even a grown man, Lord…Oh Lord, how hard it is to know what to do. I'll take him at his word…like I took you at yours, and I'll leave the rest to you…Is that okay, Lord? I need to trust someone as my husband, Lord. Is it okay?"

Although she had "the gift of fear," no one had taught her to trust it. Unfortunately, I could not teach her what I had not yet learned. I regret that I didn't at least voice my feeling that his pious words and phrases sounded phony. Discussing my negative feelings with her early in the dating process might have validated Martha's feelings, perhaps to the point where she could have been comfortable ending all contact.

I finally realized what had made Martha agree to marry him. In private, Don had repeatedly built a case that it all was God's will. He never said that in my presence or around anyone who could refute his claim. This is the very spot where he knew Martha was vulnerable, for he knew she wanted to live in accordance with God's will for her life. He had planted the idea that by rejecting him, she was going against God's will. Because she wanted to act in accordance with God's will above all else, his arguments finally persuaded her to accept his proposal.

During the two or three weeks before we traveled to Pennsylvania, Martha seemed very happy. Once we were in Pennsylvania, however, in light of her friends' questions, she could see they agreed with Kay's insights. Martha began to see the validity of their concerns. Now it wasn't just "little sister" talking. Here were four girls who were close to Martha and who cared deeply about her. They saw problems. Doubts began to surface. Martha was urged to pay attention to the problems she had experienced with Don. They convinced her that these were not insignificant matters to be overlooked. When they really laid it on the line, Martha could see through her friends' eyes that she really wasn't "head over heels" in love. She had agreed to marry Don largely because he had convinced her that it was God's will. Maybe not wanting to make Don unhappy was also a factor. Like so many other young women, she wanted to believe that he would change. She had allowed herself to be caught up in a romantic ideal. The idea of a wedding was exciting and fun, but in Pennsylvania, after all those long talks with her friends and Kay, Martha recognized that she wasn't really thrilled about the person she was marrying.

During their conversations, the girls had shared their feelings about engaging in sex before marriage. They all agreed sex was so special they would not share it with anyone until they were married. Martha confided that Don continued to pressure her, even though she made it clear she would not have sex until marriage. "How can he do that?" she asked. "He clearly knows the word of the Bible states that sex before marriage is wrong in God's eyes. He claims to believe the Bible and be a follower of Christ. His actions don't match his words." Martha had begun to realize it was not her God-given duty in life to make Don happy. Marriage had to be a mutual agreement. Here was a warning that Don wasn't in love; he was self-absorbed.

In addition to these unfavorable signs, there were other differences between Martha and Don that Martha discussed with me after we had returned from Pennsylvania. These included:

- Their differing views about marriage

- Don's parents' relationship with each other

- Their differing priorities about money and education

Another colossal warning flag was the fact that Don was a loner. If he was not capable of friendships, perhaps this could indicate that he was not a safe person with whom to be involved.

Of course, we recognized these signs too late, but hopefully those reading this, in light of Martha's experience, will not be so naïve. I want our ordeal and the suffering thrust upon us to help other families avoid having to live with the unbearable.

4

Living with the Unbearable

Now that we were fully awake, we got up and resumed the mechanics of daily life. Laurie and Gerry never left me by myself even for a minute, for which I will be eternally grateful. Laurie had a family of ten and Gerry had a family of seven. In spite of this, both of their husbands had immediately said, "Go, Sue needs you."

One full day had passed, and now there were two phone calls I had to make—one to Kay and Le, my ex-husband, and the other to my parents. Both were in Texas. However, it was still too early to call, since Texas was one hour behind Michigan. I also decided that I should wait until Daddy had finished preparing breakfast for Mother, since after that phone call no one would feel like eating. This gave me time with my friends to figure out how I could talk to Daddy without Mother also getting on the line.

I considered it necessary to talk to my father first, because Mother had become a semi-invalid some thirteen years earlier following a major heart attack. During those years, she'd also become blind with glaucoma. To make matters even more complicated, Mother was an extremely emotional woman. I was afraid the news might kill her. Since I was an only child, my daughters were her only grandchildren. As the firstborn grandchild, Martha had been very close to her grandmother. They had become even closer during her two years of college in Texas, since she had often visited her grandparents. She had spent hours sitting beside my mother's bed. Martha was a talkative young woman who delighted in giving her grandmother lively, detailed accounts of her university life.

After discussing the situation with Laurie and Gerry, it seemed a good idea to call Martha's father and Kay first. I called Austin, Texas, but there was no answer. We decided that they must have been on the way to see the grandparents. Now there was no choice. I had to call my father. (Following a brief visit to my parents in Luling, Texas, Kay and her Dad were on their way to Mexico for Christmas vacation. I was hesitant about spoiling their holiday, but I had to let them know.

To do this, I had to reach them before they left my parents'.) Now I had another problem: I wanted to be the one to tell Kay. I debated the best way to do that. I could call Daddy and ask to speak to Kay. Then I could get her to take Daddy to another phone away from the house. Even as I voiced this plan, I realized it wouldn't work. Mother had a bedside phone, so she would probably pick it up. Even if I could talk to Daddy by himself, he knew my voice so well I wouldn't be able fool him for a second. The instant I started to speak, he would know something was very wrong. His reaction would alert my mother that there was a tragedy brewing. All my life, I could depend on Daddy not to go to pieces in a crisis. He was always rock solid. I knew even then that I could lean on him for support. However, Daddy would have more than he could handle with Mother. We decided I needed someone I knew to be there on the other end of the line when I called. The first phone call was to a friend in Luling whom I knew from their church. I explained what had happened and asked if he would go to my parents' house. After waiting a few minutes for the friend to arrive, I placed the dreaded call.

It was exactly as I had imagined. My father answered the phone but was unable to keep Mother from knowing what was going on. She picked up her bedside phone on the second ring. As her weeping and wailing began to mount, I found myself almost shouting, "Daddy can you hear me?" As my frustration escalated, I lost it and spoke harshly, "Mother, stop it! She is my daughter! I need help!" The tone of my voice shocked my Mother into silence. Taking advantage of the calm, I quickly asked, "Daddy, please find Kay. Don't tell her anything. Just tell her to call me. I do not want anyone else to tell her first."

When Kay called and I explained the situation, she was stunned. I told her everything I knew. However, she is like my father in that she can be counted on in crises to hold herself together. Knowing her grandmother's extreme reaction made Kay even more resolute. Now was not the time to cry together. I asked to speak with Le, my ex-husband. I repeated the facts to him. I knew he, too, could be counted on; he would not become hysterical. True to my expectation, his reaction was subdued and practical. He told me he would put Kay on a plane back to Lansing.

"Please don't, Le," I begged. "That's a long time for Kay to be alone with thoughts that her only sister is missing. It will take hours to get from Austin to Lansing, with two flight changes and the waiting time in between. Please bring her home...come with her, please." Le was very cooperative and promised they would fly out on the first available plane. They would not arrive until Monday, the next day.

By that afternoon, my house was full of people, including friends who had heard the news that morning at church. I remember Mary Jo, a Mary Kay associate, rushing in to express her concern, as did my next-door neighbors. I was told that Don had gone to church that morning and that he had stood up and asked for prayers for Martha. Late Sunday afternoon, the police called and asked me to come down to the station. Before I agreed to go, I made sure someone would stay to answer the phone in my absence. I felt someone needed to be close to my phone at all times. *If Martha was being held somewhere against her will and she got one chance to call for help, that might be her only chance*, I reasoned. *She might never get a second one.* I could not bear to imagine an answering machine receiving her call for help. Friends agreed to remain at the house when the police car arrived to take Gerry, Laurie, and me to the police station.

When we arrived, the officers told us they had been interrogating Don all afternoon. As they were leading us into Sgt. Tucker's office, we passed the room where Don was being questioned. He looked directly at me with a pathetic, weak, helpless look—a look that seemed to be asking me to rescue him. That look merely disgusted me. When we got to the office, Gene and Elaine were already seated with two detectives.

Gene began to complain about how badly they were treating Don. He thought it was just dreadful that Don was being put through "all this questioning." Gene's attitude irritated me. *What is wrong with you, Gene? My daughter is missing! Why aren't you willing, even eager, to go through a little discomfort in order to help find her?* I thought. I was so numb I couldn't find a voice to convince Gene that if anyone had any information that could help us, it would be Don. The thoughts merely ran through my mind: *Your son is inside, warm and safe, and it has been twenty-four hours that Martha has been somewhere out in this extreme cold! Your son is safe. Why can't you see that Don needs to help? Surely you must understand that time is crucial if we are to find her alive.*

It seemed as though Gene wasn't even concerned about finding Martha, yet he continued to voice concerns about "poor Don." I was shocked when he mentioned hiring a lawyer. This was totally beyond belief! He couldn't be serious. More questions began to form in my mind. This talk of hiring a lawyer reinforced the feeling that Gerry, Laurie, and I had that Gene knew something. Otherwise, surely any father would want his son to co-operate with the police to help them find his girlfriend. As for his own relationship with Martha, Gene had always seemed to respect her. Years earlier, he had been Martha's Sunday-school teacher. He might have one day been her father-in-law. Why wasn't he more concerned about finding Martha?

When the police released Don for the evening, he spoke to me briefly. He told me that the police had asked for all of his underclothes. My first thoughts were, *That's bizarre. Why is he telling me this?* Then, I thought it odd that the police would ask Don to bring his own underwear in. After all, he could select any pair he wanted. Why wouldn't the police get a search warrant and retrieve them themselves? I also found it odd that Don expressed not one word of concern for Martha. In fact, Don never even mentioned her name. He didn't ask if I had received any new information since we had last talked. He didn't ask about anything. It was as if Martha had disappeared from his thoughts; now all he spoke about was himself and his own situation. After that one comment, he walked out with his parents.

When we were in private, the police shared the results of that afternoon's session. They told me that Don had gone over and over the same old story. They had given him two polygraph tests. Both showed he was lying, but they hadn't been able to get him to change his story. From the beginning, the police had had the same opinion as my friends and I did. No one goes off and leaves his girlfriend sitting in the snow in that kind of weather. I was told he exhibited no emotion under questioning. No rage. No sorrow. Nothing. As a last resort before releasing him for the evening, they thought he might show some reaction if he saw me at the police station. So they decided to try it. This was the reason I was asked to come down to police headquarters. But my appearance produced no results either. No one could think of anything else that could be done that evening, so we were driven home. When we arrived home, I wasted no time before I inquired about phone calls. The phone call from Martha that we had been hoping for had not come. Soon my friends and I were alone for the second night.

I felt like screaming! I felt the urge to scream, and scream, and scream. I fought this urge, because I felt if ever I did start screaming, I would never be able to stop. I would go on screaming for the rest of my life and finally be completely swallowed up, somehow lost inside the scream. I had this weird image in my mind of a throat screaming for all eternity. I would cease to exist; only my scream would remain. With this picture in my mind, I knew I absolutely could not allow myself to start. I could see myself on the verge of insanity, so I had to hold on. Somehow, each time I would feel the urge to start screaming, I would tell myself firmly, "Not now. That can wait. Not now."

With the increasing likelihood that Martha was dead, I was not interested in going on living. *My life is over,* I thought. Why wasn't it me instead of Martha? I had lived my life. She had her whole life before her. I then calmed myself with the thought that Kay was coming home the next day, and she still needed her mother. That was the first of two things that kept me going during the worst times. I felt Kay had lost so much in her young life; first, she had experienced the break-up of her family, which led to the loss of her father in her daily life, and now she had lost her only sister. She couldn't now lose her mother. If I focused only on Martha's loss, I thought, Kay might believe that her sister was the only one who was important to me. I did not want to send that kind of a message to her, because I also loved Kay intensely. I had to survive for her sake. With this thought strengthening me, I fought to retain a sound mind.

The second reason I had to survive was that the police needed me to be of sound mind to help in the investigation. I knew Martha better than anyone; the information I could give would be necessary if she were to be found. So, I had to "take captive" my thoughts and keep a sharp mind.

I was grateful to have Kay and Le arrive safely the next day. I deeply appreciated that her father had accompanied her home. I am sure that Le, also, felt that East Lansing was the place he wanted to be, for he announced he would be staying for a few weeks. That was good news. In order to help make this possible, he could stay at the house; there would be no need for him to incur the expense of staying at a motel. Also, knowing that Le's presence in the house would be a comfort to Kay, I very willingly offered him the bedroom in the basement. With an unknown menace on the loose in East Lansing, I felt good about having Le there to watch over Kay.

With Kay's return, another fear arose. Panic over her safety set in. Not knowing for sure who was responsible for Martha's disappearance, or the motives behind it, I became terrified that the same thing could happen to Kay. I was frightened to have Kay leave my sight. With all the talk of Martha being snatched off our front porch, I had this unsettling feeling that "whatever" had taken her could reach out and seize Kay as well. The media had picked up Don's story and were repeating it over and over, as if it was a fact that she had disappeared from her own front porch. Although my mind told me Martha had not been abducted from our porch, emotionally I could not be sure. On some level, however, I "bought" the story that a stranger had snatched her just outside our very own front door. Perhaps it was the constant repetition of that explanation that convinced me so. In fact, it would be years before I would return home without feeling someone might be lurking behind a bush, ready to grab me. Unlike the media today, reporters then didn't constantly barrage me with questions, trying to get their sound bites. No one was challenging Don's story, so they kept reporting it as fact. This bothered me. After I started talking to journalists, I asked them,

"Please don't say that Martha vanished from our front porch! Say instead that Don alleged that she did."

And if it was Don who had caused Martha's disappearance, what was there to stop him from taking Kay, too, in order to punish her for her influence against him? The threat that her family would suffer terribly if Martha didn't marry Don had certainly come true. Therefore, Le's presence in the house would not only be emotional support for Kay, but I knew he was as eager to protect her as I was. It was a relief to have him there. It made me feel Kay was more secure and less vulnerable. At six feet two inches, Le was a much larger man than Don, and he was strong from a lifetime of lifting weights. I did not think Don would dare harm Kay as long as Le was around. Still, one of the hardest things I had to do daily was to allow sixteen-year-old Kay to walk out the front door in the dark of the early morning and stand in front of the house next door to wait for the school bus. I was terrified. At the same time, I did not want my fears to keep her from living her life. Kay would have been outraged if she had known; after all, at her age she was convinced she could take care of herself. So I stayed out of Kay's sight as I watched from the living-room window. I opened the drape only enough to see out. When she was safely on the bus, I breathed a little easier.

I considered sending her away to Pennsylvania to live with the Bowes family for the remainder of her junior year in high school. There I felt she would be safe from the unknown threat that pervaded life in East Lansing. In Pennsylvania, Kay would have had not only Grace and Don to protect her, but also Valerie and Brian to travel with to and from school. They would be close all day and be able to look out for her. I should have known Kay wouldn't like that idea, for when I broached the subject, she quickly vetoed it. She was adamant. She did not want the person responsible for her sister's disappearance to force her out of her home and away from her friends. Kay was so enraged about losing her sister that she became defiant in the face of danger. Her attitude was, "I just dare someone to try something!" This frightened me all the more for Kay's safety. I was afraid she would throw caution to the wind and get herself into a dangerous situation.

At the same time, I understood the feeling, for I too felt if a prowler tried to get into our home or car, I would have such an adrenalin rush that I would have super-human strength. I believed I would turn into a tiger because of the rage I felt over Martha's loss. It was an extraordinarily strange feeling, for I had never been in a fight in my life and I was not particularly athletic. I remember wishing I was a man, the only time I had ever done so, so that I could give Don a good hard punch to the jaw for abandoning the search to find Martha. I wanted to knock some sense into him.

Nothing else mattered to me except finding Martha and protecting Kay. At home during those first few weeks I operated in a fog. I was unaware of time. I would have forgotten to eat if Le had not been there. He prepared food and then called to me, "It's time to eat, Sue." He made sure I joined him at the table. When we were together over meals, we talked about the case. At other times I was generally not aware of his presence in the house. When there was nothing to do to assist the investigation, Le kept busy by re-organizing my garage and doing various improvement projects around the house. While I was in the house, I stayed close to the phone. I was still insistent about having someone available to answer the phone at all times. At night, I kept the porch light burning.

The phone and the porch light began to take on great emotional importance. I had always kept it on as long as one of my daughters was away from home at night. To turn it out would symbolize my giving up hope that Martha was alive. On the other hand, if she were alive and could get close enough to see the light burning, she would know that we were home—that we were there to provide her safety.

Later on, Elaine made an odd comment about the porch light. She insinuated that I had contributed to Martha's disappearance. "What on earth are you talking about, Elaine?" I retorted.

"Well, that red light on your porch that you keep burning all the time," she answered.

"Elaine!" I blurted out, "That's a yellow outdoor light to keep the bugs away! It's yellow, not red!"

We were in constant communication with the police. In the course of the investigation, East Lansing Police Department became like family to us. My gold-colored Oldsmobile—I had not yet earned the Mary Kay "Pink Buick"—became a constant presence in front of the ELPD. I fed the meter until it was full and then Sgt. Tucker gave me a card to put under my windshield wipers in case the meter ran out. We shared information with Sgt. Tucker and Officer Rick Westgate and compared what Don had told us with what he had told them.

By the time Kay and Le had arrived on that Monday, two days after Martha's disappearance, Sgt. Tucker was confident that I was not going to pieces. He believed I could handle the first ugly piece of evidence they had found. So they told us that Don's car had been seized and searched. In it they had found blood that did not belong to Don. They were sure it was Martha's. As I listened to this disclosure I sat there, dying on the inside while maintaining a calm demeanor.

The detective continued, saying that when Don was questioned about the blood in his car, he changed his story several times.

First, he said he had a nosebleed and that it was his own blood. This was immediately challenged. Don was told that the blood pattern was not consistent with a nosebleed. This was a blood smear, while a nosebleed trickles out in little droplets. Additionally, it was not his blood type. He then changed his story, saying, "Well, one of my sisters must have been menstruating." Blood samples were taken from the Miller family. When Don was told that no one in his family matched the blood type taken from the car, he decided that Martha had been menstruating. Kay said (and her friends in Pennsylvania confirmed her statement), "That's impossible, because Martha had already completed her cycle while she was in Pennsylvania the previous week."

This was of course before the days of DNA. Martha had one of the less common blood types, AB positive. Unfortunately, the amount of blood available in the car was very small. There was enough to raise only one of the factors matching Martha's blood type, but not the second. It had to be Martha's blood, however, because no one else ever rode in Don's car. His sisters were not allowed to drive it, so it could not be one of his sisters' friends. In fact, no one drove that car except Don and his father. And according to the Millers, before Martha, Don had never had another girlfriend. He had no other friends either, so there had been no one in the car outside of his family and Martha.

After that Sunday, the Miller family stopped coming over to our house, and they were already beginning to deny access to Don. Le came up with the idea of befriending Don in order to gain his confidence. That way, perhaps, he could gain information we could use. He visited Don and sympathized with the "ordeal" of questioning that Don was going through. Le then offered the hope that "when Martha comes back," he was looking forward to having him for a son-in-law. Don became willing to talk to Le. He started accompanying Le over to our house and going downstairs to Le's room to talk. Le pursued this plan, hoping to find something. It almost backfired, however, because at one point Le told me he didn't believe Don could have had anything to do with Martha's disappearance.

The police investigation proceeded swiftly and with vigor. I never doubted that East Lansing's police department put their hearts into this case. The TV, radio, and local newspaper had been carrying the story since the first day based on information supplied to them by the police, and I had not talked to the media. During the first couple of days, they showed pictures of Martha constantly. This was accompanied by photos of the front of our house along with the story that

Don had left her sitting there in-17°F weather. By generating massive publicity, the police and I desperately hoped that somebody would remember seeing something. The detectives considered it important to keep the story in the news so that people would not forget. They needed clues. They felt it would be a good idea to offer a $1000 reward (a considerably larger sum in 1977 than it would be today) for information that would lead to Martha's recovery.

I was also convinced to participate in a press conference. At that time, press conferences were not commonplace events. I wasn't sure how they worked. I assumed the police would handle it. No, I was told, the reporters would be invited to my house, not the police station. I was fine with any idea, if they thought it would help. As the police worked on the wording of the statement, they included the phrase "dead or alive." *Oh no!* I recoiled in horror. I was afraid that "dead or alive" might actually encourage a possible kidnaper to kill her and then try to collect the reward. I wanted her found alive. In deference to me, that phrase was promptly deleted.

I expected Sgt. Tucker to announce the reward, maybe with me standing beside him, but he had a different idea. He set up a press conference in my living room, where I would read the statement. I thought, *No problem, I can read a statement*. Yet, I had no concept twenty years ago about what I was going to face. I felt supported, because Sgt. Tucker and Detective Westgate were there with me. At the appointed hour, my living room quickly became jammed with people. As I remember it, they were all very respectful and orderly. The room was so full of reporters that some stood only a couple of feet away from my face; there was no space for the two detectives, so they waited in the kitchen. Every media organization in the area was crammed into my living room and hallway. There were flash cameras, TV cameras, tape recorders, and notepads. That was fine with me, because the press would help us get the story out there, I thought. As a result, surely someone would come forward with information about Martha. A person could not just disappear off the face of the earth.

I was terribly naïve, believing I would read the statement, which summarized the facts we had, announce the reward, and that my part in the day's events would end there. The reporters, I assumed, would just pack up and leave. As we all know today, that is not how such things work. Today it is common knowledge that a press conference is about reporters asking questions—lots of questions. I had not been prepared to answer questions. As the queries began to come, I didn't have time to think about my answers. Things began to spin out of control. I started answering with the uncensored truth. "I can't answer that" was not in my vocabulary. Soon I realized I was in major trouble. I was giving information the police did not want made public, information that might possibly jeopardize Martha's life! I stopped the press conference and hurried to meet with the detectives in the kitchen. They had been listening with mounting anxiety.

"What do I do?" I asked.

"Go back in there and ask them to consider everything you have said as 'off the record,' then ask to start over.

I went back and said, "The things I have been telling you will jeopardize the officers' ability to find my daughter. Will you please take everything I have said 'off the record?' Let's start over." My home was filled with strangers, people I had never seen before. They already had my voice, my picture, and the information on film and tape. Any one of them could have used it, even though knowing it might stand in the way of recovering a young woman alive. Every single person in that room honored my request! They put my daughter's life above getting the story. Because of their restraint, the media had become part of that outpouring of support I felt from the community during those terrible days.

I had no prior connection to the media, but just as the police had done from the very first day, they responded to me with real compassion and warmth. A bond of friendship grew between the press and me. When I talk to students in journalism classes today, I say, "That experience began my 'love affair' with the media. They won my support." I told my story twenty years later in a professional journalism conference where I was one of the speakers, and all in attendance considered it a bona fide miracle that no one had scooped the story. In that room of professional journalists, no one could remember a time when at least one reporter would not have gone ahead and "leaked" the information. Because of the respect the media showed me, I kept talking to them and never refused an interview. I considered them partners in our effort to solve the case.

Kay, however, did not feel the same support from the press that I did. As a teenager, she did not want to be followed or asked questions. She did not want her home to be a part of the nightly news broadcast. I realized later that a few journalists abused my willingness to be accessible. There were occasions when I answered the phone to find myself live on the radio, and photographers came unannounced to our home. At the time, I was not upset. I just considered it part of the search to find Martha.

Of course, the media wanted to talk to the Millers also, but I was told they refused to answer questions, often hanging up on the reporters. They reported that Elaine said her son had gone through enough and she did not want him to go through any more. I thought, *What in the world has he gone through? My child is missing. What is answering a few questions? And why is she complaining? She has all of her children.* The Millers also tried to stop the police from allowing the media to show a photo in which Don was pictured sitting beside Martha. The police felt someone might tip them off that they remembered seeing Don on Friday night, even if they did not remember seeing Martha, and the Millers were aware of this.

The police still had not obtained a search warrant for Don's home. I desperately wanted to get inside that house. We had heard of accounts where women had been imprisoned in tiny compartments. If Don had abducted Martha, it was possible he could even be holding her captive there. By this time, the Millers refused to talk to the police, but we still had access. Le and I came up with a plan. The three of us would go to visit the Millers. Maybe one of us, Kay, Le, or I, would see something or some information would slip out in a conversation. Also, I had wanted to check the route Don claimed to have taken to drive Martha home. His testimony stated that he had driven her around for two hours Friday night to see Christmas lights. Earlier, at Sgt. Tucker's insistence, Don had guided the police over the area during the day. I wanted Don to drive us over the same route at night. When I requested that Don take us, Gene said that his son had been through enough. He insisted he would not allow Don to drive that route one more time.

"Gene," I explained, "we have got to do something! The police have not found Martha. Things look completely different at night. Maybe Don will see something that will trigger a memory…maybe someone followed them that night. Don doesn't have to drive. I will drive. We just want him to go along and let him tell us where to drive."

I tried to make it sound as non-judgmental as possible in order to get him to cooperate. I did not want to close down the lines of communication. I knew that as soon as I revealed my true feelings even a little, all access to Don would be cut off. Without Don's cooperation, we couldn't solve anything. Finally Gene agreed that Don could do it, but he would do the driving.

"That's okay," I said. We made an appointment to take that drive. Before the Millers came by to pick us up I told Le that if we drove around without carrying on a conversation, possibly the silence would weigh on their minds. Then perhaps they would start trying to make conversation, get relaxed by talking, and maybe we would hear something. If we entered into a conversation off the subject, we might not learn anything. Le and I got into the back seat and Don directed Gene from the passenger seat. We headed toward East Lansing Trinity Church, where Don said they had gone at 11:30 P.M. to pick up his younger sister from a New Year's party. I wondered, *Why would you pick up someone from a*

New Year's party before midnight? I kept quiet, however, because I did not want to challenge Don openly or alert him to any discrepancies. He said he had parked the car and that he and Martha had walked into the sanctuary, where people were singing a hymn. They looked around and saw that his sister was not there and left.

This, we later found out, was a lie. In checking with the church office, we found the sanctuary was not in use that night. The lights were off and the doors were locked. The only part of the church in use that evening was the basement. The basement entrance was not visible from the sanctuary side of the church. It could be entered only from the back of the building. A communion service was going on in the fellowship hall in the basement. Anyone familiar at all with churches would recognize the difference between a church sanctuary and a fellowship hall. Certainly, someone who has attended church his entire life would easily recognize a communion service.

From the church, we went back to Burcham Road and followed it down to where it went into a wooded dead-end street by the city's water-treatment plant. Don claimed he had parked in that secluded area, where they had "kissed a few times." Ken Ouellette told me that he had investigated that area while off duty. "Don's claim could not possibly be true," Ken reported, "because no car could have parked there without leaving a telltale sign. That night was far too cold to sit in a car without the engine running. With the engine running, the snow under the car would have melted into a distinctive solid-ice formation. I saw no such area of ice there."

Ken went on to state that the car itself pointed to another lie. Anyone who has ever lived in the colder parts of the country knows that in periods of sub-zero weather, there are no clean cars on the road. It was impossible, at least in those days, to wash cars during such periods. The only clean cars are those parked inside garages. The cars on the road are covered in a dirty, gray, salty crust. Pictures taken by the police of Don's car showed scratch marks dug through the mud encrusted surface into the paint. This indicated the car had been driven through thick brush. They asked Don where he had gotten the scratches. First he said he did not know. Then he stated he had gotten them when they parked by the water plant. The only tracks in that area, however, were down the center of the road. The snowdrifts along each side of the road forced the cars to drive in the center, far enough away from the tree branches to prevent a car from getting scratches. Now we had two lies about the same location.

As we continued our drive over the route Don was directing us, Gene wanted to get something to drink. He stopped at a 7-Eleven. Le and Gene went into the store. This was a chance for me to talk to Don without his father present. As I tried to think of what to say, a chilling thought occurred to me: *I am alone with a killer.* Le came back quickly, followed by Gene, and the drive proceeded.

Next, Gene turned west into Lansing and continued traveling in that direction until we came to the river. As we followed along its wide solidly frozen banks, my heart shuddered. What a perfect hiding place for a body. This was January. It would be spring, an eternity away, before the ice would thaw. If a body had been put under that ice it would be months before a search could even start. I made a mental note to ask Sgt. Tucker about this. When I did, he reassured me that the depth of the ice cover on the river would have made it impossible to put a body under it on New Year's Eve.

We headed back to East Lansing and the campus. Don told us he had wanted to see how many lights were on in the dorms so he could tell how many people had already returned to campus. A strange way to spend a New Year's Eve, I thought. Surely Martha would have wanted to do something more fun than that. As we turned into the married-housing area, my eye spotted another blood-curdling possibility—the garbage dumpster! They were large enough that someone could throw a body in and cover it with trash. There would have been very few residents around on New Year's Eve, so her body could have been deposited there. By now, garbage collection had taken place several times, so her body could have been lost forever under a mountain of refuse at the city dump. I was sickened by the thought.

We were now going north on Harrison Road. The light from my upstairs hallway was shining clearly over the roof of our neighbors' ranch house. Don had said our house was dark at two when he had brought Martha home. I did not contradict him, but I knew the hall light was on and that the window was clearly visible from the street. Any movement on the inside was so evident that those curtains were the first Martha had made when we moved into our new home. She made them of a woven fabric so that they would permit light to come through in the daytime but would obstruct the view from outside at night. Don would have seen this light if he had driven there on New Year's Eve.

We were back where we had started in just about every respect. We had uncovered nothing new, except for more contradictions, and the police could not even confront Don with these new inconsistencies. My fantasy that Don might slip up in some way did not occur; all I had accomplished was to plant another grim possibility in my mind—that the dumpster might have been Martha's burial spot.

Still another possibility was in plain sight and yet completely out of our reach. The Millers had a trailer camper parked beside their house. Could he have been holding Martha captive in there? If so, the entire family would discover that fact sooner or later. Were they all part of a cover-up? Seeing that trailer every time I passed the house was maddening. We had no warrant, so no one could get in to find out. And if Martha were not alive, the trailer would have provided a huge deep-freeze container in which her body could be held until the spring thaw, when the ground would become soft enough to dig a grave. He could take his time to choose a site where no one could discover the grave.

Eventually, after a couple of weeks or so, Le had to leave to go back to his job in Texas. I remained in a fog. The days continued to be a jumble. I still had no concept of time, yet I could function just fine as long as I was in the company of another person. Otherwise, even routine things just did not get done. It must have become evident to my friends that I was not dealing with the mail. It lay in an unopened pile, and I did not seem to notice. One day, my friend Mary asked me about it, and then she sat down with me and wrote out the checks for my bills and passed them to me to sign. When they were addressed and stamped, she mailed them for me. My friends from my Bible study were wonderful. They were frequent visitors. As they came out from time to time to check on me, they began to find other ways to help.

There were days when I was absolutely unable to accomplish anything by myself. The care of my friends was an immense comfort to me as well as very practical help. Once a large group from Bible study came over for a house-cleaning party. Not only was that helpful for me, but it really nourished my spirit. We all cleaned together. Kay was mortified when she came in that afternoon from school. "Aren't you ashamed to have your friends come to clean our house?" she asked. I was sorry she was offended, but no, I was not ashamed. I felt very grateful and supported. I refused to take on false guilt. My friends gave generously to me, because they cared, and wanted to share the load I was under. I hope I was able to convey to them just how much their actions meant.

The reason I functioned well with other people was that their presence gave me something positive on which to focus. When they weren't around, I had to work so hard to hold back the dark pictures in my imagination that I seemed to accomplish very little that wasn't connected to the investigation. When I worked on something that was related to the case, that was another matter entirely. My brain latched on like a magnet. Yet everything else seemed to slip from my memory. For example, a friend called to say that she would be over in fifteen minutes, which was great. Then another friend walked in immediately after I had hung up and asked me to go shopping, so I left with her. In an instant, I had forgotten that my friend was on her way. I began to think I was losing my mind. It was a relief when someone explained to me that our mind acts like an electric circuit: when it is overloaded, it blows a fuse. That made sense to me. He reassured me that I was not going insane; I was just on overload. In fact, he said, "You are functioning remarkably well. You are doing fine with the things that are important."

I felt warmth and support from the entire Lansing area. Many people let us know they cared. I was touched by the kindness of one neighbor, Bob Graham, who lived around the corner from us. His wife, Jenny, was a Mary Kay client of mine, but I did not know Bob very well. I remember Jenny calling me to ask if I would be upset if Bob organized the neighborhood men to search the property around the neighborhood. There was a ravine area near us filled with six feet of snow. The police had not had time to cover that area or the back of the property and the small park area behind us.

"How wonderful!" was my response. "I would greatly appreciate their help. I would be so very thankful!" Since the entire area was heavily blanketed with snow and the wind had piled up deep drifts, it was a daunting task. On a Saturday, in all that incredible cold, my neighbors spent hour after hour in the grisly task of searching for a body. Although they discovered nothing, it meant a lot to us that our neighbors cared enough to put themselves through that ordeal. Also, it was very helpful to the police, because they were able to eliminate that area and spend their time on other sites.

Support came from other quarters as well, including my Mary Kay Cosmetics "sisterhood." I'd been introduced to the new skincare company in 1967 while we lived in Dallas. My introduction came in the form of an invitation to a luncheon, where I tried the products and found I liked them. After a few months I was really impressed, because they cleared my blemish-prone skin (which was something my treatments at the dermatologist's office had been unable to do). Then I heard about the business side of the company, and it sounded like a dream—women were having fun, working flexible hours around their family, and making four times what I made as a teacher. Plus, I could promote myself by developing loyal customers and building my own sales unit of at least thirty women. These things were important to me, because I could see "the handwriting on the wall" at that point in my marriage. Knowing that someday I would need to make enough money to support my daughters and myself, I joined Mary Kay.

In 1969, we moved to East Lansing. At that time, there were no Mary Kay sales directors in Michigan, Illinois, Ohio, or Indiana. A couple of years later, I became the first director for Michigan and the surrounding area. As the area's only director, my sales/meeting room was packed with consultants every Monday morning. That first Monday following New Year's was a holiday, so nothing was scheduled. Resuming these functions presented a challenge, because Mary Kay stressed "no negativity at any Mary Kay event." The meetings were designed to provide ongoing training and to celebrate and reward the achievements of those who had advanced their businesses. They also aimed to encourage those who had not been as successful. We joked, "If you fall flat on your face, we will tell you how prettily you fell." The emphasis was upon applauding all the women to success instead of criticizing them. Mary Kay was fond of saying, "No one is ever criticized to success." In such a positive environment, women felt safe and camaraderie developed that allowed many of them to succeed beyond their wildest dreams.

Before the second Monday in January, my situation was common knowledge. Obviously my circumstances were not conducive to an entirely positive meeting. The facts were like an elephant in the room—too big to be ignored. What was I to do? I could have canceled the meeting that second week and everyone would have understood. However, if I canceled the second week, what would I do the third? Instead, I went as usual. I did change the opening though. My first words were, "All of you know what happened on New Year's Eve, and I know that you care. However, we are trained in Mary Kay to keep everything positive. That applies to me, as well. So please, don't talk to me about it before or during the meeting, or even in the parking lot afterward. You can call me at home, or come by the house, but at the meetings let's keep it positive. As long as we are talking about business, I'll have something else to think about for a change. This will allow me a brief break."

The consultants were very supportive and my wishes were respected. I remained committed to helping my associates build their businesses. In spite of the circumstances, my consultants told me that my meetings continued to be excellent. My heart, however, was not in anything outside the investigation. I felt so numb that I would not have cared if I made the largest sale in the history of the company. However, because I did care about the women who attended my meetings, I could carry on and continue to rejoice over their successes. This allowed me to focus on something besides my own pain. Planning the meetings and conducting them weekly gave me a little oasis of refreshment, a time when I didn't need to struggle so hard to control my thoughts.

That diversion ended when I left the parking lot each Monday morning. As I drove away from the meetings, my immediate thought was, *Is there any news awaiting me at home?* There was a stack of posters at all times in the passenger seat beside me. These posters reminded me of the "Ten Most Wanted" posters of criminals displayed in the post office. Only my posters had the word "Missing" and pictures of my daughter on them. After the meetings I went to see if I could place a few of these in additional stores around town. (This was before missing children's pictures were widely circulated.) The pictures I had given the officers had been turned into 8 ×11 flyers. These contained Martha's description, finger-prints, and two pictures of her, one with glasses and one without. She had left her only pair of contacts at home, so Martha would be wearing her glasses unless they had been broken. The posters had gone to every law-enforcement agency across the country. All of the police on the street locally were very familiar with the case.

I took a stack of the flyers with me everywhere. At my request, storeowners were gracious about accepting and prominently posting the flyers. I remember taking one into the East Lansing Post Office, where I went frequently to mail packages to my Mary Kay customers. Since everyone here had become my friend, all I had to do was ask. Without hesitation, the flyer was placed in the middle of the wall at the entrance, where it was visible even from the sidewalk. It was a sad reminder. Every time I approached the post office for almost three years I looked at Martha's picture. I was surprised and grateful that the picture remained as the months turned into a year, then a second, and a third. The community did not forget. Their kindness did not stop.

The chief investigators believed all possible theories needed to be explored. Even from very early on in the investigation, they considered the likelihood that Martha was a runaway very remote. Nevertheless, they needed to examine the possibility exhaustively. There were only a couple of scenarios in which I could see Martha running away from home. One was if someone had terrified her and she feared for her life trying to get home. The second possibility was that she feared something terrible would happen to her family if she came home. The only other thing I could see that could keep her from coming home was some sort of physical injury, or perhaps amnesia. Dean Tucker speculated that, if she were in hiding, she might feel it was safe to attend her college classes once the new semester began. In exploring the runaway theory, he sent an officer to attend the classes for which she had registered, hoping she would appear. When that failed, a detective contacted each of her professors from her fall classes looking for students who might be able to give them some helpful information. They looked for students who had worked with Martha on a class project. All of her professors were willing to help.

Teachers from Martha's high school days were contacted. In talks with them, a picture emerged of a teen who thoroughly enjoyed learning, was a good student, and liked to help around the classroom after school. She had been a teacher's aid in some of her classes. Martha enjoyed all of her teachers and was well liked by them in return. She participated with great enthusiasm in the chorus of the musical comedies that the drama teacher produced each spring. Martha was resourceful. For the youth choir at church, she had needed a special long dress made to a pattern that had been selected for all choir members. I did not sew, but at her request I bought the pattern and the material. Still, I was not sure how we would get it made. Martha had never made a dress before, but she took the material and cut it out according to the pattern. Then she proceeded to sew her dress on the tiny machine her grandmother had given her as a girl for making doll clothes. It turned out so well I was amazed…It was her first sewing project after her "stretch and sew" class. The finished dress looked beautiful on her. The burgundy-colored velvet was lovely with her blue eyes and long blond hair.

Because she enjoyed volleyball, Martha worked hard to prepare for the tryouts. When she did not qualify for the team, she was disappointed, but she enthusiastically accepted the position of team scorekeeper. She was as dedicated to that job as she would have been as a team member. Throughout the investigation, the authorities discovered what I already knew. She was a young woman of integrity and high principles. Her friends reported her to be genuine, caring, loyal, fun loving, and generous.

Her professors and friends were contacted in Georgetown, Texas. They also tried to help. I remembered that Martha had baby-sat for her minister and his wife. She had also gone to him for counseling, so they knew her well. I gave the police the minister's name. They traced him to a church in Arlington, Texas, where he'd moved after his term of service in Georgetown. The minister let us know that he never would have discussed the contents of his conversations with Martha except under the present circumstances. He was eager to cooperate, hoping some of the information he provided could help us find Martha alive. He told the police about the threatening letter Martha had received, which promised that her family would suffer horribly if she did not marry Don. He also related that Martha had talked to him about Don pressuring her for sex. He stated that Martha strongly rejected the idea and consequently felt threatened.

◆   ◆   ◆

Under the media spotlight in the late 1970s, we were treated very differently than victims in the decades since. The mindset in more recent times seems to take great pains to find flaws in the victims' character, so that they can somehow be blamed. The investigators and media personnel in the latter part of the 1970s did not see that as their purpose. The investigators on Martha's case came to respect and admire her as a young woman of great integrity. Martha had given her life to Jesus Christ and tried very hard to live her life in obedience to Him. Consequently, no dirty little secrets were unearthed about Martha.

The profile of Martha that had emerged inspired all of the officers who worked the case; they worked with genuine affection and caring even though none had ever met her. I was told that young policemen who had recently graduated from East Lansing High felt a bond with Martha, as though she were a younger sister. Many conducted searches and checked out ideas and hunches on their own time. Dean Tucker had a son and a daughter at home. His daughter was just two years younger than Kay. Both he and his wife, Pat, identified strongly with us and became our friends. Dean Tucker treated Kay the way he would have wanted his own daughter treated. When Kay called his office and wanted to talk to him, he would work her into his schedule.

As the days turned into weeks, I began to focus on the date of February 13. If Martha were in hiding somewhere, she would not have wanted to miss being with us on that date, Kay's birthday. In the beginning, I didn't feel I could stand to have her missing for six whole weeks. However, as the date approached, I found some hope in waiting for Kay's birthday. The big day arrived, and we heard nothing new. As this important milestone came to an end, it became harder to maintain hope.

The Lansing area community continued to express their caring and concern for us, and the support I received from my business associates extended all the way to the top, to Mary Kay Ash herself. Following my daughter's birthday, it was time for the annual leadership conference for Mary Kay directors, held in Chicago. After arranging for Kay to stay with Judy and Bob, our neighbors, I headed for the weekend conference. Since I had joined the company in Dallas when it was less than four years old, I had gotten to know Mary Kay personally and she had become my friend. After learning of Martha's disappearance, she stayed in regular contact with us. The second morning of the conference during the general assembly, one of Mary Kay's assistants came searching for me in the audience. She asked me to step outside the ballroom because Mary Kay wanted to talk to me. When I did, I found Mary Kay sitting on a sofa waiting for me. After greeting me, she asked me to sit down beside her, saying she had something important to tell me. I could only think that there had been some news about Martha. She hurried to assure me that it was not about Martha but that it was bad news. She had received a call from Lansing for me regarding the murder/suicide of one of my consultants, the consultant's husband, and their only son. When the message came through, Mary Kay would not allow anyone else to tell me. She was afraid this news would be too much for me to handle, so she wanted to be with me when I received it. She intended to stay with me throughout the morning to make sure that I was all right, and that is what she did. She sat with her arm around me, alternately talking and listening to me and sharing how she had gotten through some of her own hard times. She encouraged me to do what I was doing. "Go on working," she said. "It will help to get you through this bad time." Her concern did not end with the conference visit. Her caring letters and phone calls over the next three years were a source of comfort. I remember one particular message she left on my answering machine. She said she was thinking about me and hadn't heard from me in a while. She was concerned about how I was doing and asked me to call. When my business volume reached a low point one month, she did not tell me to work harder; she told me to take care of myself first and that my business would be all right.

Just as the investigators put Martha's life under a microscope, they did the same to Don Miller's. They talked to his high school teachers and to his college professors. They asked for a list of students from the classes that he had attended. When one of his professors refused, I thought, *How can a professor do that in good conscience when it could help save someone's life?* This was one of the few times the police were denied help. One other group was not cooperative with the police. Don had taken Martha several times to a local campus Bible study where he was a member. They talked to the staff person and a few members of the group. This group maintained that Don could not possibly have had anything to do with Martha's disappearance.

The police had kept watch on Don's movements since the first day. I was aware that they knew every time his car left his home and who was driving it, Don or his father. All the police on the street were alert to that vehicle and aware of the case. They followed Don's movements, and they became boringly predictable. All Don ever did was go to school, come home, and go to church. He never seemed to go anyplace else. In order to create a distance between himself and the police, Don's father made good on his threat and hired a lawyer. This made it impossible to do a real surveillance. I was told that Don's lawyer thought Don was being watched. The police, therefore, had to be careful not to follow him too closely, since Don could sue them for invasion of privacy. This somehow seemed crazy to me, like a cruel game. The police were expected to turn their backs and wait for him to do something else, and then turn around quickly enough to catch him in the act! It occurred to me that one of the ironic things about this case was that Don was a criminal justice major. He could use the system to his advantage. He knew the authorities were watching him, but he also knew they could not go on doing so indefinitely. He was, therefore, smart enough to do only routine things in the beginning. It was reasonable to me that he would be likely to establish a seemingly harmless pattern, knowing they would eventually simply go away and he would be free to do as he pleased.

When I first read in the newspaper that the Millers had hired a lawyer, I was astonished. I had not believed they would really do that. The article was particularly distressing because it stated that the lawyer was hired on the recommendation of the minister of his church. This was our church also! I could not believe our minister would do such a thing. He probably knew this would get a reaction from me, and before I could call him, he called me. He told me that he did not tell them they ought to hire a lawyer. Rather, the Millers came to him and wanted his help in finding a lawyer. He said all that he had done was to give them three names, after which they chose one. I let the minister know I considered that a lame excuse. He had to know that a lawyer would help shut down the lines of communication.

Open communication was our only hope of finding out the truth. Why in the world would he help close that down? Instead, why couldn't he challenge Don to do the honorable thing, the courageous thing, and the Godly thing—tell the truth! Whatever had taken place, whatever Don had done, he could do the right thing from that point on, namely, keep on talking to the police until Martha was found, or be truthful and admit what had happened.

Another theory to be investigated was that Martha had been kidnapped, as Don was eager to have us believe. That did not make a lot of sense either, because we certainly were not wealthy. As the days passed, there was no ransom note. Local hospitals and the morgue had been checked immediately. This was now expanded to "Jane Does" anywhere in the USA. A "Jane Doe" turned up in Chicago. Jo Nell Bailey, a lifelong friend who lived there, checked it out and found that the woman bore no resemblance to Martha.

Next, the police received a tip from a friend of Don's grandmother, who professed to be a fortuneteller. She said the police would find Martha in a small town about eighty miles from Lansing by a distinctive ice formation. I had no faith in fortunetellers and wanted no part of it. The police, however, were willing to act on it, particularly since the clue was linked to the Miller family. They reasoned that Don himself might have been providing a clue through this woman so that the information could not be connected to him.

I also received a strange tip, this time by phone, from a man I did not know. He instructed me (and gave me directions) to meet him, by myself, at a cabin up north, and he would give me information on how to locate my daughter. Immediately I turned this over to the authorities. Desperate though I was, I wasn't about to bite on that! I figured if I did meet a stranger in a cabin somewhere in the wilderness, I was sure to become the next missing person.

The detectives had discovered that Don had once taken Martha to a meeting of a religious organization called The Way. The police believed this group was a cult. Was it possible that Don had taken Martha there on the night she had vanished? Could she have joined this cult? The reward offer had brought disappointingly few leads. None seemed substantive, but the police were willing to check out everything.

Because we still had nothing a month into our search, Sgt. Tucker decided to take a detailed look at cults. It was suggested that I attend a meeting of parents of those belonging to The Way, which was scheduled to take place in March. These parents had come together because of the common experience of having a child alienated from their families as a result of joining the cult. As a parent, my presence at a meeting would not draw attention, although police presence would. *March*, I thought, *that is an eternity away from January.* I let the sergeant know that I could not wait that long. He gave me a way to contact one of the mothers by phone.

This mother's opinion of The Way was that though it appeared rather innocuous from the outside, its inner working were quite insidious. She claimed they turned young people against their parents. Her son had been a religion major at Michigan State when he had gotten into The Way. After this, his character underwent a negative transformation. He went from being a loving son to a violent young man. When he finally came home for a visit at Christmas, he threw their television set through the window and the police had to be called to get him to calm down. The more I found out about cults, the more I realized this did not at all sound like something in which Martha would become involved. Martha had carefully thought out her faith and accepted it on her own. Her faith taught her to honor her parents, and she felt pained when separated from her family. She had given up a lot to transfer from Southwestern to Michigan State in order to be with her family. I couldn't imagine that she would have fallen for the idea that her mother was the enemy. Somehow I never could believe that a cult was even an option for Martha.

Dean Tucker pointed out that Martha could have become an involuntary part of a sect through Don. Could Don have gotten them to hold Martha against her will? The police continued with their own undercover investigation until they became convinced that she was not there.

The Millers' hiring of a lawyer immediately became a major roadblock in the search for the truth. One of the authorities, who had conducted a search of Martha's room, was a state psychologist who had told me several important things in confidence. What concerned me the most was his assertion that the pressure had to be kept on Don in order to get him to talk. "The more time that passes from the date of the crime," the psychologist said, "the harder it will be to crack his story." This added to my panic. How could the pressure be kept on when the police couldn't even question him anymore? Sgt. Tucker and Detective Westgate were also concerned; they believed that if they'd had more time with Don at the beginning, they could have gotten more information. During my visits to the police station, the three of us brainstormed all sorts of unusual ideas. We talked about getting a policewoman to dress in Martha's clothing and walk where Don could see her. We even talked about creating a tape of Martha's voice by editing a tape she had made for her grandmother and playing it when Don answered the telephone. Maybe it would startle him into letting something slip.

Although Don would not talk to the police, he was still willing to talk to me, so I decided to invite him over to the house to talk to me alone. He agreed to come. I did not check the idea out with the police, because I was afraid they might try to talk me out it. I prepared my questions and the appeal I would make. It didn't seem wise for me to be in the house by myself, because I needed someone to be a witness to what he said. Also, there was the possibility that if I were alone I might not live to be a witness. So I asked a friend to help. I asked her to arrive at my home a couple of hours early and park her car a couple of streets over from the house. Before it was time for Don to arrive, she took her position just around the corner, out of sight at the top of the stairs. From there, hopefully, she could hear what was going on. My hopes were considerably dampened when I saw Don's younger sister accompanying him. I knew she was a champion of her brother. Just as I suspected, she started defending him the moment she entered the house. The sister answered the appeal I had prepared and Don remained silent. Soon, they left. In reporting my actions, and lack of results, to Tucker and

Westgate, we shared our increasing frustration. Somehow Don needed to be persuaded to cooperate.

In negotiations with Don's attorney, Dean Tucker succeeded in arranging one more session to question Don. The conditions under which the lawyer would allow this were as follows: all questions had to be submitted to him in writing, and Don would answer in the presence of his lawyer. Never in the fifteen years as a detective had Dean conducted an interrogation in such a manner. Since this was the only condition under which he would be permitted access to Don, he agreed. The results produced more false answers and more lies. The police were just as frustrated as I was.

As those cold winter days turned into weeks and months, the police and I spent countless hours going over what we knew, looking for new avenues to explore. Dean and Rick began to talk about feeling sure a break would come in the spring, when the snow melted.

The case was constantly on Dean's mind, even in his sleep. Around the middle of March, he had a hunch to search the Sleepy Hollow State Park area in the county north of us. I was not told that another helicopter search was taking place until after it was completed. The helicopter flew into the Sleepy Hollow area, and in a matter of minutes a body was discovered! From the air that heart-stopping first sight looked as if it could be Martha, for the body appeared to be that of a blond woman. As they approached on the ground, they saw that the body was black. Dean thought, *Is this the result of three months of extreme winter weather conditions on a body? Did the weather cause deterioration in Martha's body, which would turn the body black?* He continued to entertain the possibility that it could be Martha, until closer examination revealed that the blond hair was a wig that covered black hair. It was not Martha Sue. There was no identification on the body. Until the body could be identified, there was no way to notify the next of kin.

Because there was no identification, another idea took shape: perhaps there was a way to use the information they had just obtained to our advantage in the search for Martha or to find the killer of this newly discovered body. The plan was to release to the press only the initial finding: "Police find unidentified woman's body." The timing of the news release was typical of Sgt. Tucker's kindness to Kay and me. Sgt. Tucker didn't want me to be upset by hearing the news for the first time on radio or TV, so before pursuing this plan, I was told that a body had been discovered, but it was not Martha's. After the release, they planned to stake out the area and monitor the movements of Donald Miller for twelve hours. If he returned to the area where he had left Martha's body, the case would be solved. It did not turn out the way the police had planned, however. This was the one time I was unhappy with the press. They found the location and preceded to broadcast all of the information, which told Don they had not located Martha's body. I don't know why they did it. Perhaps the importance of secrecy during the first twelve hours was not conveyed adequately to the media.

Weeks later, as the snow slowly receded, I received another call from Sgt. Tucker. A blouse had been discovered in a field. The blouse that Martha had worn was the one article of clothing I could not describe. This is because when she had given me that final kiss before leaving, she had already zipped her ski jacket shut. Could this blouse be Martha's? Only I could answer that, so would I go with them to look at the blouse in the field? "If it is Martha Sue's," I was told, "it is important that it not be disturbed so that no clue will be spoiled." We went by the state police post to take another officer with us, since the field was out of the jurisdiction of the East Lansing Police.

The mood while driving there was somber, and there was little conversation. Each of us seemed lost in our own world, anticipating what we might find. "Oh, dear Lord," I prayed, "how many women's bodies are going to be discovered in my lifetime?" As we approached the blouse, it looked very similar to one Martha owned, but as I looked closely, I could see there were differences. Once I had stated, "No, it's not Martha's" we did not linger. To be absolutely sure, I checked once I got home, and I found the blouse that belonged to Martha. I was relieved that the blouse was not Martha's. While it would have been good to find a real clue, finding a piece of her clothing would likely mean she had been killed. I was feeling ambivalent at this point. Mostly I was sad, so sad. I couldn't shake the darkness.

During the frigid days of winter, when ideas and clues were in short supply, Sgt. Tucker looked ahead and planned for spring. We had no choice but to wait until all the snow had melted and people started doing outdoor activities again. At that time, he would enlist the aid of the media to make an appeal for help. In the spring, he had a great deal of confidence that we would find the break we needed. When the time came, a TV, radio, and newspaper appeal was made asking every person to go out over the weekend and look in areas that had not been visited during the winter months. In addition to inspecting their own property, people were asked to look inside all small structures, such as tool sheds, adjacent fields, and parks in the entire Lansing metro area. I was not as optimistic about the outcome of such an endeavor as the police were. It was a good concept, but I could not envision many people actually conducting a search. This doubt was probably the result of my personal aversion to going out to look for my daughter's dead body.

I kept my doubts to myself, because I wanted to believe it would be done. I wish I had entered into a dialogue with the detectives on that subject. I blame myself for not opening up the question. If I had voiced my concern that I could not visualize most citizens talking to their children about going out to look for a young woman's body, maybe we would have had a different outcome.

In the years that followed, I had considerable experience organizing events for the sales and marketing executives of Lansing, fundraisers for the American Cancer Society, and meetings of my own Mary Kay sales unit. I have found that it takes considerably more to get people involved than a few brief appeals carried by the news media. Consequently, I would now suggest getting various groups or prominent people to "buy in" to the idea and agree to sponsor such an effort under the supervision of the police. I would take a map of the region and divide it into sections and assign responsibility for each section, including parks and vacant lands, to the various participating groups. Farmers would naturally cover their land when planting spring crops. If we had been able to implement such a plan, perhaps we could have found her. I don't know if any local residents actually searched in their areas, but the appeal yielded no results. All of us were discouraged. Don would no longer talk to anyone, including me.

Spring also brought a significant date, April 27, Martha's birthday. I was at home around midday when a florist truck pulled into our driveway. *Who is sending us flowers?* I wondered. *How beautiful*, I thought as I looked at the long-stem red roses nestled inside the box. My name was on the envelope, so I quickly opened it. My eagerness changed to disbelief, and I shuddered. They were from Don. He had written on the enclosed card,

Martha was a rose

The flowers no longer had beauty for me. That message told me he knew she was dead. All of my instincts told me, as they had from the beginning of this nightmare, that he was responsible. And now he was sending me flowers. How cruel! I considered throwing them in the trash. On Martha's birthday, was he getting satisfaction out of causing me as much pain as possible? There I was, being reminded of that prediction again, that our family would suffer terribly. Did he enjoy seeing how much he could torture us? I had to get rid of those flowers, but I thought, *Someone can enjoy these as long as they don't know how I had obtained them.* I removed the card and took them to a neighbor. The timing turned out to be good for her, because she was a recent graduate of nursing school.

I next experienced the kindness of the community in the person of a retired gentleman. This man had trained tracking dogs for the police department. He told me that he had suspicions about a wooded area with which he was well acquainted. Because he could not get the picture of the area out of his mind and sensed that this area was connected to Martha, he had a strong desire to conduct a search with his dog. In order to act on his hunch, he came to me to get an article of Martha's clothing in order to give his dog her scent. What a generous act that was. For some reason, he wanted someone to stay with his truck while he and his dog searched. This meant that I would need to accompany him. Kay was eager to go on the search. I, however, felt a great sense of dread about it, for I knew we would be looking for a body, not a living person. While I was very grateful that he was willing to help, I had no desire to participate in a ground search. I kept these feelings to myself, however, and accepted his offer. If he was willing to invest his time on the search, the least I could do was accompany him. After the three of us performed the initial search, he continued with his dog by himself. From time to time, he would stop by the house after the search to stay in touch. He tracked diligently until he had covered the entire area, but he never found anything.

Just before Mother's Day, I received another visit from the florist. A lovely azalea was brought to the door. Thinking that it must be from Kay, I opened the card. It too was from Don! This time I just started screaming as I ran outside. At that moment, my friend Mary was turning into the driveway. Because I was obviously upset, Mary rolled down the car window as she drove to meet me. I thrust the plant through the open window as I cried, "Mary, do something with this!" As I explained why I was so upset over receiving a lovely flowering plant, Mary said, "Have you told the police?" When I said that I had not, she said, "Call them."

When I had appealed to Don to keep communicating, flowers were definitely not what I'd had in mind. I called Sgt. Tucker, as Mary had suggested. He told me that he would have a talk with Don's lawyer and tell Don to stop sending me things.

The investigation seemed to be at an impasse, but I knew there was one more group of people to whom Don still talked. These were people at my church, whom I saw Don mingling with every Sunday. In the Bible, the eighteenth chapter of Matthew describes a pattern for handling trouble between two people. The first step, listed in verses 15 to17, is to approach the person one on one. When this fails, take one or two others with you to talk to the other person. If he fails to listen, bring it before the church. Using these verses as my guide, I felt confident I would receive their support.

5

Support and Betrayal

Immediately following the disappearance, the church to which I belonged did a very lovely thing for our family. Without our knowledge, the minister and the members of our church's official board raised $1,200 for us at their regular monthly board meeting. When they brought the money out to us, I was completely surprised and deeply touched by this tangible expression of their love. I must confess, however, I was a bit bewildered by their gift at the time, as money was the thing furthest from my mind. At that moment, I could not think of a single thing that money could help us do in the investigation. Was I ever wrong about that! I had no clue that searching for a missing child would require money, and lots of it. My friends foresaw things I could not even imagine. This gift was one more reason for me to believe this was a group of people on whom I could really depend.

Even more important to me than the money were the special daily prayer services that were held specifically for Martha in the church chapel. Prayer is what held me together. At a time when I had difficulty praying, others were doing it for me. I deeply appreciated that.

In talking to the senior minister late that spring, I found out that Don had started coming by the church to talk to him. He told me that Don had expressed an interest in talking to me in the pastor's office and asked if I would be interested in talking to him. Since my access to him was now limited, I took this as a very hopeful sign. Perhaps Don was ready to tell me what had happened.

"Oh yes! Of course I would!" I responded. A few days later, I received a call in which I was informed that Don was at the church without his father's knowledge.

"Would you be able to come down right away to talk with him?" they asked.

"I will come immediately," I answered. When I put down the phone I grabbed my coat and my purse and drove as quickly as possible to the church.

What a break! I mused. *This is my chance.* My plan to talk to him alone when I had invited him to the house had failed because his sister had come with him and done all the talking. I had been unable to talk privately with Don for more than a couple of minutes at a time since Martha's disappearance. In preparation for this meeting, I made a mental note of the things I would ask and the appeal I would make to him. When I arrived, I went directly to the pastor's office. After saying hello, the minister seated himself behind his desk and Don and I sat side by side in chairs in front of the desk. My approach was to steer clear of any serious accusations and try to use reason and persuasion. I recall asking Don questions like,

"Did some stranger attack you and Martha?"

"Was there an accident in which Martha was hurt or killed?"

"Did you two get into an argument, and did you leave her somewhere afterwards?"

I didn't want him to feel I was accusing him of anything. I wanted to make it possible for him to tell us what had happened without incriminating himself. I made the statement that "a tragic accident is not murder." He maintained an unemotional expression as he kept denying every possibility I brought up. Then he again retold his bizarre story of Martha sitting down in the snow on our front porch. The authorities had already challenged this story and pointed out some of his lies. Since this approach had accomplished nothing, I didn't bother to point out any discrepancies. I could see that I wasn't learning anything new, so I tried to persuade him to cooperate in the investigation by talking to the police.

"My father will not allow it," he explained.

I directly accused him of being a grown man hiding behind his father. "Don, you are twenty-two years old! You are an adult, not a child. You claim to love Martha—you even asked her to marry you. You have a right to stand up for the woman you love and help the police find her. When you love someone, you try to help that person! Whatever has happened, do the right thing from this time forward," I pleaded. Don ignored my plea. Instead, he quoted the biblical admonition honor thy father.

Until this moment, the pastor had been a silent observer most of the time. Now, he broke into the conversation. "This would be honoring your father, Don. To tell the truth, and to live by your upbringing would honor the way he raised you. He brought you up in the church. This is the honorable thing to do."

I echoed the sentiment, asking him to do the right thing, the Godly thing. "All I am asking is that you keep talking to the police. No one has done anything mean to you. No one has hit you. You have not been abused in any way. What is so bad about just talking to the police?" I wanted to know.

"They didn't believe me," he complained.

After telling a story so hard to believe, don't you think that's to be expected? I thought.

By the end of the discussion, I hoped we had persuaded him to do the right thing. Instead, it seems he ran home and told "daddy" that he had talked to the minister and to me. The next news I heard was that henceforth, Don could no longer talk to the minister or anyone else without the presence of his lawyer or his father. This caused me to speculate further just how involved the father was. Gene Miller must have known something; otherwise, why was he so afraid to let Don talk?

I began to hear reports that Gene was saying things to indicate that I was the problem and that I was not rational but overly emotional. He made the mistake of saying this to one of my friends one day. My friend responded, "To the contrary, Sue is one of the most rational people I know."

Not long after the encounter in the pastor's office, I read a blurb in the church's newsletter that sent me into orbit. It stated that "one of our fine youths" was teaching Bible at a church youth camp for the summer. I was aghast when the article identified the "fine youth" as Donald Miller. How was this possible after the conference in the minister's office? I felt like I had entered a never-never land, the world of Alice in Wonderland, where down is up and up is down. Initially I was stunned, but not for long. Those words propelled me into action.

I was taught from childhood to have respect for those in authority. Ministers were definitely among those entitled to respect. Never had I challenged authority. That lifelong pattern changed instantly. I called the church and made an appointment to see the minister. The timid shy person in me vanished. This was too big and too important a situation to be concerned about what someone might think of me. Once in the pastor's office, I wasted little time in getting to the point of my visit. This time I was not concerned with tact. In fact, my words were about as genteel as a buzz saw!

I showed him the article in the church paper. "What does it take to be a fine youth from this church?" I questioned. "Is Don Miller a fine youth? Does someone who abandons the woman he claimed to love constitute a 'fine youth'?" My questions elicited no answers, so I continued, "How did Don get that job? Were you contacted by the minister in charge of the camp for a recommendation?" When he admitted that he had been contacted, I asked, "Well, did you recommend him?"

"No, I did not recommend him, but I didn't not recommend him," was his reply.

I can't believe I am hearing this. What kind of an answer is that? I thought, but I continued to pursue the issue. "Well, did you tell him what is going on down here, that Don is wanted for questioning about a missing young woman?"

"No, I didn't want to engage in gossip," the minister said.

I exploded. "Gossip? Dear God, I wish it were mere gossip that my daughter is missing! At the very least, Don is guilty of abandoning a young woman he claimed to love and refusing to help us find her. What kind of love is that? You have a daughter, Lana.* She was Martha's friend. Would you feel comfortable having Lana go out alone with Don, knowing what you know?" When he admitted that he would not, I asked "Well, don't you think at the very least parents should expect their children to be physically safe in the presence of their Bible teacher?" Dr. Hardy* sat there without answering, so I continued, "You would not let your own daughter go out with him. Don't you think other mothers and fathers should be made aware of the situation so they can make that decision?" Again, there was no answer. "What on earth are you going to do if some child up there is reported missing?"

It blew me away when he said quietly, "You know, I never thought about that." Finally, I seemed to be getting through to him. This was important. Other lives could be at stake! I must have talked to him for an hour and a half, trying to convince him to pick up the phone and talk to the man in charge of the camp. However, I couldn't sway him. How I wished I could confide in him some of the details that only the police and I knew. If only I could tell him about the blood, the prediction of the psychologist, the areas where the police had caught Don lying. I so desperately wanted him to understand that this was a dangerous situation. If only I could do that, surely he would see how urgent my request was. I knew, however, that I would never betray the trust the police had placed in me. So, the only thing I could tell him was that the reason I was so concerned was that I had received disturbing information from the police about Don, which I could share with no one.

This did not meet with any positive response, for he stated that he would need to hear some kind of proof. "I just can't take your word for that," he explained.

This man had known my family for over four years. He and his wife had been in my home for dinner. Kay had baked lemon pies for him after finding out that was his favorite dessert. For several years, his wife had been involved in the same small Bible study with me where the women shared their most personal thoughts. I had a reputation for integrity, and he had never had a problem believing me in the past. Even people that were total strangers trusted me enough within two days of meeting me to share sensitive information with me—and here, my pastor, couldn't trust my word!

I never succeeded in getting him to make that call. Finally, I gave up and drove directly to the police station to see Sgt. Tucker. After explaining what had happened, I asked permission to share some details about Don. The sergeant just shook his head and said softly, "Sue, you can't do that. There is nothing you could tell him that would make any difference. He doesn't believe you because he doesn't want to believe. All the facts in the world are not going to change that man's mind."

Slowly the truth of that statement sank in. As I talked to the sergeant, I couldn't help but see the contrast between two authority figures in my life: the minister and my father. Daddy was a school superintendent. He had held a position of leadership where the welfare of children was at stake. I had to admit that Sgt. Tucker was right when I thought of the way my father would have handled the situation. I told Dean, "You know, as superintendent of schools in my hometown, my father was also responsible for influencing the lives of children. He applied a very different standard when it came to their welfare. In order to get a job as a teacher, you had to have a reputation beyond reproach. A prospective teacher would never even be considered if the police wanted him or her for questioning regarding a missing person. His reasoning was that any teacher helps to mold the lives of children. Surely, someone who teaches the Bible should be held to at least as high a standard. How is it going to look if someday the children and their parents find out that their Bible teacher, Donald Miller, committed murder?" Dean Tucker agreed that this was not only a very real possibility, but actually a probability.

The investigative work reporters had done on the Watergate scandal triggered my next idea. What if I could get a local reporter to dig around? I had developed a rapport with several people in the media. Those who interviewed me often asked if there was any way they could help. I had always thanked them, but I could not think of anything they could do. Now I thought differently. I contacted a reporter named Jean whom I knew from *The Lansing State Journal* and suggested that she do some investigative reporting. She was very open to my idea. I gave her all the information I could, and she began to make a list of different people she wanted to contact. The minister's name was on the list.

Not long after Jean started contacting those on her list, I received an irate call from Dr. Hardy, because "there was a reporter down at the church asking questions."

"Yes," I replied, "she is helping me."

"Well, she has a lot of nerve. Who is she to come in here and ask me questions?"

I wanted to say to him, "Lately, the only concern you have expressed for me is over my anger. It sounds like you are pretty angry yourself right now. Yes, I am angry that my daughter is missing. But what does it take to make you angry? A reporter coming in to ask questions? Your job is not in jeopardy. Your family is not in danger. You go home every night, and your daughter is there waiting for you. Yet now you are angry. Don't you think I have a better reason to be angry?"

Jean gave up shortly afterward having failed to make any progress. I got pretty discouraged, too. Every idea seemed to amount to zero.

I could see the case closing down. We were running out of theories. We were beginning to cover the same territory for a second time, and even a third. My desperation mounted because of the terrible secret I carried from the first few weeks of the investigation. A state forensic psychologist had come to see if any clues had been overlooked. While he was there, he told me three things that sent me reeling. First, Donald Miller fit the classic profile of a serial killer. Second, pressure had to be sustained in order to get him to talk; the more time that passed since the event, the less chance we'd have of finding anything. Third, serial killers evolve, so if Miller wasn't stopped, he would become even worse. (*How could he become any worse?* I wondered.) This horrid secret knowledge and the responsibility it brought drove me even harder. Each time we reached a stalemate, those words kept ringing in my ear. I became even more frantic. I had to take action. Don had to be stopped. We had to keep the pressure on him to talk, but how? As I pondered the situation, I thought about enlisting the aid of my fellow church members for the first time. Reflecting on the issue of who still had access to Don, I realized that two groups remained. The campus Bible study that Don attended (which had been involved in the spring search) was one. I could quickly write this group off however, since none of them knew me; plus, they were convinced that Don can do no wrong. These people would be of no help.

The other group was our church. I still saw Don talking to various people every Sunday. These people not only knew Kay and me, but they had known Martha. She had been very active in the youth group and had sung in the choir. If the principles outlined in Matthew proved correct, if each church member appealed to him to work with the police, maybe he would find the courage to go against his father. By requesting that church members apply these principles, I was merely adhering to the Biblical pattern for handling disputes among Christians. I had already followed the first instruction, to get together to talk privately, when I invited Don to my house. Since he would not listen to me alone, I took the second step, asking the minister to meet with us. Only the third step remained, taking the matter before the church elders. I would ask for their help. I wrote a letter to the church board seeking their assistance. Since I had a very positive expectation, I was not prepared at all for their reaction.

My faith had been a central part of my life since my childhood. I always loved the church as Christ's instrument on earth. I felt the church was my family. During the years when churches of all denominations have been subjected to ridicule, I have felt deep pain. To this day, I love the body of believers that comprise the church. For this reason, I found it difficult to write this chapter. The only reason I have is so that others may learn from it and find a better way.

There had been such an outpouring of support from the community, and even from people I did not know, that I could not believe it when my church peers, with whom I felt such a close bond, withheld their support. The church board turned down my request. My request was a simple one: I wanted each member of the church to encourage Don to cooperate with the police until Martha was found. When they said no, they added that they would continue to pray. In light of their refusal to help, I decided that their offer to pray was an empty one. Why pray if you are not open to God's reply, since you have already decided that you will not do anything?

We continued attending church there, although my relationship with the leaders became strained. One Sunday, Dr. Hardy preached a sermon on courage. As he talked about courage, and in particular the courage of the disciple Peter, I recognized a growing disharmony between his words and his actions. Finally, I could stomach it no more. I stood up in the middle of the sermon and walked out. When I walked through the hallway to the exit, I found my daughter. My friend Mary, from Bible study, was standing there attempting to comfort Kay.

"Hypocrite! Hypocrite!" Kay was crying. She had been seated in another part of the church, so I had not seen her leave. Although Kay does not like to call attention to herself, she had found the sermon so distasteful that she had stood up and left several minutes before I did.

Although I was disappointed with the church leadership, my friends in the Bible study were incredibly kind and reached out to support me on both an emotional and practical level. Regarding my feelings about the leadership, I have to remind myself that it is not up to me to judge anyone. I need to remember my own shortcomings. In their shoes, maybe I would have been afraid to rock the boat, too. It is God's job to judge us all. I am sure they were in denial of the reality that evil was lurking in their midst. I must admit, however, that I found it harder to forgive Dr. Hardy and some of the elders than to forgive Don himself.

In fairness to those leaders, they did not have access to the information I had. I am sure they mistook my passion as the anguish of a grieving mother. They were not convinced that Don was involved in Martha's disappearance, so why would they believe that he posed a threat? It was too horrible for them even to contemplate. It was easier to believe that I had become paranoid. Because of the nature of police work, law-enforcement authorities were in a position to understand the reality of evil much better than this particular church body. The police, and their various investigative units, could more easily understand the threat to the community. Even so, what would the minister and the church leaders think if another young woman disappeared?

6

A Zest for Life—
Martha's Story, from Her Pen
and Mine

Beyond the impersonal headlines there was a real flesh and blood person, with hopes, dreams, and abilities yet to be fulfilled in her nineteen years. Behind the statistics of this missing co-ed, who vanished on New Year's Eve, is the person of Martha Sue Young. So who is this person, and what is she like?

Life began for Martha on April 27, 1957. Her enthusiasm for life was evident even in her birth, as she gave me only four hours warning before she appeared. I almost didn't make it to the hospital that sunny day in Corpus Christi, Texas. Martha Sue Young was a very welcomed baby to her parents, Sue and Le Young.

Martha was an eager child. She seemed ready to plunge into the experiences awaiting her, and at nine months she was already walking. Some time after her first birthday she and I were in the front yard of our home, and Martha started toddling down the drive toward the street. I began to call to her to come back. (We were living in a home whose driveway sloped down toward the street.) On the slope, Martha's little legs began to move faster and faster. When I realized she could not stop, I raced to catch her. I wasn't fast enough, for just as she reached the end of the driveway, she lost her balance and fell. All it took was that one fall and Martha never again had to be told to stay away from the street. Either the experience was powerful enough to remain in her memory during her grade-school years, or she had internalized my repeated warnings by that time. On two occasions, when Martha's class was assigned the task of writing their life stories, she included this incident. Martha had a flair for the dramatic, which is reflected in her writing. In the story she wrote in the seventh grade, she wrote of the incident: "One day I got tired of [my house] and ran down the steep driveway. In spite of my mother's calls, pleas, and commands, I kept on, for I couldn't stop. As I was small, the speed with which I had started increased rapidly, and losing my weak balance, I fell, skinning my hands on the rough street. My mother ran to me, lifted me up, gently scolding me, and took me inside. As long as I live, I will never forget those awful cars whizzing by when I fell!"

A snapshot of Martha's first birthday party shows her exuberantly splashing in her plastic pool. Another vivid memory I have is of an incident that occurred when she was eighteen months old. The two of us were alone in the kitchen. I stepped outside quickly to get something from the attached carport. I did not realize that Martha was immediately behind me until I heard the click of the latch on the kitchen door! I turned to see a gleeful Martha grinning at me through the locked screen door. She looked so pleased with herself as she removed her hand from the lock. Before I could speak, she turned and began to toddle across the kitchen in the opposite direction. She then proceeded to turn around, look at me, and laugh! At this point, I was too busy to appreciate her little joke, as I had to coax her back to unlock the door. After some persuasion, she was equally pleased to unlock the door and let me back inside.

In spite of my resolve to watch Martha more carefully, I one day found her chewing on a roll of what appeared to be green tape. At first this seemed harmless, but I continued to observe her as I resumed work around the kitchen. I was not concerned until I saw the "tape" crumbling. When I grabbed it from her, I was horrified to realize that it was a new strip of deodorant for the top of the garbage can. After a quick call to the doctor's office, the two of us were soon on the way to the hospital emergency room, where Martha had the unpleasant experience of having her stomach pumped.

Martha's next gastronomical adventure was much more pleasant. We had moved to Austin so Le could go back to the University of Texas to work on a master's degree in engineering. One day, my father came to Austin and took us to lunch, to a cafeteria where the booths sat next to mirrored walls. Since Daddy and I both had ice tea, there was a whole sliced lemon on the table. Martha decided she wanted to eat the lemon, so she picked up a piece and bit into it. With the first bite, Martha's face puckered into a grimace. Although shocked, she tried it again. Once again, she contorted her little face, but she didn't cry. This time, she caught a glimpse of her expression in the mirror. Instead of throwing down the lemon, she turned toward the mirrored wall beside her and continued to munch on the lemon. She watched herself intently as her face contorted with each bite. She became totally absorbed in the process until she had eaten the whole lemon! Daddy and I, as well as people seated around us, watched and laughed while Martha paid no attention to anything except the lemon and her face in the mirror.

After Martha's second birthday, we moved to Nashville for nine months so that Le and I could attend Scarritt College. Scarritt was to prepare us for our move to Lahore, Pakistan. We were scheduled to spend five years in Lahore, where Le was assigned to build a hospital for the Methodist Board of Missions. It was while we were in Nashville, just before Martha's third birthday, that her sister, Kathryn Ann, was born. We had such a heavy snowfall that night that we almost didn't make it to the hospital.

In her story for her seventh-grade assignment, Martha wrote, "My sister was born in a blizzard in the middle of February. Well, I didn't know what to think, so I offered my sister a stick of lip balm for her lips and she promptly opened her mouth to eat my present!"

Three months after Kay's birth, we sailed from New York to Karachi, Pakistan. In Pakistan, Martha became more reserved with adults. She no longer ran gleefully to people who were approaching. She stayed "glued" to my side. The Pakistani people loved children, but she was a fair-skinned, blue-eyed blonde, a novelty among the Pakistani. Some had never seen a blue-eyed blonde child and wanted to touch her fair skin or her light hair. Martha was not familiar with their custom of squeezing a child's cheeks in greeting. She didn't recognize the gesture as one of endearment and went through a brief period of shyness. Continuing the seventh-grade story of her life, she wrote, "Adults were terrifying."

When Kay was old enough to walk, we went to the Lahore Zoo. These family trips to see the animals were not very successful. Martha and Kay found themselves surrounded by throngs of people who found it far more entertaining to stare at these two little fair-skinned children than to watch the animals. Martha didn't like that kind of attention, so she tried to get away. However, everywhere the girls went, the crowds kept pace with them. The girls moved again, and the curious followed. Finally, the girls had had enough and wanted to leave.

On the college campus where we lived, the girls felt freer. Here they were a familiar sight and people would talk to them instead of touching or just staring silently. Here the girls made friends. Most of the Pakistani people around us spoke to them in English. Of course, they often heard Urdu spoken, and Martha learned some of that language. For her amusement, she decided to make up her own words; I often heard her throwing nonsense words that no one could understand into her conversations. Kay seemed to think this was great, and the girls would start giggling and laughing at each other. For ten or fifteen minutes at a time they'd enjoy their little private joke with the language.

In writing about living in Lahore, Martha wrote, "I was a very curious child when I was three...With all the children from W. Pakistan and all the families of the doctors from America living around, I soon became a member of the Great Terror's Club. (My mother says I wasn't bad—just curious.) I had my ginger head, nose, or finger into everything that I saw, heard, or felt…At times, Mother was astounded by my actions, and I deserved to be popped one.

"The Dunlaps came when I was five, and Elaine Dunlap and I were best friends. She had three older brothers, who were great at playing with us, and when the Bowes came back from the States with five children, the Ormes with two, and a British couple with five, we had swarms of kids everywhere."

During most of our stay in Pakistan, the Bowes family lived only one house away from ours. Nadine Bowes, the family's oldest child, was Martha's classmate and good friend until we returned to the States. Years later, Nadine sent me a letter to share a couple of memories from those early childhood years. Nadine wrote, "It's funny, the crazy things you remember from your childhood. [Martha] really loved her family and would brag about you when you were not around. I remember as a small child coming over to 'swim' at the little wading pool in your yard. She told me her 'Mama and Daddy' were the handsomest couple in the world, and if Martha said so, I knew it must be so. Besides, she would have dunked my head under the water if I had disagreed. She was very proud of 'Baby Kay.' I always wondered about that, because I found my younger sisters quite a nuisance. 'Baby Kay' was more like her baby than her sister."

Nadine also recalled "running through the hedges behind our house with Martha.

"One time we went through and caught our hair in the brambles. We panicked and struggled to get out. I was crying, and when we got out of the hedge I had scratches all over and my hair was all askew. Martha took one look at me and laughed so hard that she got me going, and it wasn't scary anymore."

During our first year in Pakistan, we had no car. I was, however, able to purchase a bicycle with a child's seat on the back. Martha and I were able to travel around the neighborhood on the bike. When Kay was old enough to sit in her sister's lap, Martha got into her chair first then held out her arms to take Kay onto her lap. Since Martha was physically strong, she was able to hold her sister securely. Kay never slipped from Martha's arms, and we never had a spill.

Martha loved when I read to her. As I did, she began to recognize various words in the books. She liked to play games involving words. My parents sent out textbooks so we could use them when she started school, but Martha didn't wait. Her seventh-grade paper explains, "Since my parents were busy a lot, I started to read at about four or five, so I started to school at five." Before kindergarten opened in the fall of her fifth year, she was reading to me. She had read all of the first-grade books and was eager for more. When school opened, we enrolled her in the kindergarten class. However, after six weeks, she was transferred into first grade. As a former teacher, I was concerned that putting her with students a year older might create a problem for her, but she seemed to have the social maturity to fit in with her classmates, and she loved school.

When Martha started school, Kay amused herself by following behind the workmen who were transporting dirt on the backs of donkeys for the hospital's construction. Kay had discovered that when the donkey's load was deposited at its destination, the men would lift her onto the back of the donkey for a ride back to the area where they would pick up a fresh load. Martha didn't share Kay's fondness for these mangy-looking creatures.

Toys were very limited in Pakistan. When Martha outgrew her tricycle, we were able to buy a small bicycle from a family that was returning to the States. We lived inside the walls of the new hospital compound that Le was building. There were broad areas of pavement here, and few cars were ever let into the gated hospital grounds. Learning to ride a bicycle inside those grounds was therefore very safe. Le helped Martha learn to balance by holding the bike from behind as she pedaled. Le ran behind her until she was darting around on the bike on her own. Martha loved riding. She circled the hospital, with Kay trailing on the tricycle.

"My father was a favorite of all the little children thirteen and under," Martha wrote. "Sometimes he'd get off work and he'd play tag with us. When this happened and word got around, Kay and I had more visitors than ever. My father played a different kind of tag...he was always 'it.' He'd run around the yard, roaring like a lion, and pick up two little kids. Usually, he'd tuck Kay under one arm and the Bowes' youngest under the other and run after me or some other screaming kid...We had a jungle gym, swings, slides, teeter-totters, a rocking boat, and a wading pool that my dad built."

For all of her adventurous spirit, there were a few activities in which Martha would not join. There were, for example, the animal rides at the annual Christmas Party that the American consulate held for all American children. Martha enjoyed the performers who entertained with puppet shows, birds, and other animal acts, and she enjoyed seeing Santa arrive on a camel, but when it came time to go for a ride on the camel and the elephant, she always said no. Never mind that her younger sister climbed right up on the platform and on to the elephant for a ride. She simply said, "No!" each year. On that subject, she never changed her mind. She was perfectly happy to watch her sister ride, but she wanted no part in it. On another occasion, Martha watched Kay from a safe distance when

Kay got down in the middle of the thousands of tiny frogs that hopped on our sidewalks in the fall. Kay tried unsuccessfully to catch all of them. Again, Martha was content to watch, but she never joined that effort either.

Nor did Martha have any love for flying insects. At times, locusts would descend like the biblical plagues. The Pakistanis had learned that if enough people beat on pans and made enough noise, they could prevent the locusts from landing in the area. Martha wrote, "These horrible locusts used to visit us every dry season to feast on our crops." Our small garden of flowers and vegetables could scarcely be considered crops, but that was Martha's word for it. "As I was little, I didn't have to beat pans, but I sure joined in the noise. I screeched and howled and ran about.

"When they came, it seemed like they came all at once, for the sky was black with whirring locusts. All of our cooks, family, men on the job, and neighbors grabbed anything and made as much noise as possible. I thoroughly hated those beasts, for I thought if one got on me I would surely be carried off. I am still quite afraid of them, lest one got on me." Martha might have "thoroughly hated" the locusts, but she loved being part of the action and noise to drive them away. Actually, Martha felt quite safe and secure growing up. I never saw her cry out of fear of anything in her childhood.

Martha attended the American School in Lahore for her first three years of schooling. Her teacher was, however, not an American but British. At that time, Pakistan had less than forty industries in the country. Half of these were cement companies, so there was very little in the way of supplies available. There was an art contest at her school, and Martha won first place. The prize was a box of pastels. These were a real treasure to Martha, much more important to her than her first-place finish.

In April of 1965, when Martha was eight, we sailed back to the States. The girls collected dolls from each country we stopped at along the way. Since few toys had been available to them, they were content to look in awe at all the things in the Hong Kong shops. We urged them to select some toys to take on board the ship. All they wanted were some tiny cars, which provided hours of entertainment as we crossed the Pacific to Hawaii. It was a far from peaceful trip, but this just added to the girls' fun. The captain said only one other time in his seventeen years at the helm had he seen a storm that severe. As a consequence, Le and I spent a good bit of the time on the voyage lying on top of our bunks, while our children played merrily with their cars. They fashioned a great game around the rocking of the ship. The girls sat on the floor and lined up their cars to race to the opposite side of the cabin as the ship rolled. Then they waited for the next wave to tip the ship in the opposite direction. They giggled and laughed as their cars raced back to them. Watching them happily at play was a pleasant distraction for me.

When we got back to the States, they experienced reverse culture shock. It was a grand adventure just to be taken shopping at the grocery store! Everything was new. Although they were delighted to look, they asked for nothing (to the dismay of their grandmothers). They were content to excitedly show each other what they had discovered in this new wonderland. In Lahore, a city of 1.25 million people in the early to mid-sixties, the only grocery store with packaged food was the size of a small living room. The grandparents decided the girls had been "deprived" of toys long enough, so they quickly set about to remedy the situation.

Also, in preparation for our homecoming, my father had acquired two puppies for his granddaughters. Daddy had rescued a little lost Pekinese-Chihuahua mix, so the grateful owner gave him a puppy for his grandchildren. The girls were delighted. They named this little puppy Shereen, after the youngest daughter in the Bowes family. ("Shereen" is the word for "sweet" in Urdu.) Snowball was the name they gave to the second puppy, a blond cocker spaniel. In one of Martha's art classes, she made a life-size paper-mache model of Snowball with an opening in the back in which to place magazines.

The girls rapidly adapted to the new abundance of toys. Martha was soon playing Barbie dolls with her sister. A neighborhood friend of my mother's made them beautiful doll clothing. When the girls became interested in additional clothing, their grandmother gave each of them a tiny sewing machine. With help from our kind neighbor and their grandmother, the girls created clothes from scraps of material. This was the beginning of Martha's interest in needlework and crafts.

Martha loved spending time with both of her grandparents. She would accompany my father to his farm outside of Luling, where he kept a few cows and grew a vegetable garden. Daddy taught her how to walk safely through pastureland. They walked into the pasture because Martha liked to pet the calves. Since poisonous snakes were a fact of life in the Texas countryside, her grandfather taught her how to take a long stick and swing it through the grass in front of her as she walked. A snake would strike at a foot or leg if a person walked near enough to surprise it, however, they would move out of a person's way if they were aware that someone was coming. She also enjoyed helping her grandfather pick fresh vegetables for the dinner table. Again the stick was used under the plants to ensure no snake was hiding there.

We visited the grandparents several times each year. As Martha grew, she started sitting on her grandfather's lap to "help" him drive the car on the roads inside of the farm away from all highway traffic. Her grandfather later instilled in her the qualities of a responsible driver, when she sat in the driver's seat and drove her grandfather on the country roads. Later still, when Martha took driver's education classes, she became a skillful, confident driver while adhering to the lessons her grandfather had taught her.

The year we returned to the States, we moved to Dallas, settling into a home next to a family of four. Their son, Chris, was a couple of years older than Martha, and their daughter, Cherie, was in Martha's class. Almost instantly, Martha had a new best friend. The girls often went to school and came home together. When Martha and Cherie were not together, Martha often played "school" with her five-year old sister, who was eager to start. Also, since Martha liked riding her bicycle so much, she decided that Kay needed one too. She began to save every bit of the money she earned and received as gifts in order to surprise her sister with a brand new bike. She needed sixty dollars, which in the late sixties was a considerable amount of money for a child to save. It was not an easy task, but Martha persevered until she could present Kay with her very own bike. I think Martha was even more excited about giving it than Kay was in receiving it. In our neighborhood, there were no safe areas to learn to ride, as there had been in Lahore. Kay did not have sufficient chance to practice with her father holding up the bike, so she never really learned to enjoy riding.

Martha's teacher in her fourth-grade class had transferred from teaching in junior high. I soon found that the teacher had some unrealistic expectations of fourth graders. She assigned a "theme" each night on a subject she had selected, directing the children to the encyclopedias for information. As I sat down with Martha that first evening to help her with her homework, I explained that you do not open the book and start copying the words. You begin by reading the material; then you write about it in your own words. When it took Martha until 10 P.M. that night to finish reading the number of pages required, I was sorry about what I had explained. This was too long an assignment to give fourth graders. Since I had taught that grade, I knew there was something wrong with this picture. A fourth grader should not spend every minute after school until 10 P.M. writing a paper. Every day, Martha had a similar assignment. She did not complain, but I decided to check with others in her class. I found out they were copying word for word from the encyclopedia and receiving As, as long as they had the required number of pages. Even when Martha found out what others were doing, she did not change the way she worked. At an early age, Martha had a highly developed conscience, and she would not deliberately do something wrong. She would rather spend the long hours on her assignments.

Nevertheless, I decided to talk to the teacher. I felt sure, since she had never taught that grade, that she did not realize Martha and others were not completing their work until past their bedtime. My talk did no good. The assignments didn't change. Enough other parents must have complained to the principal, however, because the following year the teacher was moved to another school. Perhaps as a result of that hard year, Martha became a very strong student. In comparison to the fourth grade, the fifth-and sixth-grade honors program was a snap for her.

While living in Dallas, she joined the Brownie Scouting program. She entered into all their activities, including their camping trips. I was unaware of even the slightest hesitation about participating in the camp program. It was not until she was in high school that she told me that she had cried herself to sleep every night she was away from home. Astonished, I asked, "Martha, why didn't you tell me? I thought you wanted to go!"

She replied, "I knew it would be good for me to go, but at night I missed home so much!" Outgoing and independent in nature, Martha later showed little evidence of homesickness when she ventured away from home. However, the attachment was there, and in college it would have a decisive effect on her life.

In October 1969, we moved from Dallas to East Lansing, Michigan. She made friends and adjusted easily to the change. Middle school seemed like a great vacation to her. There were field trips in social studies, where they would do things like comparison price shopping. She brought home almost no homework, and school seemed to be an absolute ball for her. Since there were times when I had appointments for work in the afternoon, Martha was in no hurry to walk the two blocks home. She enjoyed helping her teachers and working on scientific experiments after school.

Martha also liked our neighbors. Marilyn was a classmate who lived behind us. Like Martha, Marilyn was a good student, and the two became friends. Living next door to us were Dr. and Mrs. Andy Timnick and their two high school-aged children, Sandy and Paul. The Timnicks became like family. Sandy was a beautiful and popular high school senior who was like an older sister to Martha. In many ways, Martha was emotionally mature for her age and was very comfortable with friends older than she was. This enabled her to have a real friendship with Sandy. Looking back on that period in her life, Sandy wrote of the times the two had shared. Sandy described "sitting in the den [of their home] with Martha, talking and having a great time. We had wonderful talks. She was always interested in my stories. Martha was a great listener. She would get involved and keep me talking by asking questions about my story. I always appreciated the 'realness' of our relationship. She was a safe person to talk with. She was so sweet and fun and full of life!" Since Martha enjoyed making things, she made a craft for Sandy and gave it to her. Sandy treasured it and took it to college with her.

Sandy also remembers a story Martha told her, about drinking buffalo milk with Kay in Pakistan. Martha told Sandy that the buffaloes were allowed to scavenge for food. Consequently, the milk took on the taste of some of the weeds the buffalo ate. "At times," Martha explained, "it was really awful tasting!" So her grandmother had sent fruit-flavored "fizzes" to drop into the milk. "This disguised the taste enough to make it drinkable. That is, all except the lemon-flavored kind, which curdled the milk!"

Sandy concluded, "We laughed a lot." The year Martha became a freshman in high school, Sandy moved away to become a freshman at the University of Georgia in Athens.

◆   ◆   ◆

It was shortly before entering high school that Martha attended a weekend of activities for the youth department at our church. The program was led by a visiting group of teens from Ohio. During their visit, Martha and one of the visiting youths, Mike, developed a crush on each other. Both were dog lovers, and Mike's dog had just had a litter of collie-German shepherd puppies. He offered Martha a puppy. They corresponded for six or so weeks. During this time, they exchanged pictures and Mike gave Martha progress reports on the puppies. Even though we already had two dogs, Martha somehow talked her father and me into making the trip out of state to pick up "her" puppy. "Her" puppy soon became "their" puppy, because Kay was as enthusiastic as Martha about the new dog. We were on the road to Ohio as soon as she was weaned. As we traveled home, Martha and Kay discussed names for their new pet. Both liked the music from Sherazad, so the puppy became Sherazad, "Shera" for short. Although the long-distance "romance" soon faded, Shera became a great addition for our whole family.

◆   ◆   ◆

Both Martha and her father were two very strong-willed people. I don't remember at what point in her life Martha became Kay's self-appointed protector against all comers, including their father. When Martha observed her dad becoming angry with her little sister, she physically placed her small frame between Kay and her six-foot-two father and loudly began to defend her. Martha achieved her objective, because as she diverted her father's attention, Kay left the room. This is not to say that Martha and Kay never had a fight. As Dawn Bowes, Nadine's sister, wrote, "I felt Martha was so kind and accepting of others—except for Kay, at times. I do remember a few battles there." After one encounter with her father, Martha went to her room, closed the door, and climbed out her window. (I did not find out about this until she told me more than a year later.) She hid behind the house and waited in the dark for us to go to sleep. Then she planned to run away. However, Martha was also a very practical young lady. "Mother, I got to thinking that if I ran away I wouldn't have any place to go without money, so I climbed back into my room," she said as she concluded her story. Martha's feelings toward her father were ambivalent, which is common among children in troubled marriages. After Le and I separated, she wrote,

Dear father (Father?) we dream, we dream.

Those are words little children use, 'Daddy, Daddy, why?

Daddy, are you always going to be here? Here to rock me to sleep?

You'll never go, ever, will you, Daddy? Do ya love me, Daddy?'

'Yes, of course, sweetheart. Of course, 'Tweetie.'

It seems only slight moments ago that my Daddy was here. He tucked us into bed, told us stories…

No, never again will I love quite as deeply, nor laugh as joyously, nor scream as delightedly of any cause. A child, I'm convinced, must have two, and those two must be in love.

And now that I am no longer a child of any means, I realize the never-ending despair of life for those who have not love…" Then she wrote of "the barrels of smarting tears that well in my eyes."

When Le moved back to Texas, Martha took over mowing the lawn. This was a big job, because the yard was almost an acre. Martha had better luck starting the rider mower than I did, but at times neither of us could. If Andy were out mowing his lawn, he would walk over and start it. Sometimes Andy brought his mower over and helped Martha cut the grass. When our mower broke down, he took it apart and repaired it. Andy and Margaret often came to the girls' rescue. Margaret taught Martha how to do needlework and how to braid a rug. Martha began to make her rug out of scraps of material taken from different pieces of clothing that she and Kay had worn growing up. She was still working on this rug at Margaret's home at the time of her disappearance. Margaret finished it so that I could use it.

In high school, Martha's calendar was crammed with activities. There were the sports: swimming, ice skating, horseback riding, canoeing, football, baseball, and volley ball. As I mentioned earlier, when she wasn't selected to be on the volley-ball team, she gladly accepted the position of scorekeeper. During the winters that were cold enough to form outdoor rinks, she was an ice ranger for the city ice rink in our neighborhood. It was her job to ensure that skaters behaved responsibly so that people of all ages could skate safely. During the longer, colder winters, the city flooded some of the parks to form ponds of ice for skating. Once the city had created an ice rink, if the temperature climbed and the ice melted, they would create no more rinks until the following year. One year we had continuous sub-freezing weather for six weeks.

◆　　　◆　　　◆

Her English classes took bus trips to the Shakespearean festival in Stratford, Canada. The entry on her calendar about the festival was punctuated with the word "fun!" Greek Dancing Week each spring was always a time Martha eagerly anticipated. Each year's musical production from a popular Broadway show was another favorite. She enthusiastically participated in the exacting rehearsal schedule in order to be in the chorus. If you missed one rehearsal, you were out. Martha never missed one. To this list of her activities, Martha added the school newspaper and yearbook.

In addition to school activities there were the church-related events of the Methodist youth fellowship—the folk choir, hayrides, and retreats. There were also Campus Life meetings, Girl Scouts, and, in her junior year, the Rainbow Girls (which she joined because Kay was involved and she wanted to support her sister). Pursuing her interest in sewing, Martha enrolled in a "stretch and sew" class at a local fabric shop.

Sprinkled throughout her calendar were the names of friends with whom she shared activities and interests, birthday parties, and dances. She jotted reminders to write letters to friends out of state and to her grandparents. She also included lists of ten to twelve books she was reading or wanted to read.

Martha took all her activities in stride until the spring of her senior year. In April, my father contracted a life-threatening case of pneumonia. Since my mother was blind, it was necessary for us to fly to Texas to help out. Following my father's recovery, we flew home, and in May I entered the hospital for major surgery. With final exams, and Martha's high school graduation, a few weeks away, this was an overwhelming load for a seventeen-year-old. The only sign of this enormous stress that Martha exhibited however was facial blemishes, which she experienced for the first time. When I came home from the hospital after five days, Martha's face began to clear up. During my recovery, Martha "mothered" me by driving home each day to have lunch and to be sure I ate.

Fortunately, I recovered sufficiently that I could attend Martha's graduation. With the help of my daughters, we were able to throw Martha a joyous gradua-tion party. Life was looking good again for Martha. With her scholarship to Southwestern University in Georgetown, Texas, in place, Martha looked forward to a bright new chapter of her life in the fall.

Being a very social person, the idea of joining a sorority appealed to her. Many of her new friends were in Phi Mu. When she pledged, she sent home pictures of her sorority sisters and the profusion of flower arrangements she had received that lined her dorm room.

When Martha arrived at Southwestern, she already knew one person. He was the oldest son of some longtime friends and an upperclassman there. They con-nected soon after Martha arrived, and Tony* was very attentive, helping to get Martha involved with various campus and church activities. Through frequent letters and phone calls, Martha let me know she was having a great time. It was not long after the semester started that Martha began to fall in love with Tony. It seemed to be mutual from the conversations I had with my daughter. The follow-ing note, delivered by "campus mail," that was found among Martha's things also suggests that he loved her. The "campus mail" allowed students to place notes in others students' boxes anytime, enabling them to communicate with each other quickly. After all the correspondence we found had been turned over to the police, only one note from Tony remained:

Dearest Martha,

I wept a little and grew a lot.

Thank you for lifting me up this morning with your letter.

You are God's special gift to me.

God bless you again and again.

With all my love,

In Him,

Tony

I do not know the significance of this message. I do know that Martha reported that everything was wonderful for a few months; then the age difference began to get in the way, and Tony began to date one of Martha's girlfriends. I could not believe the maturity Martha exhibited in not allowing her feelings for Tony to break up her friendships with either friend. I know I could not have handled it as well. She allowed the agony she felt to surface only in her writings and prayers, such as the following written prayer:

"Oh, Lord, I know that pain kills but, I realize that it can only kill my spirit & quest for life, which is the most dangerous.

> Oh, Lord, bless and keep my heart from unhealing scars. Yes, Lord, I know I'm only seventeen. I still bounce when thrown to the ground…But, Lord, keep me moving in your direction no matter if I'm crawling or riding.
>
> Lord, I don't know whether meeting and loving Tony was your will or not. I only know that he came so very close to being the very one of my heart. Yet, I know too that it would not have worked. Lord, I just pray that I have not hurt or offended anyone in trying to love him. I know I am not ready for any serious relationship.
>
> Tony is. And, Lord, I am happy about his new "interest." Lord, you know better than any that I'll always care for him. But I want your will. I know you care for me and are planning the timing perfectly. I just pray I make it to that time! I am very grateful to you for giving Tony the sense to tell…that he was being sensible about our ages.
>
> I am sorry for ever being angry and frustrated about this. I have behaved like a spoiled child. Yet, Lord, if I may ask, please find me a man that can love like I have and do love Tony. With all those attributes I love so much in him."

As she was facing the loss of her first real love, I marveled at the way she accepted it and vowed to go on with her life with no bitterness in her heart. Few people, even those much older, would handle a situation like this with such grace.

Martha might have had a premonition that she would die young, for in her papers, I found a note asking me to give Tony the rest of her college fund for his graduate school "if anything happened." (That did not happen. Instead, all these funds, and more, were committed to Martha's rescue effort.) This breakup with Tony may have contributed to her increasing homesickness and may have prompted Martha's decision to return to Michigan.

◆   ◆   ◆

I had noticed that it was becoming harder and harder for Martha to say good-bye to us when she came home for visits throughout her two years at Southwest-ern University. During the winter and spring of her sophomore year, she began to talk seriously about transferring to Michigan State University for her junior and senior years. In the spring, she decided she wanted to come home to stay, so I went down to Georgetown. We loaded her old Buick convertible to the brim. With only enough space left for the two of us to sit, we started back to East Lan-sing.

Once we were home, Martha and I unloaded enough of her things to fit Kay into the car, and then we headed down to the church where Kay was attending a youth meeting. One of my favorite memories is the squeals of joy and the broad smiles my daughters had on their faces when Kay spotted her sister and ran into her embrace.

Even after she returned home, Martha was still debating whether to return to Southwestern in the fall. This is reflected in the letter she wrote to her major (and favorite) professor, Dr. Reynolds. The letter gives flavor of Martha's personality. I carefully saved a copy of her letter all these years. I wanted to include it here, in Martha's handwriting. Unfortunately, while taking it to be professionally copied, it was lost. I made no back-up copy before I left the house. Martha wanted Dr. Reynolds to know how much she appreciated her and valued her friendship. She shared how excited she was to find that Michigan State rated Dr. Reynolds' French courses a semester ahead of comparable courses at State. Martha was thrilled that her transferred credits were the equivalent of two and a half years' worth of work, as opposed to two. She was excited about being able to take grad-uate-level classes while in her last year and a half of college. She gave Dr. Rey-nolds' excellent teaching credit for that. She expressed her gratitude for the way Dr. Reynolds had opened her home to groups of her French students and for her wise counsel to students who were sometimes "homesick and confused."

After Martha set things in motion to stay in Michigan for the remainder of her undergraduate work, she seemed to blossom even more. At home, she began to take an interest in cooking and healthy eating. She lost the few pounds she had acquired eating dorm food. She seemed especially thrilled with living her life.

In writing about Martha's college years, her friend Nadine concluded her let-ter by writing, "Later, when we were older, I remember how concerned Martha was about you [her mother] and Kay. She told me once she would never live far away from you." Nadine described her most lasting memories: "I especially remember that contagious laughter of hers…Martha was what I always considered a 'joyful person.' She was enthusiastic about even the most mundane tasks. She was emotional and had a genuine concern for others. Your pain became her pain, your problems became her problems, and your smiles became her smiles.

"She always seemed to have a twinkle in her eye, as if she were up to something…she laughed so easily and found the silliest things so funny…she was one of those people who always made you feel special; she laughed at all my stupid jokes. I could feel her presence in a room even when I hadn't seen her yet. (My sister Valerie is like that.) I just remember so much laughter with Martha. I can't even count how many times we would race to the bathroom because we had been laughing so hard…"

I have my own poignant memory from that last fall that she went to MSU. Martha had always been a beautiful girl. Yet, I remember thinking that she looked more beautiful than ever before. Strangely, in retrospect, I connect it to the feeling I've always had about autumn in Michigan. In Texas, where I grew up, the beautiful flowers and vegetation of mid-summer scorch and become gangly at summer's end, long before the first frost kills them. In Michigan, this doesn't happen; the flowers are not parched at summer's end. They are at their most beautiful just before an overnight freeze destroys their loveliness. This perfectly describes the last days of Martha's life—intensely beautifully, vibrantly alive one day and then lost in the frost before the next dawn.

Young Family
Kay, Martha, Le, with Sue Standing

Kay (16 months) and Martha (age 4)

In front of United Christian Hospital, Lahore, Pakistan

Martha and Friends in Pakistan

Martha age 12

Martha Sue (16 years).

Martha (18 years)
Student at Southwestern University
at Georgetown, Texas.

Martha Sue (19 years),
Christmas Day 1976,
Danville, Pennsylvania.

7

A Major Discovery

When the spring searches produced no real clues, I sensed that the investigation was drying up. Then the summer passed without any new leads, and the moment I feared most had arrived. One day, Dean announced, "Sue, we have done everything we know to do. We have exhausted every possibility. While we will never close the case, there is nothing at this time we can actively do. We just have to wait for something new to turn up." I knew what he said was true, since for some time we had been going over and over the same ground. I did not blame the East Lansing Police. So, by the fall of 1977, nine long months after Martha had disappeared, I began to have a hopeless feeling that I would never know what had happened to my daughter, that we had come to the end, and that there were not going to be any more clues. I feared that I would go to my grave with no answers.

Sgt. Tucker had made it a priority to keep me up to date with the investigation all the way through. Even at this point, someone from the police department continued to drop by from time to time, just to touch base and see how I was doing. They wanted me to be aware that they had not forgotten Martha. On a Thursday evening in October, I received a call from the sergeant asking if he could stop by. Since this was not unusual, I wasn't expecting any news when Sgt. Tucker and Detective Westgate came into the living room. I was getting them a cup of tea and making small talk when Sgt. Tucker stopped me with the words, "We have a major discovery; Martha's brown leather purse has been found."

As my heart raced, I questioned, "What makes you so sure it is Martha's?"

"It has her driver's license inside." Sgt. Tucker answered.

The questions poured out of me:

"How did you find it?" "Where was it?" "Was it in the trash somewhere?"

I wanted to know everything at once. It was so hard for me to settle down that the detectives were barely able to answer my questions.

"We didn't find it," Dean and Rick explained. "The purse was found by two hunters. While the two men were out hunting pheasants, they stumbled onto a small weather-beaten purse in an area of thick underbrush and grass. Fortunately, they picked it up and began to look around the area to see if they could find anything else. There was a lot more. There was women's clothing. After making this discovery, the hunters called the police."

It was Martha's clothing—every article of clothing that she had been wearing. The clothing was meticulously laid out in a manner unlike any these veteran detectives had ever seen. The clothing was arranged as though a body were still inside, as if the body had just floated out of the clothing. The undergarment and leotard Martha was wearing were inside the trousers, the bra was inside the sweater, and the sweater was inside the jacket. Her shoes were at the bottom of the pants, and the scarf was at the neckline of the jacket, but Martha's body was not there. It was as if her body had just vanished from inside her clothing. There would be much speculation later as to the reason for such a strange act, but at the moment the detectives were focused on using this information to flush out the killer.

The discovery of her clothes all but confirmed that Martha was dead. This had been my intuition from the first day, for I knew there was no way anyone would have gotten those clothes off of Martha while she was living. Also, with absolutely nothing to protect her from the extreme cold, she would have frozen to death very quickly. Now we had to put this information to use. The police had the area "staked out" and told the press that evening only that Martha's purse had been found, indicating that it might have been moved from its original location. They did not disclose where it had been found in the hope that the perpetrator would return to check the area where the clothes had been. Don's house was watched to see if he would drive out to the area. Also, the police wanted to search the area thoroughly before the press arrived. I was told where the discovery had been made. However, I made it a point not to pay attention to the exact location. I did not want to have the image of the area where Martha died engraved in my memory for the rest of my life. My mind already had too many dark images stored there. I did not want to add anything to that terrifying collection.

I was glad that I had glossed over that detail, because a reporter called me from one of the TV stations saying he had been down to the ELPD. Since he found only a skeleton crew there, he concluded something important was happening.

"No one will tell me where the police have gone," he said, and he wanted to know if I knew.

I thought, *Good, the police are doing what they are supposed to be doing. Why would you think I would tell you?* Fortunately, I did not remember, so I simply said, "No, I don't know."

The entire next day, I felt as though I were suspended in time. I felt Martha's body had to be close by the area where the clothes had been found. Now it was just a matter of hours until they found her, I felt sure. I knew the search was in progress. No matter what I tried to do, a part of me was listening for the phone. I wondered at what minute they would come and tell me they had found her body. All the time I was waiting, I knew that the major search was scheduled for Saturday, but still the discovery could come at any minute. They had to be very, very close.

As the purse had been discovered in another county, the state police entered the case. From that point on, this was treated as a homicide rather than a missing-person case. Later, I was told by one of my friends in the East Lansing Police Department, Rick Little, that although he was off duty at the time, he had a hunch to check out an area near where the purse was discovered. This was typical of the officers at the ELPD; they gave hours and hours of their own time. Because he was off duty, Rick was not aware that he was searching in an area that the state police had staked out. Consequently, he had ended up handcuffed before a fellow ELPD officer identified him. Friday morning, while the state police dogs and detectives covered the ground, I heard the familiar sounds of a helicopter being brought in for an aerial search. Nothing additional was found, so the plans for the massive search scheduled for Saturday went forward. Fifty volunteers from the Tri-county Community Radio Watch and the National Guard were called upon to assist the ELPD and the state police. These people went through the area on their hands and knees.

Emotionally, I could not stand the idea that I might be the one to find my daughter's body, so the idea of helping with the search repulsed me. If I were the one to stumble upon her body, the memory would be seared into my brain forever. It would haunt all my days and terrorize my nights. Fortunately, the police did not want me there. Kay however, ended up driving out to the area because that was the day that Le flew in to pick up Martha's car. She will never forget the moment she and her dad entered the car for it was at that time news was being broadcast of the search. Kay had not told her father about the discovery. Since Le was coming to East Lansing anyway, she wanted to tell him in person when he arrived. Upon hearing the news, he was upset and wanted to drive out to the site immediately to talk to Dean Tucker, which they did.

Since Kay was with her father, and I did not want to go into the woods with the searchers, I found myself sitting at home waiting for the news. In these times of peak crisis, I couldn't stand being alone so I went where people were. A Mary Kay workshop had been planned for that Saturday. I had planned to be one of the teachers. I knew they could get along fine without me, but I did not know how I could survive just waiting. I decided to go, "but don't expect me to motivate anyone today," I said. "I can teach technique, such as time and money management." So that is what I did, and as long as there were people in front of me, I could maintain my focus on what I was teaching. Although I received praise for the outstanding job I did, all day I expected to be interrupted with news of a discovery. To my surprise, the workshop ended and the search had turned up nothing. I went home to resume my vigil. How could they not find her?

The search area presented a major obstacle, of which I was not aware until the conclusion. In the days following the unsuccessful search, Sgt. Tucker and I talked about a possible reason she had not been found. The reason: a large body of water in the area near where Martha's clothes were found. When Martha disappeared, that water would have been frozen solid. If a body had been placed upon the frozen ice, and was not disturbed by animals, it would have stayed there until the spring thaw. Then, first, the body would have sunk to the bottom, and after a time it would have floated for a while and then sunk to the bottom permanently. It had been over five months since the ice had changed to water. If it had been on the ice, now it would be at the bottom. In that case, the water would have to be drained in order to find it. The area was huge, so the cost would be prohibitive in all likelihood. The idea that Martha's body might be lost forever at the bottom of that lake cut me like a knife.

The search of the area had come to an end. The clothing had been taken to the state crime lab, where they would be identified. "Oh, no!" I groaned, when the thought hit me that I would have to identify them. I asked, "Will I be needed for verification?"

Dean Tucker could sense my dread. He replied, "Don't worry, I'll make the identification." The police had in their possession the jacket that belonged with slacks of the pantsuit that Martha had worn that night. I had given them a description of the blue ski jacket with the gray fake fur collar. Jacobson's, the store where Martha had purchased her jacket, had also provided details regarding the garment Martha was wearing. I had given Kay's shoes to the police because they matched the ones Martha was wearing, and they had taken a picture of them. I had also taken Kay's bracelet watch to be photographed, as it was a duplicate of Martha's. In addition, Dean Tucker had the woolen cap that matched the design of the scarf Martha had worn. "Besides," he added, "there won't be room in the lab for you." I knew he was just saying that to let me off of the hook, and I was grateful for his kindness.

After the search failed to find Martha, I became depressed. I was in a kind of suspended state of grief. There had never been any closure, so I could never give myself the time to grieve and deal with her loss. I tried to put my mourning on hold, nevertheless grief sort of oozed through me and a great sadness settled over me. I still felt like screaming yet I continued to hold it in check, fearing that if I ever started there would be no one around who could get me to stop. I still had an intense desire to be around people all the time.

Although I loved my Mary Kay clients and consultants, a sales career depends on staying motivated, and I was not. It was wonderful when my customers stopped by to order things. I functioned quite well when another person was standing before me, but I could not initiate the customer-service calls. I lost a lot of my customers during that time, because people "did not want to bother me." What they didn't realize was that, instead of "bothering me with their business," they were part of my lifeline. Not to mention that the Mary Kay business I had built provided the money that sustained Kay and me.

I almost lost my livelihood. In October, I received a warning letter from the legal department of Mary Kay saying that I was in danger of losing my sales unit and the directors that I had developed. (Mary Kay Ash, the chairman of the board of Mary Kay Cosmetics, responded quite differently. She was always very supportive personally, and she kept up an encouraging correspondence with me throughout the ordeal.) I had continued to conduct my weekly sales meetings for my consultants and never missed a single one. All the way through, my colleagues told me that my weekly sales meetings were good, even though I knew I was not at my best. I was pleased, however, because I felt their comments were genuine. If they had not felt that way, the consultants would have said nothing. Because of my constant need to be around people, I considered getting a second job.

For a time, I wished I had a job where I could just show up each day. I considered looking for a job where I could greet people, perhaps as a hostess in a local restaurant. That way I felt sure I would see and talk to many people that I knew. I thought about asking some of my business contacts if I could work for them part time for a while. I didn't even care if I got paid. I never followed through, though, for I knew in the long run I could not afford to lose the business I had created. Somehow I had to rebuild it, regardless of my lack of motivation.

As the days began to pass by again, the major discovery of the clothing appeared to be just one more dead end. The ordeal seemed endless. Kay and I would think that things were becoming somewhat normal again, and then we would be sucked right back into the center of a whirlpool, where we would have to fight to keep from being submerged. This was Kay's senior year at East Lansing

High School, and she deserved to have some normal, happy experiences associated with this important time in her life. With the constant publicity, particularly in the beginning, this was not possible. When Kay first went back to school following Martha's disappearance, her friends would see her from a distance and actually turn around and change direction to avoid speaking to her. This was not meant to be cruel; they simply did not know what to say. If their parents had realized what was happening, I am sure they would have encouraged their children to support their friend with kind expressions, such as, "I'm so sorry" or "That's awful." One group of her friends was particularly helpful. They were the Rainbow Girls, an organization to which Kay and Martha had both belonged. I recall some of the older former Rainbow Girls, who had already graduated from high school, coming by the house to visit her from time to time. I particularly remember the time they stopped by to make plans to take Kay out to a nice restaurant to celebrate her birthday.

Each time the girls visited they brought along a single long-stemmed red rose. Following Martha's disappearance, either one of the girls or one of their leaders would always come by our house after the meeting to bring Kay the rose and just visit for a few minutes. Even when we were not at home, they would leave the rose inside our storm door. After Kay went away to college, they continued to deliver the rose to me. It was a simple act, but a powerful statement of concern. I shall always be grateful for the way they expressed their affection for Kay. The rose said, without words, "We know you have not forgotten Martha; we have not either, and we care about you."

Even with the additional manpower from other law-enforcement agencies that had joined the investigation, after the clothing was discovered, there seemed to be nowhere else to go once again. I keep remembering the words of the forensic psychologist, who considered Don a ticking time bomb. In addition to my own pain, I felt fear and anguish over what he might do next. Somehow he had to be stopped. I didn't want any other family to go through this. Nothing we could do seemed to be enough. In the meantime, Don was free to go about his life. He was finishing his degree in criminal justice and was going to work for a security company as a guard. All this time, I had the feeling that he could simply wait it out until he was no longer news and no one was watching him. He could simply play the waiting game until he was free to strike again.

Copyright *The Lansing State Journal* 1977.

Martha Sue Young still missing

By MARK NIXON
Staff Writer

Margaret Young awoke from a dead sleep around 6:45 a.m. that day, and was almost immediately overcome by what she later described as "a horrible feeling."

She had been to a dinner party the night before, and upon returning home quickly retired for the night. She slept soundly, hearing nothing through those long hours, and that is what worried her.

Normally she heard her daughter, Martha, open the door and pad about the house following a date. It was either that or the sound of a car pulling into the driveway that usually stirred her into consciousness. That would be Don Miller's car. Don and Martha were engaged.

Yet she heard nothing that particular night, and the horrible feeling persisted.

She checked Martha's bedroom. The bed had not been slept in. Quickly now, Mrs. Young went from room to room inside the stylish, two-story house at 1978 N.

Harrison Road. Martha was not there.

Her concern growing, Mrs. Young telephoned Martha's fiance. It was approximately 7 a.m. when Don Miller came to the phone to say, no, Martha wasn't there. (Miller lives with his parents only a few blocks from the Young household.) No, he told her, he didn't know where Martha was. He had said goodnight to Martha on her doorstep, sometime around 2 a.m.

It was 7:35 a.m., according to an East Lansing Police log, when a distraught Margaret Young called to report her daughter could not be found. The desk officer logged the complaint: Missing person, Martha Sue Young. Caucasian female. Age: 19. Five-feet, five inches tall, blonde hair, blue eyes. Last seen: 0200 hours in front of her home, 1978 N. Harrison Road.

It was New Year's Day, 1977, and Martha Sue Young had disappeared.

* * *

IF YOU were to compose a

mental portrait of a young woman about to run away from home, it would take some stretch of the imagination to place Martha Sue Young on the "most likely" list. In the days and months before her disappearance, she lived a relatively secure and untroubled life.

Returning from two years of schooling the previous spring at Southwestern University in Georgetown, Texas, Martha was planning to resume her studies at Michigan State on Jan. 5. She was enthralled with the French language; it was her major avenue of study as a junior majoring in Romance Languages. She had planned to take a waiver exam at MSU on Jan. 3. She had pre-registered for the winter term, and paid for her tuition in advance. A part-time job awaited her beginning Jan. 8 at the American Bank and Trust.

Moreover, when Martha vanished, she took no extra clothes, had only pocket money in her purse, had no credit cards and left $125 in cash in a dresser drawer.

Yet as the days dragged on into

weeks without a clue as to her whereabouts, East Lansing Police investigators pursued the runaway theory, if not enthusiastically, at least with vigor. There were, simply, no other leads to follow.

"We took her photographs around to rail stations, to air lines, showed them to cab drivers working that night," said Sgt. Dean Tucker, who has headed up the investigation from the beginning. Friends and family were questioned. Don Miller was interviewed repeatedly.

The result of all that police legwork proved fruitless. No Martha Sue.

Article courtesy of *The Lansing State Journal*, Copyright 1977

8

How Many More Must Die?

The months dragged on with no more developments, and I was haunted by the thought that I would never know what had happened. I had an odd feeling as I traveled through different areas of Michigan. Since Martha could be any place, her body might be lying beside the road that I used that very day. The eerie thought persisted that perhaps one day, I would be the one to discover Martha's body in a field somewhere. Silently I questioned, *How could I handle such a discovery?* Later, I discovered that Dean Tucker had a very similar feeling. Dean liked to hunt in the woods around his home. "All through the months of the investigation," he said, "I never crossed an open field without looking for a body."

The state's forensic psychologist's words, "Don Miller fits the classic profile of a killer, and he will become even worse," continued to haunt me. His freedom allowed him to move easily among people who could not possibly understand the danger he posed. Would another young woman die a violent, senseless death?

Although a second spring was nearing its end since Martha's disappearance, we seemed no closer to solving the case. The police had stopped observing Donald Miller's daily activities months ago. All efforts had ceased, but there was no way that Kay and I could just walk away. Jan Williams, a friend of ours, had an idea. She had been talking to her friend, Leo Farhat, a highly respected lawyer and former president of the Michigan Bar Association. While he was a student, Farhat had become acquainted with a murder trial where no body had ever been found. That defendant had been found guilty! Since that time, he had become interested in researching the few cases that had ever been tried without a body. As a lawyer, he was not allowed to seek me out, but he asked Jan to ask me if I would be interested in talking to him. Since I was not wealthy, I said to Jan, "I don't know if I can afford to pay his fee." Jan assured me money would not be a problem. So I went downtown to his office. I told him in confidence all that I knew. He said he was convinced that he could build a case against Don Miller without

Martha's body, and he believed it would result in Miller's conviction for murder. I asked about his fee and he set a modest sum, which I am sure for him was only a token. He immediately got to work. When he completed it, we turned it over to the Ingham county prosecutor, who would be the one to bring the case to trial. For months, there was no movement on Leo's work.

Then, on June 14, Marita Choquette, a WKAR-TV editorial associate, vanished. Strange as it seems—although I believed and agonized over the prediction—I did not associate Marita's disappearance with Don Miller at the time. In fact, at the time this was happening, I paid as little attention as possible to the details of any new crime that was committed. This was one of my coping mechanisms, I suppose. Emotionally, I couldn't handle anything more. Later I would learn far more than I ever wanted to know about the events surrounding her disappearance, which occurred a year and a half after Martha had vanished. Marita had last been seen meeting with a friend for an early dinner. The two had parted at 7:30 P.M. after her friend drove her to her home in Grand Ledge. She had been seen around 8 P.M. dumping trash outside her apartment, confirming her arrival home. After this, Marita was never seen alive again. However, shortly after eight o'clock the next morning, her yellow Opal was found parked in the WKAR lot, as if she had come to work. It was not in the usual spot near the entrance, but farther back in the lot. The car contained no clues. Her friends and family reported her disappearance immediately, knowing it was out of character for Marita to miss work without any explanation and to be out of contact with those close to her. Thirteen days after her disappearance, Marita's mutilated body was found in Okemos, a town adjoining East Lansing. A farmer dumping his trash in a woodlot a short distance from his residence came upon the grisly scene. This area was more than thirty miles from where she had been seen last. At the point where speculation began in the media about a possible connection to the Young case, Kay began to hide the newspaper and turn off the TV when news concerning the case was reported. I dismissed the idea that there could be a connection. I did not want to believe that Don Miller was guilty of deliberate multiple murder, in spite of the prediction of the forensic expert. I can't explain why I refused to entertain the possibility. My mind just refused to go there. It would be much later that I would start to pay attention to the parallels in both cases. Marita was exactly Martha's height, and about ten pounds heavier. She had slightly darker hair and was said to bear a striking resemblance to Martha when Martha wore her glasses.

The body, with its multiple stab wounds and its amputated hands at its side, had been placed near a pile of concrete blocks and other discarded items. Several of the cement blocks encircled Marita's body. Her legs and feet were tucked under her, as if she had fallen while praying. Was the position of the body significant? I would never know for certain.

Two weeks from the day that Marita vanished, a blond Michigan State co-ed named Wendy Bush was reported missing. The day Wendy disappeared was the day Marita's body was discovered. This time, the press was quick to compare the woman's appearance to Martha's. They claimed that the two bore a striking physical similarity. I disregarded this as somebody's attempt to further sensationalize the story. Although, I could have asked the police at any time—and I feel sure they would have told me—I did not ask until much later if they suspected that these disappearances were connected to Don Miller.

Wendy Bush was twenty-one years old. She had long blond hair (Martha had worn her hair long all of her life until she entered college) and green eyes, she was a couple of inches taller than Martha, and she weighed 145 pounds. Wendy was last seen after an evening class, at around 10 P.M., as she was walking with an unidentified tall white man on the Michigan State Campus. They had been seen walking between the library and MSU Administration Building. Unlike Martha and Marita, Wendy did not have strong ties to the community. Since she was known to be impulsive, friends thought it possible that Wendy had left on her own. On the other hand, her belongings, including her purse, pictures, and cherished mementos from family and friends, were left in her dorm room. Also, the morning after her disappearance, two paychecks were discovered. A student loan had also been cleared for Wendy, yet it had never been picked up.

Three young women had now disappeared. The last two women vanished within two weeks of each other. The campus, and the entire Lansing area, was gripped with fear. The disappearances were never far from the minds of young area women and their families. Women became very afraid to venture out in the evening. Volunteers were recruited on campus to escort co-eds to evening classes and the library after dark. Ironically, during this time, Don worked for a local company as a security guard.

With all of these new investigations going on, there was no way I could just stay at home and worry. I needed to work to keep up with the house payments, living expenses, and Kay's university expenses in the fall. Consequently, I made plans to attend the Mary Kay annual seminar in Dallas. First, I made sure that Kay could stay with my neighbors. She was not pleased, since she felt she was old enough to stay by herself. It was an affront to a college-bound eighteen-year-old. Nevertheless, I would not leave until she agreed to stay with Judy and Bob, and I knew that they would ensure she kept her promise.

While I attended the seminar, I planned to stay with my senior sales director, Idell Moffett (who later became my national sales director), and her husband, Herschel. Because they were friends, they were interested in the investigation. Prior to my visit, as we were discussing the lack of progress in the investigation, Herschel recalled a client of his in El Paso. (Herschel was a top salesperson for Rockwell International, so he often traveled to El Paso.) His client had told him about a private investigator who was somehow able to track down and bring home people that no one else could find. This investigator had found Marlon Brando's son after he disappeared somewhere in Mexico. Idell suggested, "If you want to go, Herschel will set up the appointment, and I will go with you."

This discussion came at a crucial time. Throughout the preceding months, the media had reported gruesome details about young blond girls being abducted, taken outside the States, and sold as sex slaves. The news also broadcast the grisly details of a woman being buried in a coffin-like container, her only lifeline a small pipe that extended above ground. Even after Martha's clothes were found and all the evidence pointed to a near certainty that she was no longer alive, someone close to Kay suggested to her that Martha was being held in a similar way. These two possibilities were the worst things that Kay could imagine happening to her sister. When Kay told me, she said, "Mother, we have got to find Martha. We are her only hope. She is praying right now for us to find her." Logic did not always win over emotion where Martha was concerned, and I refused to give up. However, I had run out of ideas. Herschel's suggestion had come at just the right time; here was something we *could* do.

Also, for months, friends had asked if I had considered hiring a private investigator. I had not, because I knew I had all fifty-two members of the ELPD dedicated to solving the case. I didn't think one man could do as much as an entire police force. Now that there was nothing else they could find to actively investigate, I felt differently. This private investigator had a legendary success rate for cracking unsolvable cases. I was excited about being able to do something. If he had found someone in a foreign country, I thought, surely he could find someone in this country. We encountered a problem, however, in that El Paso is a thousand miles from Dallas. However, we found that by taking an early-morning flight and returning on a late-evening flight we could do it in one day. The appointment was scheduled for the day following the conclusion of seminar.

The client who knew the investigator met us at the airport in El Paso. He took us to a unique building, which housed the offices of private investigator Jay J. Armes. Vehicles were kept at a distance from the building by huge triangular-shaped concrete barriers, which jutted high into the air from the concrete paving.

We entered the building, which had the strength of a bomb shelter and featured secret rooms and two-way mirrors. We seated ourselves in the waiting room, where we were secretly observed through a mirror. Later, we were told this was all part of Armes' elaborate security system, implemented to protect his life from the various organized-crime figures he had been responsible for capturing. The concrete spikes between the street and the office building were to prevent vehicles from driving close to the building; they could even stop a tank, he boasted. We were kept under surveillance until it was determined, from the background check they had conducted on both of us as soon as the appointment was made, that we were indeed the persons we represented ourselves to be. We were then ushered into an interior office. When our escort took out a card, slid it into an invisible opening in the solid wall, and the wall moved to reveal a secret elevator, I felt like I had just entered the world of James Bond. This, however, was the day-to-day world of Mr. Armes. The wall of the elevator opened again, and we stepped into a huge room the size of a small theater. The elevator vanished behind us, and we turned to see the only person in the room.

J. J. Armes was seated on an elevated platform behind a huge crescent-shaped desk. When I saw the control panel built into the desk, I felt as though I had stepped out of the world of James Bond and into a *Star Wars* movie. We just stood there taking in our surroundings. We were invited to advance past the large sofas near the elevator to the comfortable chairs at the foot of the desk. Comfort does not accurately describe what we felt as we sat there, however, for Armes told us there was a gun hidden inside the desk that had been trained on us from the moment we entered his office, just in case something had escaped the security check. Since Armes had lost both hands, a hook protruded from each sleeve of his shirt. He used the hooks very deftly, and he told us that they served him better than hands in certain situations.

Behind all this high-tech security was a man with a very friendly demeanor. This friendliness was necessary, I felt sure, to compensate for the bizarre and frightening surroundings in which he conducted his business. He expressed great confidence that he could find Martha for me. Since he was a master of disguise, he explained, he could get information that no one else could. When he was in disguise, he wore lifelike prostheses that he had learned to use as effectively as others used their hands. He carried a handgun at all times. It was hidden in the sleeve of his shirt and would drop down into a position where it could be fired, if the occasion warranted it. He said that if later we recognized him someplace we were not to speak to him. Although this would be our only meeting, he promised that once employed he would never quit working until he had solved the case.

This promise was wonderfully reassuring. He also told us about some of the hard cases he had succeeded in solving, cases the police had thought were unsolvable. Since I had no alternative, I was ready to believe he could do what he claimed he could do.

His fee of $25,000, however, was discouraging. In 1978 that was an awful lot of money. Nice homes sold for little more than that, and a brand-new Buick could be purchased for $7,000. It was more money than I was making in a year. I did not have the money to hire him, and I didn't know if I could even borrow that much. I said I would have to see if I could get the money. At the conclusion of the appointment, the same man who had met us took us back to the airport. He gave us a little tour on the way, so that we could see where Armes lived with his wife and children. In keeping with the security at his office, his home was set well away from the street and surrounded by a high fence. The zoo on the grounds served a dual purpose. It provided entertainment for his children, and it provided a unique means of security: instead of guard dogs, lions and tigers were allowed out of their cages to roam the premises. I doubt that he had any uninvited guests!

On the plane back to Dallas, Idell and I discussed our impressions. She kept the possibility of hiring Armes alive when she offered to help raise the money in the "Mary Kay world." With Mary Kay's approval, she spread the word among directors and consultants. Before we could engage J. J. Armes, however, two more shocking developments had taken place in the Lansing area during my absence. Yet, another young woman had disappeared. I would not find out about this until I returned.

In the meantime on the day following our trip, I received a phone call with more startling news. This time the appalling news involved Donald Miller. We found out that he had been arrested and was in jail, and it wasn't because of Martha's disappearance. He had raped, stabbed, and almost succeeded in strangling a fourteen-year-old girl to death, and he had also tried to kill her younger thirteen-year-old brother. This time there were eyewitnesses, as the teens were expected to live. More of the forensic psychologist's prediction was coming true! When I returned home I heard the reports. Later the details would be filled in by family members and court documents.

Don had driven to the west side of Lansing along a road that headed into a rural area. When he came to the last house built along that road, he stopped in the driveway. Both of the teens had returned from school, but neither was inside when Miller managed to slip into the unlocked house.

It was broad daylight, a little before three in the afternoon. Each day, Lisa and Randy were required to call their stepmother, Donna Irish, at three o'clock at her office to let her know they were both safely home. Since it was close to the time to make their daily call, and since her brother was playing on the other side of the creek at the back of their property, Lisa had stepped outside and gone behind the house to call him. (It would take him ten to fifteen minutes to walk the path around the creek to their home.) As soon as her brother started along the path beside the creek, she turned and walked around the house into the garage entrance. As she did, she noticed a brown car parked in her driveway that had not been there a few minutes earlier. She thought it was a friend who owned a similar brown car. When she reached the bottom step leading into the house, she saw a man standing inside the screen door of her home. As soon as she noticed him, the man asked her in a mild-mannered voice, "Is your father at home?"

Neither the presence of this stranger inside her home nor his question about her father alarmed her, since she was accustomed to seeing workmen in their home. Although they had been living there for some time, a number of small jobs remained to be finished. She assumed that he was just one of the workmen and that he wanted to ask her father about the job he was there to do.

"What time will he be home?"

When Lisa told this stranger that her father would be home at "a quarter after six," the man asked if she had anything he could write his number on. Without hesitation, she stepped inside and walked directly to the cabinet beneath the phone where they kept their pencils and paper. While she wrote down her father's number, suddenly the stranger's left arm gripped her in a chokehold around her neck. At the same time, she saw the flash of a knife in his right hand and felt its sharp blade at her throat. He forced her into the master bedroom. There he blindfolded her, bound her hands with her father's ties, gagged her, and raped her.

After committing the rape, Miller tied Lisa's feet together, picked up her belt, and wrapped it around her neck to strangle her. Fortunately, the belt was made of plastic and it broke under the pressure. This slowed Don only momentarily, for he immediately resumed choking her with his bare hands. During his attack, the girl's brother had been making his way home, unbeknownst to Don. Fortunately, Don had not locked the back door. It was at this point that Randy, knowing nothing of what was happening inside, came into the house. The screen door slammed shut behind him. At the moment he entered the home, his fourteen-year-old sister was only seconds away from death. Lisa was no longer moving, so when Don heard the kitchen door open, he got up and walked outside the bedroom to investigate. When Don saw the boy, he said, "Hi," as he walked past him as if to leave. Once he was behind Randy, he grabbed him with one arm and put a knife to his throat with the other. Then he dragged Randy up the stairs.

As Don was slashing him in the chest and throat and trying to strangle him, Lisa could hear her brother's screams. Fortunately, Lisa's feet were not tied securely. She was able to spit out the nylon that had been stuffed in her mouth, dash outside screaming for help, and run onto the road into the path of an oncoming pickup truck. The driver, James Regan, a supervisor at Oldsmobile, recounted, "I was coming home from work and this little girl ran out into the street, all bloody yelling, 'Help me! Help me! A man in there's trying to kill my brother.'"

Regan knew he needed to get to the boy fast, so he drove past Lisa into the driveway and stopped behind what he identified as a brown 1973 Oldsmobile Cutlass. As Regan was bringing his truck to a stop, he saw the red cutlass of the local fire department chief arriving from the opposite direction. Ken Dorin, the local chief of the fire department, recognized the "little Gilbert girl still running down the road," realized she was in trouble, and stopped to assist. By now, Regan was out of his truck and shouted to Dorin, "Pick up the girl!" as he headed toward the house. When Regan approached, he saw "this guy [with sunglasses on] come flying out of the house." Regan told him, "Stay where you are! Is there a little boy in there?" Without slowing down, the stranger mumbled that he didn't know. Regan persisted, "Is he upstairs?"

The man answered, "I guess so."

As Regan pursued him, he asked, "Is he all right?"

As the man bolted past Regan, he responded, "Yes, I guess he's all right. Why wouldn't he be?" When the young man reached the Olds, he jumped inside, locked the doors, and started the engine. As Regan yanked on the door handle then beat on the window, this "guy" backed into Regan, knocking him into the dirt before "hightailing it" down the road. As the car sped away, Regan memorized the license plate and kept repeating it over and over. Later, Regan said, "That was foremost in my mind. I kept saying it out loud so I wouldn't get the damn number wrong."

While Regan was dealing with Don, Dorin put a hysterical Lisa into his car. She pleaded, "Help me! Help me! I've been raped!" While trying to calm her down, he got on his radio and told the dispatcher to send the sheriff and an ambulance. As he was untying Lisa's hands, she looked back toward her house, saw Don coming through the door, and pointed him out as her attacker.

Family friends, Mrs. Krapf and her mother, saw the disturbance as they were driving by and stopped. Dorin felt Lisa would be more comfortable with the women. After transferring Lisa to their car, he turned his attention to the man escaping in the brown Cutlass. He flagged down a passing motorist to chase the fleeing car.

As Regan picked himself up, he kept shouting out the license number over and over so that it would be stamped into his memory for the police. Then he ran into the house to check on the condition of the boy. He found him lying at the foot of the staircase. He was so quiet that he was afraid he had gone into shock, so he covered him with a rug and waited by his side for the ambulance to arrive. Thankfully, both teens survived their physical injuries. Lisa was in the hospital for three days and Randy was there for five. Their emotional scars, however, would last for decades.

The driver who had pursued the Cutlass from the scene had lost him in traffic. However, when the plate was called in, the dispatcher traced the license to Donald Miller of East Lansing, and he contacted the East Lansing Police Department. They staked out the home of Miller's new girlfriend and waited for him there. It was around four o'clock, an hour after he had fled from the West Lansing neighborhood, when he arrived at his girlfriend's house. Rick Westgate was waiting to arrest him.

When I found out Don had a new girlfriend in spite of all the publicity surrounding him, and that he had been arrested at her home, I shuddered to think of what could have happened to her. I also wondered what on earth that girl had been thinking when she started dating him. Right after he was arrested, she defended Don; she didn't believe he could do such a thing. Later, however, she became so afraid of him that she left the area, leaving no forwarding address.

Finally, Don was in jail! While he awaited trial, no bond was posted. Whether this was the case because he feared for his life if released into the East Lansing community, I cannot say. I did hear rumors that some individuals were considering taking justice into their own hands, and for that reason he was advised to stay in jail. Although the police held him in their custody, the charge was not related to Martha; therefore, he could not be questioned about that case, and so we learned nothing about her.

Once I got home, I also learned that on August 14, two days before the teens were attacked and Miller was arrested, another woman, Kristine Stuart, had disappeared. Kristine was five feet six inches tall and weighed 120 pounds. She was almost exactly the same size as Martha. She had green eyes and shoulder-length brown hair. Once again, questions arose about a possible connection to Martha's disappearance. Mrs. Stuart was a thirty-year-old woman who lived in an area of East Lansing close to where we did. I was so grateful that I had insisted Kay stay with Judy and Bob. Mrs. Stuart vanished shortly after 9:30 A.M. while walking down the street a few blocks from her home. She had dropped her car off for repairs and was walking the short distance to her home. She was last seen by a workman who was employed by her husband's company.

Now the Lansing area was becoming a very scary place. The fact that Mrs. Stuart had last been seen in the daytime just a few blocks from her house in a very nice neighborhood added to the pervading sense of fear. The attacks had started at night; now they were occurring in daylight! And now there were three missing women in addition to the unsolved murder of Marita Choquette. Along with everyone else in the area I was wondering, "What in the world is going on?"

In the months that followed Don's arrest, I paid very little attention to the news reports about the change of venue and the other events leading up to his trial. The trial was moved to the extreme western part of the state, St. Joseph, Michigan, and scheduled for the spring. I did not attend and was only made aware at the time of his defense that he was "pursuing demons." In writing this book, I was allowed access to the transcripts of that trial.

Because Don was now in jail, J. J. Armes said it would be a less difficult case to crack. He reduced his price and, with the help of the "Mary Kay world," I hired him.

9

A High-Stakes Gamble

During the first year of Martha's disappearance, I decided to go to the Ingham County Prosecutor's Office, in downtown Lansing. I hoped they might be able to help me in some way. I was granted an appointment and subsequently an investigator was assigned to Martha's case. During my visits to his office, I felt encouraged by his wholehearted dedication and the ideas he put forth. Suddenly, I discovered that he had been removed from the case. No one was assigned to take his place, and I never understood what had happened. I knew that no trial could transpire until it was presented to a grand jury. So perhaps he wasn't replaced because a judge had put a moratorium on the convening of a grand jury in our county. Whatever the reason, I was extremely disheartened.

After Leo Farhat prepared his case against Miller and turned it over to the prosecutor's office, I heard nothing from the prosecutor's office until the fall of 1978. In September of that year, following the arrest of Miller in mid-August, Farhat sent a memorandum to the chief of the criminal division, Lee Atkinson (who was in the prosecuting attorney's office) that set the process in motion. In a letter dated November 2, 1978, my lawyer informed me that the prosecutor had decided to move forward with the case once again. This was the first action they had taken since removing the first and only investigator from the case a year earlier. It had been almost two years since Martha disappeared. With this letter, Farhat enclosed a copy of a letter sent to him by Lee Atkinson.

In that letter Atkinson stated that he was supervising the prosecutor's investigation! He went on to state that he had reviewed the material that Farhat had supplied them with and "was particularly thankful for [his] memorandum of September 18, 1978." Then he added, "As you are well aware, grand jury secrecy provisions would preclude me informing of any progress made by that body should it undertake to investigate these matters."

So, Prosecutor Peter Houk was now giving thoughtful consideration to using the material that Farhat had prepared to bring Miller to trial. What great news.

From the tone of Atkinson's letter, I felt certain that at last Martha's case would go before the grand jury!

I had confidence in Leo Farhat. He told me that despite the lack of a body, he could get a conviction with the evidence he had assembled, and I believed him. I trusted his judgment, so I felt ready to take the risk of prosecution earlier than my friends in law enforcement. As I'd mentioned earlier, Prosecutor Houk shared the same feelings as the police. Both were acutely aware of what the consequences of losing would be. Following a not-guilty verdict, even if Martha's body was discovered the next day, and with it evidence beyond any doubt that he had murdered her, he could never be held accountable. An article published by *The Lansing State Journal* a year later, on Monday, September 3, 1979, underscored the high risk he had considered. Houk stated, "In the one reported Michigan decision dealing with a homicide prosecution where no body or body part was recovered, the Michigan Supreme Court said, 'We think under the authorities cited, it should be held that the people have failed to show beyond a reasonable doubt that the defendant is guilty of manslaughter.'" Although Houk was aware of this court decision, I surmised that he had decided to set the process in motion by convening the grand jury. This required a good deal of courage, for he was well aware that this was a high-stakes gamble. My hunch proved correct. It therefore came as no surprise when I was called to testify before the grand jury. While all of this was taking place, Don awaited his trial for assaulting the two teens. On August 17 of that year, Don had been arraigned on four felony charges: two counts of assault with intent to murder, one count of criminal sexual conduct including a weapon, and one count of breaking and entering an occupied dwelling with the intent to commit a felony.

In February, I was to testify before the grand jury. The day of my testimony, Dean Tucker accompanied me for moral support. We sat in the hallway outside the room where the grand jury was meeting. I had assumed Dean would stay beside me while I testified. To my dismay, I discovered that the rules governing grand jury testimony would not permit Dean to go inside with me. I would have to testify alone—but it was a relief to know that Don would not be in the room. Dean assured me I would do fine. After my testimony, I resumed the waiting game to see what would happen next.

Would the grand jury indict Don for Martha's murder? I would have to wait until spring to find out. I received my answer in the form of a summons to testify at the arraignment. The summons told me that the grand jury had found sufficient cause for the case to advance to the next step, which was a weeklong court hearing before a local judge who would determine whether the case merited being brought to trial. Once again, on the day I was to be a witness, I was not allowed in the courtroom until it was my turn to testify. This time I waited in a jury room until I was called, and this time I knew I would be facing Don Miller, who would be seated at the defense table. I returned to the jury room during breaks in the testimony. I was grateful I did not have to wait by myself. A friend drove me to and from court and waited with me.

I recall three distinct images from that day. The first was the sight of Don. I had not seen him since he had been jailed for attempting to murder Lisa and Randy. Now the defense attorney positioned himself so that both he and Don were directly in my line of vision as I was being questioned. I could not avoid looking at Don. The entire time I was on the witness stand, he glared at me with cold, hard eyes in a clear attempt to intimidate me. Others in the courtroom noticed that Don's demeanor was vastly different the day I testified from the rest of the week. I was told that on days when I was not in the courtroom, he tried to appear as if he were not aware of what was going on around him. As he sat at the defense table, he seemed to try to scrunch into a fetal position.

My second memory is my response to Don's look of hatred. In spite of his glare, I felt an amazing sense of calmness and confidence as I faced his lawyer. It almost seemed as though I were observing the scene rather than testifying in it. Obviously, I had been anxious while anticipating what the hearing would be like. As I discussed my feelings with my friend Flo Allen, she told me that when she was faced with an awful circumstance she had visualized Jesus standing between her and the bad situation. She suggested that I do the same.

On the day of my testimony, as I faced Don's stare, I did as my friend suggested and pictured Jesus standing between us. It was a most unusual experience. I seemed to sense how the defense was trying to handle me as a witness. I could "see" the defense dealing very gingerly with me. They needed to appear gentle with me because of the sympathies of the court toward me, the victim's mother. At the same time, the defense lawyer needed to discredit me. Apparently, his goal was to make it appear as though I did not really know my daughter. As he asked the first innocent-sounding question, I clearly saw the trap he was setting.

Without hesitation, the right words just came out of my mouth. Ordinarily, it takes me time to think of the way I ought to phrase an answer. Sometimes I even ponder over things I have said the next day. But that was not the case that day. My answers came quickly and confidently, and they stopped the defense's line of questioning cold. One of the questions was, "Were you aware that Martha was looking for another place to live in East Lansing?"

When I answered, "I suggested it," I could see immediately that I had caught the defense off guard. They had anticipated this information would come as an upsetting surprise, which would help him establish his theory that I really had not known what was going on in my daughter's life. I guessed that he had planned to follow up with some related questions, because he appeared shaken, hesitated, and scrambled to find a new direction for his queries. I certainly did not smile in court, but I remember thinking that the scene was almost funny, for the same thing kept happening over and over. He asked another question, and again I answered promptly, once again throwing him off.

The third and most painful memory, however, is not related to the defense attorney; it came from "our" side, the prosecution. For this I was totally unprepared. Martha's small Western-style leather purse was brought before me to identify. It was the one that the hunters had discovered the year before. I couldn't understand why that was necessary. Obviously, it was Martha's, because it contained her driver's license and other items that identified it as hers. Nevertheless, I was asked to look at the contents. As the purse and it contents, which I had last seen in my daughter's hands, were displayed, I no longer felt a feeling of detachment. Instead of touching them, I shrank back. Now my emotions were raw. They only got worse when they brought out her clothes. When the hunters had found them, I was not asked to identify anything. Mercifully, Sgt. Tucker had been able to make the identification, because he had a match to the trousers, scarf, watch, and shoes. Her ski jacket had been identified by the store where we'd purchased it. I had never wanted to see her clothing, which provided tangible evidence of her gruesome ordeal. Until this day in court, I had been spared the sight.

As her clothing was thrust toward me, I was told to "look." There was no need to tell me to look, because I could see nothing else. My eyes were absolutely riveted on them. Still, I was repeatedly told to "Look! Look!" As her clothes were pushed ever closer toward me, I shuddered. I felt like yelling, "I am looking!" I suppose he wanted me to hold them, but I wasn't going to touch them; just the sight of Martha's things made me recoil. Instead of handling the items, I started to cry as I pleaded, "What do you want me to do?" Judge Tschirthart, seeing my obvious distress, ruled that the clothing had been identified sufficiently and to move on. I didn't view this as a deliberate act of cruelty, but unfortunately our justice system often deems it necessary to re-victimize survivors in order to convict the perpetrator.

The pastor of East Lansing Trinity Church also testified. Don had claimed that he and Martha had stopped by the church looking for his sister. The minister, however, refuted this, testifying that he had not seen Don there. Another witness, Ernest Boillard, had shared a cell with Don while in jail. He testified that he had heard Don say, "I should have done away with [the teens] the way I did my girlfriend."

Nancy Daniels of East Lansing was called to testify in the Kristine Stuart case. She had witnessed the abduction of Kristine while driving past Don's car, but although she contacted the police knowing that she had seen something, the images did not come into sharp focus until she underwent hypnosis. Then she was able to assist the police with a composite drawing that strongly resembled Don. Under its influence, she also recalled seeing Don hold Kristine down on the seat of his car while he plunged a knife into her.

The arraignment took place the week of April 18. At the end of the week, Judge Tschirthart bound Don over for trial for second-degree murder in the deaths of Martha and Kristine. The news had been a long time coming, and I welcomed it. However, before this trial could take place, the case in St. Joseph had to proceed. The St. Joseph trial was scheduled for the first of May, to be presided over by Eaton County Circuit Court Judge Richard Robinson. At its conclusion, a date could be set for the case involving Martha's death. In the meantime, I could not make plans in either my business or personal life, as I had no idea when the next trial would start.

I was told to expect a very long court proceeding, one that would last months. While I wanted Don to be tried for Martha's murder, I was dreading the experience of living through it. Having recently experienced being a witness, I could only imagine what was in store for me during the actual trial. To make matters worse, the defense would likely be able to get a change of venue, moving the trial far away from the community. There was a precedent for the change, since it had been granted in the preceding trial. Community emotions were certainly running high with regard to Martha and the other three victims, so a change of location seemed inevitable.

This would make things incredibly hard on me, since I would be removed from all my support systems. I was told my presence would be required every day in the courtroom. What would it be like to go by myself and take up residence in a strange community? How was I going to survive? Facing Don Miller each day was a daunting prospect. I still had a bitter taste in my mouth from the previous experience. I knew that he would once again do all he could to intimidate me. I had never wanted to speculate about all the excruciating details, and so far the police had shielded me from them as much as possible. To me, the most awful part of all this was that at the trial I would no longer be shielded; I would see and hear everything. I could only imagine what it would be like to be totally immersed, day after day, in all the gruesome details, without friends or even my business to distract me. My Mary Kay business was already in trouble; I had received a standard warning letter that I had failed to meet production quotas for one month, yet during a trial in another city I certainly wouldn't be able to get any business done. How was I going to survive without an income? With a daughter in college, would I lose my livelihood? How was I going to pay for months of motel bills and meals in restaurants? I couldn't help feeling, "Where is the justice here? Is it right to keep on punishing the victim and forcing her to sacrifice in favor of the 'rights' of a murderer?"

Yet, I knew that I had to do everything necessary, no matter the emotional or financial cost. On June 4, 1979, I received a letter from Ingham County Prosecuting Attorney Peter Houk updating me on the status of the *People v. Don Gene Miller*. It advised me that the criminal trial docket ran only from September to June. "None of your vacation plans or other plans will need to be altered because of your status as a witness," it said. "However, I would ask that, if possible, you avoid scheduling activities or events which would interfere with your appearing as a witness from the first of September through December 1979."

After reading the letter, I decided to put thoughts of the trial out of my mind until the end of the summer. I would treat the time as a brief reprieve. I could actually have three whole months when I could focus on other things. I would have a peaceful summer in which to concentrate on my business. During this time, I would need to generate enough momentum in my business to compensate for my absence during the fall. Plus, I somehow needed to gain strength for the ordeal that lay ahead. Kay had decided to attend the summer session at the University of Georgia, so there was nothing to prevent me from planning an August business trip to a conference in Indiana. A month later, my plan for a peaceful summer was interrupted.

10

Battling Demons

During the last week of May in 1979, Don was tried for the assaults upon Lisa and Randy. Defense Attorney Thomas Bengston established the defense's strategy in his opening statement before the Berrien County Circuit Court. He stated that the defendant "lived with an angel and devil inside, co-existing, but not aware of the other's existence."

Following the state's opening remarks, by Assistant Prosecutor Michael Hocking, the first witnesses were called. It took three days for the state to build their powerful case against Miller. First, Hocking reconstructed the crime through the testimony of the two teenaged victims. Lisa and Randy were able to give a clear, detailed account of the calculated manner in which Don carried out his assaults. Lisa was called to the stand first. Testifying was an uncomfortable and embarrassing experience for this sheltered young lady of fifteen. For this shy girl, who had not even discussed the details of the assault with her family, testifying merely added to her nightmare. Years later, her stepsister, Laura, who had shared the same bedroom at the time of the assault, told me she used to hear Lisa crying at night when the lights were out. Lisa's embarrassment was evident in her testimony. Her voice was so soft that she often had to be coached to "speak up." Even so, her testimony was solid. Starting from the beginning, she explained how Don had instructed her, "Lie down and put your face down to the floor," so he could tie her hands. He then covered Lisa's eyes, but before he proceeded, he remembered that the front door was open, because it was a hot summer day. He stopped to shut and lock the door. When she was questioned about how she knew what he was doing with her eyes covered, she replied, "I heard the front door close and heard it being locked." Then, while the assault was in progress, he stopped again and she heard him go to the bedroom windows and draw the drapes.

Randy's testimony followed Lisa's. He described being forced upstairs and fighting for his life while his assailant attempted to cut his throat. Randy described how he grabbed the knife and threw it under the bed. Don then proceeded to strangle him with his hands, and Randy blacked out. When Randy came to, he discovered he had been stabbed in the chest and was covered with blood. His assailant was no longer in the room, so Randy somehow managed to get down the stairs. The front door was now open, and he saw a "commotion taking place" in front of the house. The impact of the two teen witnesses' testimony was powerful. Hospital records substantiated the accuracy of Lisa's and Randy's accounts. In addition, their testimony was corroborated by the two men, Dorin and Regan, who stopped to offer their assistance at the scene.

Following Randy's testimony, these two men were called as witnesses. Both could provide eyewitness identification of Don, as they had seen him running out of the house to his car. Their testimony could not be impeached. They were solid citizens and reliable witnesses. One of them, as a fire chief, was trained in remembering pertinent details. Regan had memorized the license number. That number, called into the fire department dispatcher from the scene, was the same one used to trace Don and arrest him. Chief Dorin also testified that he had gone inside to check on Randy, as he was concerned about his condition. He had a personal interest because he knew the family; Randy had even gone on a camping trip Dorin had led. There was so much blood that Randy appeared to be severely injured. As Randy lay covered in blood, Dorin tried to reassure him that he would be all right. He told him, "You are a strong boy," even though Dorin was uncertain whether Randy would survive.

Other witnesses who arrived at the scene were also called to testify. The evidence was overwhelming. In fact, Assistant Prosecutor Hocking stated he had never seen a stronger case.

Consequently, the defense did not argue the facts in the case; their defense was based on a "not guilty by reason of insanity" plea. To support this position, the defense had psychologist Rudolph Bachman from Garden City, Michigan, take the stand. His conclusion was that Miller suffered from multiple-personality disorder, that his psyche consisted of a "good" side that warred with an "evil" side. Following Bachman's testimony, Bengston requested that the charges be reduced to assaults with intent to do great bodily harm rather than attempted murder, and second-degree criminal sexual conduct rather than rape.

In denying the request, the judge stated there was good reason to believe the assaults were attempted murders. The second defense witness was Dr. Dennis Koson, a psychiatrist in private practice in Ann Arbor. His testimony was based on a three-hour interview with Miller that he had conducted plus a video he had watched of Miller under the influence of sodium amatol (truth serum). In the video, Miller talked of demons. Based on the interview and video, Koson concluded that Miller's memory of the attacks had been repressed. Koson continued that it was the intensity of Don's belief (when he looked at Lisa and saw her as a demon) that evoked "the fear and rage that put him in that house." The doctor's scenario didn't exactly match the established facts. Don hadn't stopped because he had seen Lisa as a demon. He stopped and went into an empty house. He saw Lisa after he had entered it.

During Prosecutor Hocking's cross-examination, he asked Koson if it was possible to lie under the influence of sodium amytol. The doctor admitted that the use of "truth serum" provided no guarantee that a person would tell the truth. He acknowledged, "People can tell bald-faced lies" under its influence. Pursuing that line of questioning, the prosecutor asked if Miller could have invented the demons he had been speaking about as a defense tactic. Koson sidestepped a direct answer by implying that Miller's reluctance to talk about demons when not under the influence of the serum indicated he had no conscious knowledge of such information. Hocking suggested that Don had not talked about demons at first because he hadn't had time to develop his defense strategy.

Hocking reminded Koson that Miller had engaged in deliberate acts to avoid being caught. These included interrupting his assault on Lisa to shut the door and close the drapes, disposing of the knife that he had used, and changing into clean clothes before arriving at his girlfriend's home.

Koson answered with a question: "Because a person closes a drape or changes clothes, that can only mean that they know that they are doing something wrong. Is that what you are saying?" Koson purposed that Don could have had a completely different motive for taking such actions other than concealment.

The third defense witness was Dr. Gerald Briskin from Wyndotte General Hospital, which is located just outside Detroit. Dr. Briskin agreed with the first two expert witnesses that Miller was an angry, tightly controlled psychotic. From inkblot tests he conducted on Miller, he characterized him as having a distant relationship with his father and ambivalent feelings toward his mother and other women. Another inkblot interpretation suggested he was "leaking" sub-conscious memories of the crime. He painted a picture of Miller as a religious fanatic who saw himself engaging in a battle against "the forces of Satan." The fourth witness was Dr. Arthur Hughett, the director of the Wyndotte psychiatric unit. He concurred with Briskin's assessment that Miller saw himself as a force for good, fighting to save souls from Satan.

The prosecution presented two rebuttal expert witnesses, Dr. Lynn Blunt, of the state Center for Forensic Psychiatry at Ypsilanti, and psychologist Dr. Harley Stock, also from the forensic center. Dr. Blunt testified that Miller was "psychologically intact." He stated that Miller invoked religion inconsistently and used religion to justify his actions. With regard to the videotaped session with Miller under the influence of sodium amytol, Blunt stated that he saw evidence that Don was "feigning an inability to remember." He saw inconsistencies in Miller's story and holes in his testimony due to a withholding of information. He stated that Miller was "certainly aware of reality" during the attack. Dr. Stock also testified that Miller had been sane when he committed the attacks and that he used religion only when it suited him. (Earlier, Dr. Stock had aided police in prosecuting another killer in nearby Oakland County.)

In the closing argument, Hocking began by asking jurors to use their common sense, stating, "The facts speak for themselves." He enumerated actions that demonstrated Don had been fully aware of his surroundings and had calculated his acts to avoid detection. He pointedly asked the jury, "Can a person slip in and out of acute psychosis to suit his needs?"

After the closing arguments, the judge instructed the jury on verdicts that they could render and the consequences of each. It took the jury less than two hours to find Miller guilty on all counts.

I was grateful to the six-woman, six-man jury. Hailing from the farming community of St. Joseph, Michigan, they had their feet planted firmly in reality. They were not easily influenced by a fanciful defense that portrayed Miller as a man fighting the forces of evil, embodied in two teenagers in their own home.

On behalf of his client, Bengston filed a petition for a new trial on the grounds that Judge Robinson had prejudiced the jury when he told it that a "not guilty by reason of insanity" verdict would mean that Miller would be sent back to the Forensic Center for another evaluation, and, if judged sane, would be set free. The defense claimed they had a right to limit the information that the judge could give the jury regarding what a "not guilty by reason of insanity" verdict would mean. The defense wanted the judge to say instead that the evaluation would determine the "course of further legal action." It seems to me the judge would have been misleading the jury if he said so, at the very least. Once a person has been tried and a verdict has been handed down, there can be no further legal action. It's over. The case is finished. Any further legal action would be double jeopardy. The "not guilty by reason of insanity" verdict puts the accused outside the criminal-justice system and into the mental-health system. I think it should be illegal for the jury not to be told what their sentences could mean. Why should a defense attorney be able to exploit a citizen's ignorance of the law? If it is legal to do so, we certainly need new laws to level the playing field. Fortunately for the citizens of Michigan, the jury's verdict was upheld.

On May 31, Judge Robison sentenced Don to thirty-to-fifty years on each of the three charges. These sentences, according to Michigan law, were to be served concurrently, rather than consecutively. This meant that he would be eligible for parole in thirteen years! Still the sentence was stiffer than a "life sentence" at that time, for I was told a life sentence would mean an even earlier potential release. (In fact, Don's first parole hearing was in the eleventh year instead of the thirteenth. Maybe that was due to the automatic "good time" prisoners begin to accrue the instant they set foot in prison.)

Although I was grateful to have Don off the streets that last day of May 1979, the St. Joe trial had answered none of the questions about my daughter. Consequently, I was focused on the one that lay ahead, when Don would finally be tried for Martha's murder. This trial, however, was one that would never take place. In July, I was asked to come down to the East Lansing police station to speak with Dean Tucker, who was now Lt. Tucker.

11

It's Over—or Is It?

When I walked into the conference room at the ELPD, two other people were there besides Dean Tucker. I recognized Ingham County Prosecutor Peter Houk (who later became Judge Houk), but I had never seen the other man before. When I was introduced to Ernie Stuart, I recognized the name immediately. Ernie was the husband of Kristine Stuart, who had disappeared in 1978. When the press had begun suggesting that there was a connection between Martha's disappearance and those of the other women, I considered it wild speculation on their part. The police had never mentioned a possible link to me, but then I had never asked about the stories that were appearing.

Although I believed in my heart that Don would commit other murders, I didn't want to accept the fact that it had already happened. I didn't want to be proven right. Strange as it seems, I still did not want to believe that Don was a serial murderer. Somehow, there was something in me that still didn't want to believe he could be that evil. Now it hit me. The only possible connection I could have to this man, whom I had never met, was Donald Miller, so I didn't need to be told why Mr. Stuart was sitting there. *It is true*, I thought. Without being told, I now knew for sure that Don had committed more than one murder.

The reason the two of us had been asked to meet was that Don's lawyer had initiated talk of a plea bargain! Don had suggested that if he were given "a truth serum," perhaps a psychiatrist could help him "remember." If he could recall his actions, it might be possible for him to lead police to the bodies of Martha and Kristine Stuart. In exchange, he would plead guilty to manslaughter in the deaths of Martha and Kristine, and he would not be charged in the deaths of Marita and Wendy.

Prosecutor Houk wanted to know if Mr. Stuart and I would accept a plea bargain. My immediate thought was, *Why would we want to do that?* The police department had worked Martha's case with great passion for such a long time that I felt I would be betraying them if I agreed. I looked at Dean (Lt. Tucker) to see if I could get some sense of what he was thinking. Since I couldn't, I asked, "Would there be anything for us to gain by taking the case to trial?"

The answer was, "No, there really isn't anything to be gained." Peter Houk explained, "Michigan law does not allow for consecutive sentences. We already have a thirty-to-fifty-year sentence. If we take the case to trial, as scheduled in the fall, the most we can get are second-degree murder convictions, which carry about fifteen-year sentences." I was told we could not get a first-degree murder conviction without the bodies. A second-degree sentence, therefore, would be less than the sentence we already had. The hard fact was that we could not get one day added to the sentence that he was already serving.

"How unjust!" I fumed. Prosecutor Houk's resigned response left me almost speechless. "So according to present Michigan law, after I kill one person, anyone else I kill is a 'freebee'?" I looked at Dean Tucker incredulously, and his expression confirmed what the prosecutor was saying. At this point, I knew for certain that Michigan law needed to be changed. *Why do we protect the rights of murderers over those of the victims?* I wondered. This went against common sense.

Ernie Stuart sat silently while I did all of the questioning. His first priority, I found, was recovering his wife's body, so he stated that he was in favor of accepting the plea agreement. Next, I was asked, "Would you also accept the plea bargain?"

Before answering, I turned to my friend Dean and said, "What do you think? I know you and the rest of the East Lansing Police have put your heart and soul into this case."

His response was, "There is nothing to be gained. It will save you from the trauma of a long, drawn-out trial, and in the end we will not be able to add one day to the sentence. This way you will finally be able to bury Martha Sue."

As I hesitated, Peter Houk told me he was willing to take the case to trial if that was what we wanted. He went on to state that if we did take the case to trial, however, there was no assurance we would win. I already had learned from my lawyer, Leo Farhat, that very few cases had ever resulted in a guilty verdict where no body was found. Circumstantial evidence was all that we had to link Don to Martha's death. We had no physical evidence at all in Kristine's death, and the only link between Don and Kristine was an eyewitness whose memory had to be refreshed under hypnosis.

To be sure we knew what we were up against, Houk reported, "In the most recent appellate court decision involving the attempted use of evidence obtained through hypnosis, that evidence was deemed inadmissible. If we can't use this woman's testimony, we have no link to Don. On the other hand, if Don confesses and leads the police to the bodies, this will be on his record with corrections officials. If, instead, he is tried for the murders and is not convicted, they will not become part of his record." I certainly agreed that this record was important when it came time for parole. The way Michigan law worked, parole seemed to be inevitable at some future date. It was essential that the board know that he had done more than attempt to kill. The parole board needed to know that he had succeeded in murdering four women. The way I saw it, after Don had led authorities to the bodies of these women (whom no one else had been able to find), there would be no reasonable doubt that he was their killer.

In accepting the plea bargain, I wanted to make it clear that I would say no if there were anything to be gained. Also, if the ELPD wanted the case to go to trial, I would also say no. However, considering the way the law was at the moment, I could not see anything to gain by insisting that the case be taken to trial. I could not fathom putting myself through the ordeal of a trial and accomplishing nothing in return. Plus, it would take the time of the police and prosecutors and cost the taxpayers a lot more money. Considering all these things, I didn't think we had any choice but to accept the plea bargain, so I agreed.

I went away wondering what Don would get out of this. Why would he offer such a deal? Surely, he had to have known about our inability to add to his sentence. For years, I puzzled over what Don thought he had gained by doing this. Finally, it occurred to me that the picture could change for him if the bodies were ever discovered sometime in the future. By striking a plea bargain, he could eliminate the possibility of being charged with first-degree murder. I knew for certain that the murders of both Martha and Kristine were, in fact, premeditated. He had three days to plan Martha's murder. In Kristine's case, he prepared beforehand and looked for someone to kill. By ensuring he would never stand trial for first-degree murder, he figured that he would get early parole. All he needed to do was be a model prisoner until he became eligible for parole in eleven years. By the time he reached age thirty-five, he could walk out of prison a free man.

At the conclusion of our meeting, Peter Houk said he would contact Don's lawyer, who would arrange for him to see a psychiatrist. I left the meeting feeling certain that we would finally find Martha's body. I felt absolutely sure that the request for truth serum "to unlock" his memories was nothing more than a ruse. *What a charade*, I thought. *How could he plea bargain to find the bodies if he had no memory of his action?* Sometimes the law seems to ask one to lay aside common sense. (Later, after the plea bargain was in place, Don admitted that he had found Martha's glasses the next morning in his car. He went on to comment that if the police had searched his car that day, they would have found them before he had a chance to get rid of them. I knew Martha would have never left her glasses behind when she was not wearing her contacts. This admission seemed to add to the proof that Don knew exactly what he was doing.) Following the meeting, I talked to Dean, who said we would probably know something by the end of July. After that, I received no news of any progress. The waiting game continued.

On the afternoon of July 13, I received a call from Lt. Tucker asking if it was all right for him to stop by the house. A few minutes later, his unmarked car arrived. As I went to the door, I saw that four officers, all of them dressed in suits, were getting out of the car. I knew something was up immediately. Never before had four officers come at the same time. Never had they all appeared in suits. As I greeted these men who had become my friends and invited them into the living room, my stomach was going into knots. I didn't know what to say, so I offered them tea. They declined. Dean asked me to sit down. "Sue," he said, "we have some bad news."

Before coming to my house, the police had carried out a grisly mission. The lieutenant led the group that had followed Donald Miller into a brush area of a park in Bath Township, which adjoined East Lansing to the northeast. There they had found Martha's body. As this seasoned detective with twenty-nine years on the force stood looking down at the remains of someone he had once described as a "beautiful young girl," by his own admission, he cried. He described to reporter John Schneider feeling "a mixture of sadness and anger." It had been "a hell of an emotional thing to go through," he stated in the interview.

They had put their feelings aside before entering my home so they would be able to support me when I heard the terrible announcement:

"We have found Martha's body," Dean said.

I was numb. I didn't cry, but from that point on I don't remember exactly what was said. I know I was told that Don had led the police to the area where he had left her. Although they were sure it was Martha, they would need to prove it conclusively in the forensic lab, where they had taken her body for an autopsy. I remember Dean asking who I wanted him to call, for they were not prepared to leave me in my house by myself. I decided I did not want to wait for someone to come to me. I thought that my next-door neighbor, Judy, would be home. I wanted to go there. Even then, Dean didn't want to leave until he saw for himself that she was home, so he walked next door with me. When Judy came to the door, he stood there and talked to her for a minute. Only after he was satisfied that she was going to stay with me did the officers depart.

I had kept my emotions in check until I got to Judy's. Now that there was no longer any reason to hold back, the two of us stood in her kitchen, hugging each other and crying together. Finally, we sat down in her family room…sometimes crying…sometimes Judy just listened as I talked. She was my sounding board, and I don't think I moved from the sofa all afternoon. I did not want to go home. I did not want to be by myself. If I went home the phone would start to ring, and I didn't want to answer the phone. There was nothing I wanted to do. I knew the press would be calling for a statement, and I did not have one. I certainly did not want to talk to the media.

Finally, I realized there were decisions to be made and things that would have to be done. I couldn't just sit there. My minister, Dr. Bob Williams, from Plymouth Congregation, the new church I'd attended the last couple of years, was out of town on vacation, so I had not tried to call him. Around quarter to five it suddenly occurred to me: it was Friday afternoon and I had to call the church before its offices closed for the weekend. However, the phone there only rang and rang. The office had already closed. Since I couldn't reach the church, I thought maybe I should call the Williams' home and leave a message on their answering machine; perhaps they would have someone come in and look after things while they were gone. Possibly that person would know how to get word to Bob. To my surprise, their son, Mark, answered my call. The pastor's teenage children had just walked in that minute, as the phone was ringing.(What extraordinary timing. If I had made that call any earlier, I would have received no answer. I would have assumed the children were with their parents and not called back.) I asked Mark if there was any way of getting in touch with his dad. He said he was sure there was, and then he paused.

"Hang on! He is just walking in right now." he said. I felt like this was a miracle. Earlier in the afternoon, I'd had no inclination to call, but the moment I did was the moment the pastor returned.

Bob told me he would come over that very evening, and he did. When he arrived, he let me talk, just as Judy had that afternoon. I talked and talked in what seemed to me to be all sorts of odd circles. I didn't know what to do, so I depended a great deal on Bob's help. He very kindly took over many of the details for me. He asked about my wishes concerning flowers for the funeral. My feeling was that my beautiful daughter had been left outside to die, and I could not stand the thought of one more beautiful thing being left to die under the hot sun. However, I wanted long-stemmed red roses on her casket from her family, so I asked Dr. Williams to have individual roses placed on her casket, each in its own vial, rather than a funeral spray. I wanted them removed when people had left and taken to hospitals or shut-ins. In sensitivity to the feelings of the sick, I asked that they not be told where they had come from. I knew that Martha would not be in that grave, so I thought flowers in a hospital or home would be a more fitting tribute to her than those left in the sun to die. Ever so gently, from time to time, Pastor Bob would bring me back to what had to be done. One after another, we dealt with the details. I told him that the forensic lab would have the body for the weekend. It would not be released before sometime on Monday, so services were planned for Tuesday. Finally, Bob said, "Have you talked to the press?"

"Oh, Bob, I don't want to talk to anybody, not now. I don't have anything left to say," I pleaded.

He persisted, "You need to make a statement to the press and get it over with. You know you are going to have to do it sometime. Come on," he coaxed, "I will help you write it." I knew he was right, so we composed a statement. I considered the media my friends and I would have welcomed them to come to the funeral, because I felt they cared about Martha. Kay, I knew, wanted it to be private, not wanting attention focused on her at such a time. My first concern was for Kay, so I told the press it would be a private service. All of the media honored my wishes; none of the press came, and no one took pictures from a distance. I cannot remember anything about the statement that we wrote except for the last sentence. Bob told me to conclude with, "I will have more to say later." The reason I remember that part so vividly is that, at the time, I was absolutely certain that I would not have anything to say to the press again, ever! I did what I was told, however, because I trusted my pastor. It turned out he was right. At that moment, he knew me better than I knew myself, because a few short days later I had a lot to say!

Judy's husband, also named Bob, came home from work, and I had supper with them. They gave me the downstairs study for my bedroom. I greatly appreciated their graciousness. As I was not sleepy, I didn't bother to get ready for bed. But it was a comfort to know there was someone in the house. Since there was a pool in the backyard, Bob came down for his routine midnight swim. When he came in and saw that I was still up, he sat down to talk for a while before turning in for the night. Kay would be coming home from Georgia, and I had called my friend Grace in Pennsylvania and asked her to come. Grace is the type of person who makes things better by just walking into the room. I certainly needed that.

I don't remember much about the next little while except that the days between Friday and Tuesday were sunny and gorgeous, yet cool. They were the kind of Michigan summer days I especially loved. God was so kind to provide us with great weather. I was particularly grateful that Tuesday, the day of the memorial service, was also sunny. A gray day would have been much harder on me. On

Sunday, my friend Jan had us over for a luncheon. She had taken great care to make it especially lovely. The kindness of Grace, Kay, Jan, Judy, and Dr. Williams made those days poignantly beautiful.

Dr. Williams had told me that the church committee that ordinarily sent food to funerals was gone for the summer and asked if I wanted food sent in. I told him we didn't need for anyone to go to that trouble. Food was the last thing on my mind. Judy knew, however, that many people would be coming in from out of state. So when she observed that no food was being brought in, she mobilized the neighbors to take care of the situation. She did this even though her mother was suffering from terminal cancer and she would have to leave to be by her bedside before the memorial service. She brought everything to the house the morning of the services and left Grace in charge.

Le flew in the morning of the service. That day was one of the hardest of my life. I told him I didn't think I could stand it. Perhaps that is the reason Bob Williams had the three of us come into his study before the memorial began. Emotions often defy logic. I knew that Martha's body had been outside for over two years, and I knew that she had been safe with God for those years, yet I couldn't stand the thought of putting her in the ground. Bob's advice was very practical and very helpful. He said to remember that all the people in the service had come for us and to concentrate on the details and listen to the words.

Kay had made a collage of pictures depicting Martha's life and placed it on a table at the church entrance beside the guest registry. I was glad she did, as I would not have thought of doing that. As the memorial began, Le, Kay, and I walked down the aisle together and sat down in the front row. I did pay attention to the details and the words. I am grateful for that suggestion, as they gave me comfort. A family friend, Reverend Carl Staser, opened the service with the prayer of Francis of Assisi, which begins with the familiar words, "Lord, make me an instrument of your peace" and concludes, "It is in pardoning that we are pardoned, and it is in dying that we are born to eternal life." Dr. Williams continued the service by saying,

> Most young people die violently. They die as the victims of recklessness, as the victims of adult-created wars, as the victims of harsh illness, as the victims of crime. I was not privileged to have known Martha personally. Yet, through her mother, Sue, and through several things Martha has written, my perception of her feels remarkably clear.
>
> She experienced a world of feelings in her young life—pain, loneliness, sadness, anger, frustration. But, by her own testimony, she also experienced beauty, delight, love, and laughter as both a giver and a receiver. She had

opportunities to express compassion, concern, and love for others. And this she did in magnum quantities. In her young life, she experienced more of lightened shadow than most adults who live a fuller span of years.

Dr. Williams read a prayer Martha had written and then continued,

She would quickly say that the way she died was not God's will, but a horrible abuse of the freedom God has given us. Martha writes, "God is the creator and lover of the universe. Man was born of God, yet when given the choice of God or earth, he chose earth." Not believing God's way to be all powerful, but choosing to be all loving, she wrote that in the worst happenings, "God intercedes for me in all things."

What we believe to be true about God can make a literal world of difference in how we meet life, in how we come to feel not only about God but about ourselves and about others. Martha's emerging theology was moving towards a mature grasp of truth. By joining Martha's quest, by joining Martha's faith, we shall be comforted.

The gift of Martha herself—her life, her strength, and her beauty—are perceived anew through the intensity of our deep feelings in this hour.

There is the gift of new sustaining relationships. Martha knew peace quickly. For Sue, for Kay, for Le, for friends and loved ones, for concerned and compassionate police officers, for Carl Staser, and for myself, only now does peace have its opportunity with us. The deep unknowing, the uncertainties, the foreboding anxieties of possible trials, the quest for truth—as agonizing as it has been—has yielded new friends and the perfecting of God's strength through these friends in times of great need.

As the minister continued, Kay cast a quick glance up at her father and saw his eyes brimming with tears.

And there are those gifts of the spirit developed by the sheer burden of it all. As St. Paul said, "Suffering produces endurance, endurance produces character, and character produces hope." If we fail to perceive it, we will have let Martha down in ways that she would find inexcusable.

A beautiful photograph of Martha is before us. But something transcends her, draws her up into it.

The Bible, in all its humanity, witnesses to an emerging reality of life that transcends death.

The two candles remind us of the dual nature of Christ: One reminds us of the humanness of Christ, who died violently, as did Martha. The other candle represents the divinity of Christ, that which is of God—loving, transcendent, healing, restorative, everlasting.

The Cross, in which the divine is savingly wed to the human. As Martha said, "The Cross is my hope." It is ours.
Today we will be thankful:
Thankful for Martha's life.
Thankful for Martha's faith.
Thankful for the living God who meets us here today.

Today we grieve, for we love. We will mourn, we will cry, for we are hurt. But if we are to please Martha and to honor her, we shall soon let the Lord God, who swallows up death forever, wipe away tears from our faces, and rejoice in God's salvation.

Following the service, we made our way to the cemetery. On our way, we passed a golf course, where golfers were playing in the brilliant sunlit day. As I watched, the game ceased while the golfers placed their hands over their hearts in a silent salute as our procession wound past. Approaching the grave, I saw long-stemmed red roses fanned out across Martha's casket. They were just the way that I had requested, so that they could be given to the living to add beauty to their days. Afterward, I was grateful to have friends follow us back to the house for lunch. The ache remained, but finally the ordeal was over—that long black nightmare of the soul, the glimmers of hope followed by despair, the struggles, the work of seeking the truth, the waiting, the wondering, and the endless searches. There was nothing else to be done. It was finished.

My feeling that it was finally "all over" lasted through the night following the funeral. It didn't last much longer than that. Almost immediately, I realized it was not over! There was still much work to be done. In thirteen years, the killer could be unleashed upon society once more. The public was incensed about the plea bargain. Irate letters appeared in the paper. Women looked ahead to probable release dates, frightened for themselves and their children. The fury over the plea bargain grew. The daily paper's editorial staff reflected the views of the community when they expressed the opinion that under Michigan's laws, justice had not been served. I shared their frustration. I was told by our prosecuting attorney, who was running for election, that people were so angry with him that they slammed doors in his face. The truth of the matter was that the plea bargain was not Peter Houk's fault. Peter didn't make the laws. Under the current law, as it had been explained to Mr. Stuart and me that afternoon a few weeks earlier, there was not a single day that could have been added to Don's sentence. The law itself was defective. However, I felt that change to the law was possible. Human beings had made those laws, so human beings could change them. There had to be people who could find a way to address the situation. I had no idea how. I didn't have a law degree, but I felt sure there were those who did and who would be willing to come forth. Again, I realized that I indeed had something to say, and now I was ready to say it. Amazingly, I was invited to speak on Lansing's CBS affiliate, Channel 6 TV, for a news special to be aired locally, and I was allowed to say exactly what I wanted to say without being edited. I also gave a copy of my remarks to *The Lansing State Journal*, which published a great deal of the text. The statement I gave them was printed verbatim:

> I have kept silent for months, going into years, because I did not want to jeopardize the case. Now I want to speak!
>
> I identify with the people of Lansing who are outraged! I have been furious for months. Let me implore you not to waste that outrage, but to channel it and use it for good. Laws need to be changed to protect victims…to protect the whole of society. Let me remind you, my fellow citizens, that we, the people, are supposed to make the laws (through our elected legislators) and that the laws are supposed to be a reflection of the majority opinion. If you don't want multiple murderers out on the street, find a way to change the law. Do something about concurrent sentencing, which means one sentence does not add to another. So we have Martha Sue, Marita Choquette, Wendy Bush, and Kristine Stuart, plus two attempts, for a total of thirteen to nineteen years, or two to three years apiece for each crime! I don't know how—I don't know where to start—but there are people out there who do!
>
> I have felt all through this horror that we bind the hands and the feet of the police and then say, "Protect us." Why couldn't the police get a search warrant for Don's house while it was early enough to do some good? Lt. Tucker called for people to search areas near them. If this had been done thoroughly, if a body had been found, there would have been no reason to plea bargain. The police can't do it all.
>
> I don't want Martha Sue's death to have been in vain. If we can learn something from the tragedy so that we can stop compounding tragedies, it will not have been in vain. Let's take a hard look at the home, the church, the schools, and our society that develops this [type of] person. Don't excuse it with words like "sickness" or "demon possession," as the defense would have us believe. We allow people not to take responsibility for their own acts. I am sick of murderers being referred to as "religious" because they mouth nauseating religious phrases and go to church. Tell it like it is! As one psychologist told me early in the investigation, this type of personality hides behind the "safe" professions of religion and law.
>
> Martha Sue was religious, but that gave her a conscience and a desire to add to the goodness and beauty of the world. True religion adds integrity, real goodness, and justice to society. Look at the prophets of the Old Testament, who gave a ringing call to righteousness, justice, truth, and honesty. See in the New Testament what Christ had to say about those who hide behind religion

in Matthew 23: 23–24. Don't leave it up to God to deal with the messy, unsightly tragedies in your city, and don't leave it up to the other person.

The most effective prayers in this situation were from people like Lt. Tucker, Detective Westgate, and Officer Ouellette of East Lansing Police, to name a few. [These men] worked without pay when a job needed to be done and no funds were allocated, worked overtime, and gave up vacations all because of their dedication and integrity. They included people like my neighbors, who organized a search on a bitterly cold day, and people who were witnesses in the Gilbert case and cared enough to stop, offer help, and see it through. These were responsible acts; these were godly acts of concern for their neighbors. My opinion is, don't pray for a situation if you aren't willing to do anything about it.

Yes, I am angry. I am angry that my daughter was murdered. I am angry for the deep hurt my other daughter feels in the loss of her only sister. I am angry that my life has been so completely disrupted. It would be easier not to speak out, but that would be a copout. I would be letting down the memory of Martha Sue and the chance that her death could do some good. I would be failing Kay in living up to the highest standard that I know. I want to use this anger to effect change for the public good, so we will have neither anarchy nor a return to lynch law.

On Friday, friends told me about an Old Russian proverb that states, "Those who are left behind are responsible forever for doing the good others would have done had they lived." Let's act on this idea, lighting candles rather than simply cursing the darkness. Please, let's start lighting candles.

I was appalled when I listened to an interview that preceded my segment on that same show. In it, a psychologist stated that he felt Don Miller could be rehabilitated and ready for release in two years! Thankfully, the judge did not agree with his assessment.

My appeal went out. Afterward, I awaited a response. No one stepped forward, and gradually the community settled down. I did not know of anything more I could do. At that point, I knew we would have at least ten years before parole hearings would enter the picture.

◆   ◆   ◆

In the fall of 1979, Kay went back to the University of Georgia and I started to rebuild my life. Both of my parents lived to see me through the ordeal. My father, who was rock solid with a strong voice in the beginning, had faded as the months turned into years. Over the course of time, I could hear in his voice what his beloved granddaughter's disappearance had done to him—it grew weaker and weaker. Eleven months after Martha's body was discovered, in June of 1980, Daddy died of a stroke. Mother lived for only six more weeks. Soon after the funerals, Kay and I handled the sale of my parents' property. Then the two of us returned to East Lansing before Kay returned to the university.

I had felt I was managing my emotions just fine when Kay and I went home to East Lansing. Shortly after Kay left, however, I went to bed with the flu. Once in bed, I began staying there twenty-four hours a day. I recovered from the flu, but I did not get out of bed, even to eat. All I wanted to do was sleep, and there was very little to stop me from doing just that. I slept, roused a little, and promptly fell asleep again. One day as I awakened, a single thought invaded my peace. It was so strong it pierced through the semiconscious fog that had enveloped my brain: *If you don't get out of this bed, you will never be able to get out of it again!*

That got my attention, but I did not have the ability to just get up and go on with my life. After that, whenever I awakened, I forced myself to get up and fix something to eat. Then I'd time myself to stay out of bed for at least thirty-minute stretches before I allowed myself to go back.

About that time, my friend and business associate Flo Allen began to call me from Ann Arbor. She wasn't aware that I was not getting out of bed. She didn't know I had been sick. The purpose of her phone calls was to urge me to sell my home and move to a different house. Based on her own experience, she was absolutely convinced that it would be good for me. (Flo's daughter had died the year before and her mother had died the following spring.) Flo believed that the move had really helped her get over her depression. She was convinced that I needed to do the same. My response was, "I am not depressed, and I don't want to move." I thought, *A move sounds like an overwhelming amount of work. Where on earth would I move to? I can't even get out of bed! How on earth would I walk through all those houses? Even if I found one that I liked, I don't have the energy to move!*

Moving sounded like torture to me. Flo couldn't see that I was in bed every time she called, so she persisted. I could not convince her to drop the subject and leave me alone. Finally, her persistence annoyed me so much that it got me out of bed. I decided the only way to stop those phone calls was to look at something—anything! Then I could at least tell Flo I had looked and hadn't been able to find anything. I called Gloria, a friend of mine in real estate, and told her I wanted to look at a condo in my area. I figured since I didn't have the strength to climb stairs, I could walk around the ground floor and then walk out. I told Gloria there was only one area in which I would even consider buying. She found two listings in that beautiful area around the lake. I had ridden my bike around that area for years. When we arrived at the first condo, I walked not only through the main floor, but the second floor and even the basement. Suddenly, amazingly, I was interested. The only trouble was, there were two condos to choose from, and each had its own special feature that I really liked. I could not choose between them. Since I was having a hard time deciding, Gloria took me to see a third condo in the neighboring suburb. One look at the beautiful home—which was nestled in a forest and had three bathrooms, four bedrooms, and three balconies—was all I needed. The living room had a cathedral ceiling and fireplace. My bedroom extended the width of the condo and included a separate dressing area, plus the two bedrooms downstairs that I could use for my Mary Kay offices.

"I'll take it," I said.

From the day I found my new home, I was not only well again, I had energy! It was like someone had given me a shot of adrenaline. Only then did I realize how much living in my home, surrounded by memories twenty-four hours a day, had depressed me. In my new environment, no longer would I have to walk past Martha's room every day or pass Don's street in order to get out of the neighborhood. My depression was gone. I was ready to live again.

The beauty of my new home and the surrounding forest enveloped me with a feeling of peace. Life seemed good again. When Mary Kay first started giving out cars, she gave only Cadillacs. In order to qualify for one, a director needed to be in the top ten in the company, although the Buick could later be won by any director who met a certain quota. My father and mother had lived long enough to see me win my first car with Mary Kay, a pink Buick. Years earlier, Daddy had worried that I had thrown away my master's degree by getting into Mary Kay, Inc. I learned this from my mother, since daddy would never say anything to discourage me. This time she shared with me, "Your Daddy said, 'You know, I think she'll make it in that business after all.'" After moving into my new home, I won my first pink Cadillac.

Then, one day, the darkness of the past reasserted itself in the present. It began when I opened the mail. That day's mail contained a large plain brown envelope. Inside, I found a single large sheet of paper with a very strange drawing, which included a picture of a cross. I could find no note or letter. To be sure, I turned the envelope upside down and shook it. Nothing fell out. Since there was no return address and I did not recognize the handwriting, I wondered who had sent it. I examined the drawing again. I studied the back carefully as well as the front. This time I detected an almost microscopic signature on the back, at the very bottom of the page. The name written there was Don Miller!

Why? Why would he do this? When he went to prison, I was still living on Harrison Road. How had he gotten my new address? I took it down to the police station and gave it to Lt. Tucker. Both of us were uncertain about what Don was trying to accomplish. I figured perhaps he just wanted me to be aware that he knew exactly where I was, even after I had moved. Did the drawing mean something? Was it a warning? We never got an answer to our questions. Dean did tell me that he would see to it that the prison officials knew about this and would make sure that Don ceased contacting me in any way.

The drawing re-enforced what I already knew. Before Don was released from prison, I would have to disappear. I would need to leave my home, my friends, my community, and my business and relocate. I would need to change my name and leave no trail. It would be almost like being in the witness-protection program. However, I would have no government agency to help me. I would have to accomplish this on my own, and at my own expense. How could I hide and continue my business? If I could not advertise in a new location, my clients and customers would not be able to find me. I contacted Mary Kay Inc. and discussed the situation with them. How could the records for Sue Young be taken out of the company database and entered under a different name without leaving a trail? If there was a record of a name change, someday an employee could unwittingly give my location to someone connected to Don! Since we had no release date, there was no way that we could put a plan into action until a few months prior to his release. It was an uncertainty that would hang over my head for more than twenty years.

Unbeknownst to me, a great number of lives had been profoundly affected by this case over the years. It would be many years until I realized the extent of the help that was being germinated. During the years before Don was eligible for parole, the only public official I knew who was concerned that he might be set free was a newly elected representative named William Van Regenmorter. He was elected to the Michigan House in 1980. Carolyn Toles, a friend of mine, was his assistant. She knew that Van Regenmorter had campaigned on issues related to victims' rights, and Carolyn suggested that I talk to him. Of course, I wanted to do so, because I was still adamant that the law needed to be changed. Bill was a man who understood the law and was in a position to make changes. So I made my first trip down to the state capital. Over the years, Bill became a true friend to me, as well as to all of Michigan's crime victims. The victim's rights legislation he sponsored in 1985 was among the very first such legislation in the country. In the letter he wrote accompanying the bill, he stated, "The loss, hurt, and fear often experienced by these victims is only made worse by a system which provides extensive legal rights for the criminal and almost none to the victim." He stated that under the provisions of this bill, "For the first time, crime victims [would] be given the legal right to notification, education, consultation, protection, and participation." The National Organization for Victims Assistance has called this legislation "a model for the entire country."

Bill Van Regenmorter has never ceased fighting for victims. He organized an evening of remembrance for all Michigan's murder victims, held each year in the state capitol. He works with victims groups and hands out the Victim's Advocate of the Year Award for Michigan. He is a part of the group of prominent leaders who fight to keep serial killers from being set free to kill again. He was part of the group I refer to as my "White Knights."

In 1993 another state senator, Michael Bouchard, offered his support to me regarding parole hearings. At the same time, he asked Senator Van Regenmorter to place his consecutive sentencing bill on the Senate Judiciary Committee agenda. The subsequent passage of this bill was a tremendous help.

◆   ◆   ◆

Eleven years passed. In February of 1989, thanks to the victims' rights bill initiated by Bill Van Regenmorter, I was notified that Don Miller was eligible for parole. Prior to the passage of this bill, victims and their loved ones did not have to be notified. This was one of Kay's biggest concerns. Her fear was that I wouldn't be aware of Don's release until I received a "surprise" visit, one she was afraid I would not survive. The victims' rights law gave Kay a measure of reassurance. It gave me hope too, because I would have a chance to appeal to the board to deny parole. By making sure the parole board knew how dangerous Don was, perhaps I could affect its decision. When the notification came, it gave me the choice to contact one of the parole members by phone, send a letter, or appear before the full board on the date scheduled.

I had no idea what to expect at a parole hearing, but I considered it imperative to make an appearance. This was too important an issue simply to ignore or to address with a mere letter or phone call. Ever since Martha's disappearance, I found myself with no one to instruct me, so I was continually walking into unknown situations. This was one of those times. Without any facts to guide me, I was left with my own speculation about what to expect. I assumed that Don would be present (and possibly his lawyer) to present his arguments. I considered what it would be like to face him, and once again testify against him. I believed that by doing so I would be singling myself out and putting myself at the top of his revenge list. But who was I kidding? I came to realize. Don had not forgotten me. I was already at the top of that list, so I really had nothing to lose.

Although this was only the eleventh year of the thirty-to-fifty-year sentence Don had received, he was already eligible for parole. To answer my question, "How could this be possible?" I was told this was because "good time" had been awarded to him. Those words conjured up in my mind some kind of extraordinary progress in rehabilitation. "Good time," I soon came to realize, had nothing to do with rehabilitation. What then did these words actually mean? In order to receive these automatic reductions in one's sentence, one is not required to do anything at all. Therefore, day by day, Don's sentence was being reduced. Only by breaking certain prison rules would any of his "good time" be taken away.

I knew no more about a parole hearing than I had known about the meaning of "good time." Would I be the only person in front of the board to testify against Don? Would I be facing his relatives pleading for his release? When I entered the room, it was much to my relief that I found out the prisoner was not allowed to be present. It was explained to me that "his presence might intimidate victims and their families." I saw then that I had allies. I was surrounded by support. We were all there to voice opposition to Don's release. My friends from the East Lansing Police Department had sent two ELPD officers. Then I met people who would become new friends, people whose names I recognized but had never met. Michael Hocking, the former prosecutor of Eaton County, who had successfully tried Don and had won the thirty-to-fifty-year sentence, was there. "Oh wow, it's great to have him here," I said to the officers from the ELPD. It was at the hearing that I first met Donna Irish, who would become my ally and good friend. Donna's stepdaughter and stepson were the teens who had been Don's last victims. Following the trial, Donna had stayed in touch with Michael Hocking in the Eaton County Office as long as he was there. When Jeff Sauter became the new prosecutor, she wrote him asking for an appointment. Donna made quite an impression on Jeff, for he became our champion. In Jeff, Donna had discovered a man who would come to share our passion for keeping Miller from killing again! Although I knew nothing about Jeff before the parole hearing, when it came time to address the parole board, both Donna and I agreed that Jeff should speak first. When I heard him speak for the first time, I knew we had made the right choice. He was extremely knowledgeable, sincere, passionate, and brilliant as he made the case that Don Miller continued to pose a threat to the lives of young women in the community. I was absolutely thrilled that he was on our side. He set the stage perfectly for those of us who would speak. In the years that followed, the admiration Donna and I have for this man has continued to grow. I told him after hearing him for the first time, "Jeff, you can speak for me anytime." I have never changed my mind about that.

Donna made a tremendous contribution toward keeping this killer off of the street. Each year, she and Shirley, the mother-in-law of Don's last victim, collected hundreds of letters from people all over the Lansing area to put before the parole board at the yearly meeting to help keep Don behind bars. They amassed as many as 750 letters a year. I was of course deeply touched and grateful for all that they did.

Knowing my deep concern, Donna found it natural to ask me if I would collect signatures from residents on the east side of town. Emotionally, I just could not do it. I hated to disappoint Donna, but this was more than I could handle. To collect signatures would require spending months re-exposing myself to traumatic memories. In order to get people to sign letters, I would need to explain repeatedly why those signatures were needed. Then I would be subjected to questions—endless questions—that people would ask. It was too disturbing for me to spend hundreds of hours each year re-living the horror of my daughter's death, even in the service of a noble cause. If I allowed myself to fall into a full-blown depression again, it could take months to crawl out. And then it would be time to start the process all over the following year for the next parole hearing.

We were alerted six weeks to two months prior to the annual hearing date. During this time, I was forced to deal with the agony of Martha's death until the hearing was complete. This yearly event was all I could handle psychologically and financially. My ability to earn an income in sales was directly related to my attitude. Each day I had to create business for that day. If I did not make calls, I didn't work and I generated no income. If I was depressed, I didn't make calls. I explained this to Donna and she understood my situation. Her experience with the way these hearings affected Lisa gave her insight into the suffering involved. Because Lisa became depressed each year around the time of the parole hearing, Donna could appreciate my feelings. I also did not want Kay's life disrupted any more than it had been, so I did not broach the subject in our conversations. Kay always grew anxious around the time of the hearing. Each year, she expressed fear for my safety and talked to me about moving out of state.

In the period between the yearly hearings, I tried to return to a normal life, but the loss of Martha and its aftermath still affected my decisions, even on the most mundane matters. When considering replacing worn furniture, I wondered, *Should I spend the money when Don might be released this year and I have to leave everything?* Even with the passage of years, an annual appearance at the hearing, and the painful memories that preceded it, was all I could handle.

In 1995, we learned that Don had received an additional two-year sentence because he had been found in possession of a weapon in his prison cell. That was also the year that, in deference to the victims and their families, we were spared a parole hearing. It was great to know with certainty that at least he would not be released that year or in 1996—but I also knew that time was running out. At the 1997 hearing, we were told that there would be no more hearings, because in February 1999, Don would have completed his sentence (due to accumulated "good time"). However, before I had time to set relocation plans in motion, I received a life-changing phone call.

The
Thursday
State Journal

Lt. Dean Tucker, East Lansing Police Department, holding a disturbing
painting by Don Miller.
Photograph by Bruce Corneilus, *The Lansing State Journal*, 1979
Copyright *The Lansing State Journal*.

12

Arrival of the White Knights

The phone call was from a Frank Ochberg, a man who had been a stranger to me up to that point. He explained that a group of local people had gotten together because of their concern over the imminent release of Don Miller. The name they had adopted for the group was the Committee for Community Awareness and Protection or C-CAP. He invited me to a C-CAP meeting. During that first conversation, I was not able to figure out what this group was all about. I thought maybe it was some kind of victims' support group. After so many years, I found that idea depressing, but since he was only asking me to attend a meeting, I agreed. It was to take place at one o'clock in the conference room of the police department in my own township. Well, that's a safe enough meeting place, I concluded, so I decided to check it out. Although I entered somewhat apprehensively, I was blown away by the high profile people in attendance! I discovered that Dr. Frank Ochberg, the man who had issued the invitation, was a psychiatrist world renowned for his work with victims. I found Frank to be an incredible man, as well as the catalyst without whom C-CAP would not have come to exist.

Our host for the meetings was the Director of Public Safety Jay Kohl. As the chief of both the police and the fire department in my own town, he not only knew about the Don Miller case but was vitally concerned over the prospect of his release into the Lansing area. As Jay later stated, under the leadership of Frank Ochberg, we "started out as a small group who got together to find out where we stood and what our options were." The committee had been purposefully secretive in the beginning for two reasons: first, in order not to rouse opposition from Miller's lawyers, and second, to avoid promoting panic in the community over the prospect of Don's release. We had good reason to fear the reaction of the community if Don was released. Over the years, I had heard a consistent sentiment expressed by a number of husbands and fathers who had always been law-abiding citizens. Each told me that if the law failed to keep Miller locked up, they would take the law into their own hands and "deal with him." One grandfather told his son, "My life is almost over, so if Miller is freed I will take care of him, so that my loved ones and the women and children of the community can be safe." I feared something like this would happen, adding one more tragedy and one more destroyed family. Since everyone in this group was aware of these sentiments, a key focus of C-CAP was to develop a plan to inform the public, prevent vigilantism, and keep the community safe if the committee could find no way to stop Miller's release.

As I noted regarding my first meeting, I was totally amazed by the quality of the group and their dedication to the cause. I had had nothing to do with its formation, but here it was, an answer to my prayers! In 1979, I had prayed and pleaded for one person to come forth, and here was a roomful of individuals dedicated to my cause. And what a group it was! These people were movers and shakers. The meeting was an incredible experience. I left feeling an almost euphoric sense of gratitude. The group had invited me to join, and I was more than willing. When I signed on, there were three police departments involved, two sheriffs, a prosecuting attorney, a judge, a senator, representatives from the Michigan Attorney General's office, forensic experts, corrections officers, mental health professionals, victims' advocates, and victims' families. In the presence of such talent, I felt I would have little to contribute. Yet, regardless of my feeling of inadequacy, the group immediately made me feel "at home." They were just as open to my questions and ideas as they were to the experts in their particular fields. Each member's ideas and opinions were treated with genuine respect. The committee operated on the principle that by assembling a group of diverse backgrounds, more creative ideas would emerge than would occur in a group of professionals who were all from the same background.

After such an experience, I found myself yearning for one of those wonderful chats Martha and I had enjoyed so much. I longed to share every detail about this group with her. I knew she would have found every person fascinating. She would have peppered me with questions and then listened in rapt attention to every detail. I know it's absurd, but I remember thinking, "She's been gone long enough; I want her back now!" I have found that when we miss someone dearly, our minds surprise us with irrational—but at times curiously comforting—thoughts such as these.

Years before C-CAP was born, and possibly even at the time I was praying for someone to come forth, the lives of many of these individuals were being shaped by a variety of life-altering circumstances. They were from different locations and had various backgrounds. They were largely unknown to each other before the crimes of Don Miller brought them together. Bonnie Bucqueroux was one of the earliest persons affected by Don's violent acts, as Marita's body was discovered in a field behind her home. Bonnie would be the person to get the ball rolling when it came to the formation of C-CAP.

Long before I met Bonnie, however, another killer had affected her life. Her introduction to the term "serial killer" came while she was living in Ann Arbor, Michigan. As Bonnie stated, "I was there attending the University of Michigan during the reign of terror of Norman Collins." (He was the good-looking young man who preyed on and murdered co-eds attending the university. Currently, he is serving a life sentence here in Michigan.) "While I was alone in my apartment, because my husband was a patient in the University Hospital, Collins was abducting young women in Ann Arbor. I was especially concerned, because it seemed that women were facing a new kind of threat. This emergence of the serial killer, a new kind of predator beyond anything I had known before, was cause for alarm." When Collins was finally apprehended, Bonnie could not have imagined that this kind of threat would ever again arise in a community where she lived. However, years later, after moving to the East Lansing area, she "again felt fear rippling through the community." She related, "Young women were disappearing from the area, and it appeared that they had fallen prey to a similar kind of predator. This time it was chillingly close. The body of Marita Choquette, the second young woman to disappear, was discovered in the wooded area behind my home." She felt an even greater cause for concern since her daughter, Kim, was a high school student. Typical of that age is a sense of invincibility that engenders recklessness, and Kim was no exception. Bonnie continued, "Since Kim's bedroom was a tiny loft, she was accustomed to having girlfriends over during the summer months, when they could all sleep outside in the travel trailer. The girls loved the privacy that the trailer provided." The threat disrupted Kim's plans for the summer, because Bonnie refused to allow the girls to sleep out there. This was met with fierce protest by her daughter. Kim's response sounded so much like what Martha's reaction would have been in her situation. When Bonnie described the situation, I could practically hear Martha stretching out the word, "Mo–theer," the way she did when she felt exasperated by my caution.

Stuart Dunnings III was also extremely concerned for the safety of young women in the Lansing area. Stuart had lived in Lansing all his life. In the late seventies, when Don was committing his murderous acts, Stuart was attending law school in Ann Arbor. "It was all over the news down there," he remembered. "It was frightening, just chilling, because I had sisters in Lansing." These memories remained with Stuart as he returned to Lansing to practice law. In January 1998, when Stuart became Ingham County Prosecuting Attorney, Jeff Sauter wasted no time in inviting Stuart to C-CAP.

Bonnie remained acutely aware of the vulnerability of young women after Miller was arrested and sentenced, and she was among those furious at the Ingham County prosecutor over the plea bargain. She voiced her vehement objections to a friend of hers who was an assistant in the prosecutor's office. Her concern, like that of so many others in the area, was that someday Don Miller would be let go. Unlike the others, though, Bonnie was a passionate crusader whose interest did not wane. She vowed that she would not forget, and she kept her vow.

She carried this passion with her when she went to work with Bob Trojanowitcz, who was director of the National Center for Community Policing and director of the School of Criminal Justice at MSU. In Bob, she gained an ally for her cause. Bonnie became the associate director of the National Center for Community Policing. Trojanowitcz persuaded FBI profiler Robert Ressler to help in his assessment of Miller. After performing the analysis, Ressler stated emphatically that "the question was not whether he would kill again, if released, but when." Ressler suggested that they bring another expert, Richard Walters, into the discussion. Both men cautioned Bonnie to keep her participation quiet, since Miller had a real problem with women and he might make her a target. Walters suggested that Don's pattern of attacking only women could be used against him. Richard suggested that, if all else failed, because women were a protected class under civil-rights laws, it might be possible to find a U.S. attorney willing to bring civil-rights charges against him. In effect, they planned to use the same law that prosecutors had used to try murderers of blacks decades before.

Nevertheless, persuading a U.S. attorney to undertake such an effort would present a real challenge. Such a case would require a new use of old laws, and it might be hard to persuade them that the time and money required to build such a case would be worth it. Therefore, it seemed wise to exhaust other strategies first.

"Watchful waiting" was therefore the plan until a firm release date was scheduled. Then Trojanowitcz wanted to bring together community policing personnel and collaborators from the community to work on the problem. "By taking action too early, we risked alerting Miller and giving him the opportunity to derail the community effort," Bonnie noted.

With the sudden death of Trojanowitcz in 1994, we lost a local champion with an appropriate platform to pursue solutions. This was when Bonnie went to work with Dr. Frank Ochberg with the Victims and the Media program in the School of Journalism and Critical Incident Analysis Group (CIAG). She also became executive director of the Michigan Victim Alliance.

Frank Ochberg is not only an internationally known psychiatrist but also the former Michigan director of mental health, an adjunct professor of criminal justice and journalism, and a clinical professor of psychiatry at MSU. Frank would play a tremendous role in the fight to keep Donald Miller from terrorizing our streets again. He had worked with "Trojo" on CIAG.

After working with Frank for some time, Bonnie approached him about taking up the leadership of the cause. "After all," Bonnie thought, "he was committed to helping victims, and he had worked with Trojanowitcz on several initiatives." But Frank's interest had always been focused on helping victims. As he did not want to focus on the predators, he initially said no to the idea.

He could not, however, dismiss the problem from his thoughts. Consequently, one night at the regular monthly board meeting of the Michigan Victim Alliance, Frank asked Bonnie to tell the board about the threat that Miller's release posed. As Bonnie spoke, the group realized that both the president and the vice president of the Victim Alliance lived within a mile of the Miller home. Both had families to consider. Obviously, both were tremendously concerned about the potential danger, not only to their children but to all the young women in the area. The members agreed with Bonnie that their organization had an obligation to try to keep him behind bars and, if all else failed, to prepare the community for his release. Frank was eventually persuaded to lead the group. Without his leadership in assembling and directing an incredible team from the community, we would not have succeeded in our fight to keep Miller out of the community. Frank's dedication and expertise were essential. His credentials enabled him to attract the experts we needed to the table.

Once Frank made the decision, he gave nothing less than total commitment. He was a tireless worker, and he realized that time was short. There was a sense of urgency, because in the spring of 1996, Don's firm release date was less than three years away. Frank put together an impressive group of people and held private meetings in his home. Bonnie was not included in this initial group, for reasons related to her safety that are noted above. In spite of this, before the group had grown to ten people, Bonnie became the first female at the table.

While Bonnie was working with Trojanowitcz in 1992, a young lawyer named Pat Shannon was pursuing his master's thesis at the University of Michigan. Pat's ideas were ahead of his time, as evidenced by his thesis, *Intentional Violence as a Public Health Threat*. This was the first time such a concept had been explored within the U of M community, and they found it foreign to their way of thinking at first. Pat recalled he was made to feel very uncomfortable. His thinking was "just too radical." The basis of his thesis was that "there are some really evil people who need to be identified." Pat concluded that such unredeemable and dangerous individuals actually pose a public-health threat. At the time of this writing, the Centers for Disease Control existed solely to deal with disease. Later, a branch was added to focus on alcohol-related automobile accidents as a public-health threat. Today, the CDC fully acknowledges Pat's conclusion, as there is a branch that deals with intentional violence. Pat commented recently, "These people are certainly more dangerous to public health than the West Nile virus."

While Pat was attending college, Jeff Sauter was also a student there. The two never met, however, both men later became prosecutors. They finally did meet in the Michigan Prosecuting Attorneys' Association, and both, at different times, became president of the association. Later, Jeff would invite Pat to join various C-CAP efforts.

The numbers began to grow as the group continued to identify people with reasons for involvement. The first order of business for C-CAP was to study the problem, learn as much as possible about serial killers, and then assess and analyze. We continued to study and learn throughout the life of C-CAP. Richard Walters added greatly to our understanding of the serial-killer mind and the continuing threat Miller posed. Richard was the psychologist for Michigan's state prison and a Viduex society member. (The prison is located in Jackson, thirty miles south of Lansing.) During a meeting in February 1997, Richard Walters gave a lecture with slide illustrations. Frank wrote notes on Walters' reflections concerning the exchanges he had with Miller. Frank observed, "Walters knows this diabolic subject intimately." Walters believed that there were more than four murder victims, noting, "There are evolutionary stages of serial killers."

In his notes, Frank went on to reflect on the differences between the psychotic killer, who is usually hospitalized "for a very long time, past the prime killing years," and the conscious psychopath. The lone killer is the one who "evolves from a voyeur to an obsessed stalker." His first murder is, perhaps, impulsive. Thereafter, this type of killer proceeds with great cunning. Toying with and torturing his victim and leaving tantalizing 'signature clues' are characteristic of the serial killer. Finally, he becomes a necrophiliac and a cannibal. Both from a psychiatric point of view as well as a common-sense point of view, I have often heard Dr. Ochberg pose the questions, 'Can this be sanity? Can that be beyond the public expectation of psychiatric care?'"

Frank's notes go on to point out that obsession is at the heart of the disease. These killers, according to Walters, need no radio or TV to entertain them. Their minds display increasingly sadistic acts and images, and their fantasies exceed the scope of their previous criminal actions. They become insatiable. Theoretically, they can tell right from wrong, and they can delay the acts that give them their bizarre sense of gratification. They can even abort a plan to avoid detection. This qualifies them for criminal prosecution and precludes a verdict of "not guilty by reason of insanity." However, once they have begun the killing pattern, they are dangerous until death or very old age.

Listening to such graphic details of human depravity, I couldn't help reflecting on how far I had come from those leisurely, peaceful bicycle rides Martha and I had enjoyed, rides where we had shared our hopes and dreams. Martha would have been completely amazed at what her mother was doing now. However, she also would have been completely supportive, knowing I had to take such a stand alongside my friends.

The phenomenal dedication to our cause among C-CAP members continued. His preoccupation with the thought of Miller's release led Jeff, in a casual conversation with his friend Tom Robinson, to share his frustration. Here again was a remarkable coincidence. Tom had recently read about a law that allowed for criminal prosecution of a prisoner caught with a weapon in his cell; if convicted, the prisoner could receive a five-year sentence. Tom knew that Miller had been caught with a weapon a couple of years earlier, so he suggested that Jeff investigate prosecuting Miller on a weapons charge. Deducting two years from Miller's good time was an administrative action taken by the warden, yet he had not filed a criminal charge for the weapons offence. Could that charge be filed now? Jeff had thought Don had been disciplined because of drugs rather than a weapon, so this was new information to him. Weapon possession put things in a completely different light. Armed with this knowledge, Jeff headed a group to explore the possibility of bringing charges against Don on behalf of Eaton and Ingham counties.

During a spring meeting in 1997, Mark Blumer, a C-CAP member from the state attorney general's office, reminded us of an appeal pending before the U.S. Supreme Court. The state of Kansas had petitioned the Court to uphold its right to civilly commit sixty-two-year-old Leroy Hendricks. He was a serial rapist who had said that he believed it would be impossible for him to stop molesting children. In order to prevent Hendricks from victimizing more youngsters following the completion of his jail sentence, Kansas held a civil trial. As a result, Hendricks was committed to a mental-health facility. I heard no more about the case until shortly after my birthday in June of 1997. The wonderful news came as I was returning home from a weekend trip. I remember the exact location. I was listening to the radio after turning onto the Okemos exit. The Supreme Court had upheld the right of the state of Kansas to confine a serial sex offender to a mental hospital after the completion of a criminal sentence! Although it was a five-to-four decision, the dissenting judges indicated there was a way that a law could be written which would satisfy their constitutional concerns. In the majority opinion, Justice Thomas stated, "The decision by Kansas to afford such procedural protections does not transform a civil commitment proceeding into a criminal prosecution." He also stated that Kansas law did not contain "either of the two primary objectives of criminal punishment: retribution or deterrence," but he noted, "Incapacitation may be a legitimate end of the civil law." Findings were based on a 1902 Supreme Court case which had ruled that involuntary confinement of persons with highly contagious diseases, even when there was no treatment available, was permissible. "It would be of little value to require treatment as a precondition to civil confinement of the dangerously insane when no acceptable treatment exists." Additionally, Judge Thomas stated, "To conclude otherwise would obligate a state to release certain confined [individuals] that were both mentally ill and dangerous simply because they could not be successfully treated for their affliction." I considered this development a wonderful birthday gift. After the June 1997 Supreme Court ruling, I wanted to see such a law passed in Michigan. The ruling seemed to satisfy common sense. How could anyone oppose it?

By the summer of 1997, our research had not produced any solutions—and the clock was ticking. It was now only a year and a half before the prison doors would swing open. We needed help fast. We considered holding a nationwide "think tank" of persons experienced in the subject of serial predators. With Bonnie leading the way, this first-of-its-kind nationwide serial sexual predator conference was organized. The date was set for April 1 to 3, 1998. Michigan's Democratic State Attorney General Frank Kelly agreed to be our keynote speaker. The conference was designed to bring together groups that had never met before, including local law enforcement, legislators (several Michigan senators attended), corrections officers, psychiatrists, prison psychologists, victims and victims groups, prosecutors, and forensic experts. The FBI's Critical Incident Response Group and the Department of Justice's Office for Victims of Crime agreed to help.

In line with Richard Walters' thinking that serial killers go through evolutionary stages, we investigated the possibility of finding a fifth murder victim of Don Miller. Based on the traits that Miller displayed in Martha's murder, other experts agreed with Walters that this could not have been his first murder. Several forensic experts tried diligently to find another Miller victim. To date, they have found nothing.

Since we were planning a nationwide conference and there was slightly more than a year and a half left on Miller's sentence, C-CAP decided to go public. Director of Public Safety Jay Kohl announced a press conference for July 28, 1997. At that time, he welcomed the reporters and those new to the group, and then Frank explained its purpose and gave an overview. Various subcommittees then gave progress reports, and Bonnie outlined plans for the national conference.

Bonnie suggested that since we had so much talent in town, we needed to have a meeting that would involve members of the community outside the criminal justice system. In order to fund Marc Klaas' participation in the community night, I asked my Zonta Club of Lansing to sponsor him. They graciously agreed to do so.

Megan Kanka's mom, Maureen, also came to share the experiences she had fighting for Megan's law. Of course, Michigan's criminal laws had been of deep concern to me for twenty years. I was therefore surprised to learn that from the time C-CAP began trying in earnest to get a bill passed by the legislature, a few of the city and state employees involved in C-CAP began to feel uncomfortable about "getting into politics." I did not feel that we were being political; all we wanted was a bill to protect the women and children of Michigan. I certainly did not see it as a partisan issue. After all, we had the support of the top law-enforcement person in the state, Attorney General Frank Kelly, a Democrat, as well as the support of Republicans. I was greatly encouraged by Kelly's opening speech to our conference. In it, he gave his strong support to the legislation, stating, "Michigan needs a civil-commitment law similar to the Kansas law." He then went on to quote John Locke's statement: "Each citizen gives up some rights in order to live in a civil society." He continued, "In those rare cases—like the Miller case—society has the right to curb individual liberty to keep people safe."

On the opposite side of the aisle we had the vigorous support of Republican Senator Bill Van Regenmorter, chair of the judicial committee. Bill was the architect of the legislation we supported. He had senators on both sides of the aisle co-sponsoring his legislation. With this strong bi-partisan support, I was optimistic.

To set the stage for the community night, Frank explained the work of C-CAP and the Serial Killer Conference that came as a result of its work. Since I was asked to be one of the speakers, Frank introduced me. I wanted the audience to be aware that the purpose of my involvement in these issues was to do whatever I could "to keep [them] from ever having to stand [there] in my shoes." I didn't want them to experience what I had endured for over twenty years, a tragedy that would continue to have a bearing on my entire life. However we wanted to be sensitive to members with concerns about entering the political arena. I agreed to make it very plain that I was not speaking for our organization when I talked about legislation. To make that point, I began by saying, "Tonight I am speaking to you as one voice." After my speech, I turned the podium over to Marc Klaas and Maureen Kanka. Each of them spoke with only one voice as well, but their impassioned pleas encouraged thousands of others to join the chorus.

A second emphasis for the evening was prevention. To avoid becoming a victim requires that you know how to protect yourself and your children. Part of this knowledge is a constant awareness of your surroundings. We wanted to help our audience of 450 people develop a game plan for individual and family safety. For the safety of their children, we suggested implementing a kind of "fire drill" for various danger situations, both over the phone and in person. Marc Klaas and Bonnie Bucqueroux covered this in detail. Through interactive exercises, Bonnie emphasized the importance of paying attention to our instinct of fear when we encounter potentially dangerous situations. "Forget about being nice if you are afraid of someone," she said. "Later you can apologize for being rude if your fears prove to be unfounded; but if you were correct in your assessment, you'll have saved yourself suffering or death."

While most of the delegates came from Michigan, we had others from Virginia, California, and even Washington, whose assistant attorney general attended. It became an international conference with the arrival of representatives from Taiwan and Great Britain. All the delegates were there because they were deeply interested in listening, learning, and sharing ideas. This was the first gathering of its kind to bring together different disciplines in one setting—police, prosecutors, corrections officials, forensic specialists, psychologists, psychiatrists, senators, a judge, and victims. I heard some incredible facts, such as, as prison guards are not even informed of the crimes for which the different prisoners have been incarcerated. Also, female guards aren't told which inmates have raped or murdered women. This, to me, is unconscionable. It's a tragedy waiting to happen. If guards know which prisoners have perpetrated violent crimes against women, they can take precautions and call for backup before getting themselves into dangerous situations. Also, I believe male guards should know which inmates have been convicted of violent crimes so they too can avoid putting their lives in jeopardy.

It was an outstanding conference. Bonnie did an incredible job of organizing it from the ground up. The participants agreed that this process had led to valuable exchanges of information and ideas that could be built upon in the future. However, we did not develop the "breakthrough idea, the one solution" which we were hoping for as a result of the conference. Where were we to go from here?

Jeff was working on bringing up the charges for Don's weapons violation. However, there were numerous hurdles, some perhaps insurmountable, to be faced before that became a reality. Even if he succeeded in bringing this to trial, at that moment the best we could hope for was ten years; taking "good time" into account, we could expect to net about six years. Of course, we would be delighted to have those six years, but we also needed a long-term solution. Our best long-range hope seemed to lie in civil-commitment legislation. Someone suggested we contact the CBS television show *60 Minutes*. Perhaps we could persuade them to carry our story before the nation; surely that would carry weight with Michigan's legislature.

In the meantime, Bonnie Bucqueroux had written an article about the community effort that was taking place here. As it was published in one of the Detroit newspapers, another coincidence was about to unfold. In New York City, an assistant CBS producer, Laura Levin, picked up the article and was intrigued. She decided to investigate the possibility that we had a story her CBS newsmagazine, *48 Hours*, would be interested in telling. She placed a call to Bonnie. So, instead of trying to contact *60 Minutes*, we were approached instead.

At the conclusion of Laura's call, Bonnie phoned me. She said that a CBS producer had requested my phone number and that I should expect her call. Shortly afterward, my phone rang.

Levin wanted to fly to Michigan to interview us. Bonnie and I agreed; this sounded exactly like the kind of story that we had hoped to persuade a TV news program to produce. We were thrilled! Since we felt our best hope would be to get the Michigan legislature to pass a civil-commitment law in time to stop Miller's automatic release, we thought that a TV story could be a great lobbying tool. However, one woman would position herself to block our efforts and to squash the will of the majority of Michigan voters.

13

Against the Will of the People

Surrounded by my friends at C-CAP, I became emboldened. With their encouragement, I started doing things I would never have imagined. Some of the time I initiated action, and at other times, Frank, Bonnie, Bob Dutcher, Jeff, and others became my coaches, prompting me with phrases that began, "Sue, why don't you...?"

After the Supreme Court ruling that allowed states to confine serial predators, I waited through the summer months for the Michigan legislature to take action. I didn't realize that they were in recess for the summer or that bills needed to be approved by a particular committee by as early as May 19 in order to be passed by both Houses before the holiday recess at the end of the year. Also, I had assumed that the legislature would automatically pass such a bill on their own without outside promptings. So I waited. In the fall, I became aware that several members of the House were interested in exploring ideas for a serial-predator bill for our state.

Subsequently, I was invited to the capital to testify before the House Mental Health Committee. This was a new experience for me. I had never been involved in a discussion whose aim was to create a new law. I had no idea how to prepare. I was told simply to go to the office of the representative who had invited me. When I arrived, his assistant invited me into the representative's office to meet him. He made me feel very much at ease as he expressed interest in hearing the details of my story. After listening intently, he left me in the care of his assistant while he went to the committee hearing.

Shortly before it was time for me to testify, I was escorted into the chamber. The presence of the nine representatives comprising the Mental Health Committee dominated the room. As they sat on their U-shaped platform in front of a large U-shaped table, the sense of separation from the rest of the room was striking. The setup seemed designed to intimidate those there to testify.

As I entered I observed that another person was delivering his testimony while seated at a table below the platform in the center of the room. He was reading his speech from prepared notes that he held in his hands. I was struck by the conspicuous disrespect many of the representatives showed. These "public servants" seemed to be paying no attention to him. Throughout his speech, various aides stepped upon the platform, walked behind the chairs, and carried on whispered conversations with the representatives. This seemed rather rude, I thought. The man might as well have been reciting the alphabet for all the impact he was making. I noticed that some of those testifying had prepared material to be handed out to the representatives. I carried nothing with me; I had simply come to tell my story and appeal to them to pass the legislation. I had brought no information to leave behind, so if they did not listen to it, my coming would have been in vain.

When it was my turn to speak, I relied on the lessons I had learned in twenty-five years of speaking before various-sized audiences for my Mary Kay business. That training taught me I had to gain the attention of my audience before I could get their support. Consequently, when I was called to speak, I took my seat behind the witness table and sat in silence while I gazed at the representatives, seeking to make eye contact with each person. I waited patiently until the conversations ceased. When I had their attention, I began to speak.

During my speech I continued to reach out to them by making eye contact with each representative, gazing from one end of the table to the other. After I had gained their attention they listened intently; however, I failed to persuade them. I could tell by their questions and comments.

"This should have been dealt with at the beginning by the criminal-justice system," said one representative. She was full of comments about things that "should" have taken place more than twenty years before. In the process, she was absolving her committee, according to her way of thinking, of any responsibility for the present situation. Silently I wondered how a woman who considered herself an intellectual could render such a childish interpretation of the situation. I wanted to scream, "You are crying over spilt milk! No one can undo any action of the past. The task at hand is to deal with the present reality. The present is the only time over which we have some control. Human beings make laws, so human beings should be able to change laws that threaten the public."

Other comments followed: "Funds for mental health are too short now; we don't want funds to be diverted from the mental-health patients we have now. We don't want serial killers mingled with other patients and killing them. It is double jeopardy to keep a criminal locked up after he has served his time." I reported my experience to Frank Ochberg. I found it tragic that some lawmakers were so territorial, and consequently so narrowly focused on their own committees, that they failed to see the overall needs of the citizenry. He felt that the chairwoman of the Mental Health Committee was sincerely trying to overcome the objections of her fellow committee members. He felt that she was really interested in helping draft the legislation, which would take into consideration all the opposing viewpoints while providing a well-crafted, narrow law that would protect the public from serial predators. Occasionally, she sent a staff person from her office to C-CAP meetings. Frank and others spent countless hours designing a law that would be acceptable to the opposition arising from the controlling Democratic committee members. He also had meetings with the chairwoman, Laura Baird.

While Frank worked with those crafting the bill, I looked for ways to win support for it once it was ready. Since attorney generals from thirty-six states (including Michigan) favored a bill like the one in Kansas and had petitioned the Supreme Court to hear the case, I decided to visit the Michigan Attorney General's Office. I got an appointment to see Bob Ianni and received a favorable hearing. He told me, however, that in order to get such legislation passed, we needed the involvement of the governor. I left thinking, *I need to find a way to get our case before the governor. Who can help me do that?*

I remembered that Governor Engler's wife had sponsored a fundraiser for my friend Priscilla Peterson when she ran for a seat in the legislature. At the close of that event, I had the good fortune to have a five-minute conversation with Michelle Engler. We had talked about her San Antonio, Texas, roots (My hometown, Luling, was only fifty-five miles from there.) On the chance that she would remember me, I decided to write to her. Mrs. Engler is a mother of three small daughters, so I appealed to her as one mother to another. She is also a Christian, so she would be familiar with the story of the Jewish Queen Esther.

On March 16, 1998, I started my letter to Mrs. Engler by referring to the brief meeting I had had with her, and then I wrote,

> Perhaps you are aware that the Lansing area's only serial killer is due to walk out of prison in less than eleven months, to resume his killing of women and girls. For years, we had no tool in the law to prevent this from happening. That changed in June, when the Supreme Court upheld the Kansas law.
>
> Since that time, a number of states have enacted laws to protect their citizens from the release of violent predators into society. In Michigan, much to my amazement, that is not happening! I understand the excuses the legislature is putting forth. What I cannot understand is why they are allowing these

excuses to stop them from enacting a very narrow law against these most violent predators, a law that would be enormously popular with the people who elected them. (I have not found one single person in Michigan who wants a person like Don Miller to move in next door to them!) It strikes me as amazing that the legislature would be that out of touch with the will of those who elected them, particularly in an election year! We need a leader in this.

It is too late to save my daughter...Truthfully, I would like to be able to walk away from this whole issue. It makes me angry that I have been asked to deal with the ugly facts of my daughter's death over and over and over for twenty years. Now I would like it to stop! (In fact, I cried again as I drafted this letter.) However, in obedience to God's call on my life, I cannot do that when there is still something I could do to save someone else's daughter.

One of the agonies I suffered in the almost three years before Martha's body was found was having learned details from the police, such as the blood found in Don's car, but having to keep them secret. Having been told he could kill again, I was forced to watch powerlessly as he did exactly that!

Today we are not powerless! The Supreme Court has opened the door!

I was told in my conversations at the State Attorney General's Office that this legislation will not happen without the governor making it his top priority (and we have less than eleven months) and leading the legislature to create a sense of unity and urgency.

Also I appealed to her as a woman of faith, saying she could become an "Esther-like" figure for our state. As the Biblical figure had saved thousands of Jewish people, she could be instrumental in saving thousands of women and children in the future of Michigan. I added that she, like Esther, might have been placed in her position for such a time as this.

I ended with the question, "Will you help?" I also invited her to be our honored guest at the community awareness night on April 2, which was part of the Serial Predator Conference held on the campus of MSU.

One of her assistants answered my letter, saying she would "look into the issue." I also wrote to the governor. I told him, "Since I lead an organization of businesswomen in various parts of the state, I know the hearts of these women. We all would be most grateful to you for providing the leadership needed to give Michigan a law to keep deadly predators from becoming free." Senator Van Regenmorter suggested that I give him the letter I had written so he could personally hand my letter to Governor Engler. This way it would not get buried in a mound of mail. I was grateful for that generous offer. As a result, I received a letter from the Governor rather than a member of his staff. His letter was encouraging, stating that his staff was working closely with the senator in fashioning legislation for civil commitment.

The Mary Kay directors and consultants in this area came out in force to support community awareness night. If we had a serial killer on the loose in this state, it would affect the entire Mary Kay world, plus their children and grandchildren, as well as our customers. After the conference, Mary Kay friends enlisted the aid of their friends across the state of Michigan in support of the legislation. I spoke to the local American Business and Professional Women's Club, and they took it to their statewide convention. Hundreds wrote letters, e-mailed, signed petitions, and made phone calls to their respective legislators, senators, and the governor.

Our friend Senator Van Regenmorter, chairman of the senate judicial committee, and his legislative assistant, John Lazet, had been working consistently with our committee to draft a bill. In May I was asked to testify before the committee. This time I knew what opposition we faced. I designed my speech to overcome the opposition's points before they had a chance to state them. I practiced my speech over and over again. I needed to present a strong and persuasive message. Bill Van Regenmorter was going to have me testify first.

48 Hours sent a crew to my home to film me as I was putting the finishing touches on my speech. The producer and film crew were my first audience as I practiced my speech. Following the filming, they left and met me outside the capital. They started filming as my friend Carol Peterson and I walked up the capital steps, entered the elevator, and walked down the hallway and into the committee room. To the people in and around the capital, we must have presented a rather unusual picture. I noticed that people cleared the way for us and turned aside to watch the camera crew following us everywhere we went.

Frank and Jeff were also there to testify. As I entered, I noticed that our support team filled all the available seats in the visitor section. These individuals included other C-CAP members, a sizeable group of Mary Kay consultants and directors, church friends, the pastor of my church, and my friend Judy Bloss from Ann Arbor, who had brought several people with her. After greetings were exchanged, I took my seat to await the opening.

As I began to testify, I expressed my thanks and deep appreciation for the sponsor and co-sponsors, plus all those who had worked on the civil commitment bill. Then I began:

> On Wednesday, December 29, 1976, my daughter Martha Sue Young broke her engagement to Donald Miller. At the time, Don talked Martha into the idea of remaining friends. Two days later, on New Year's Eve, Martha walked into the kitchen and kissed me goodbye for what would be the last time. Don had come over and wanted to accompany her while she babysat. Since Martha

did not want to be rude to anyone, she said yes. When the baby's parents came home, they became the last people to see her alive. For the next two and a half years, I was not to know what had happened to her.

So I began the battle. I fought with myself not to give in, not to allow the tidal wave of agony to pull me under. I had to stay in control of my feelings. My daughter was out there—perhaps abandoned, badly hurt.

We were experiencing six weeks of below-zero weather, and Martha was out there in the cold. I had to stay focused. I had to help the police. I knew Martha better than anyone else in the world. My mind needed to focus. I would say to myself, "Hang on—you've got to hang on. Think! Think!" I had to survive for my daughter, Kathryn, who at sixteen had lost so much. She couldn't lose her mother, too.

During those two and a half years, three more innocent young women died violent, brutal deaths. Finally, after the attempted murder and rape of the fifth and sixth victims, Donald Miller was caught and sentenced.

This law is about the ultimate women's issue. Women should be free not only from sexual harassment but also from a rapist who tortures and kills his prey. Therefore, I have come to talk to you today, representing women and mothers of Michigan, to ask you to give Michigan a law for civil commitment which will quarantine from society killers who are due to be released from prison.

History has set a precedent in isolating people who have deadly diseases. The disease I am talking about is an illness of the spirit and soul that makes them kill. Attorney generals from thirty-six states, including Michigan, petitioned the Supreme Court to hear the challenge of the Kansas law, which opened the door for all states to protect their citizens. So far, sixteen states have walked through. Now Michigan is standing before that open door.

Let me address some of the concerns that have been expressed. To the concern about whether it is constitutional, first, it is constitutional, as evidenced by the ruling of the Supreme Court in ruling for the State of Kansas. Our own attorney general, Frank Kelly, in opening a conference this spring at the Kellogg Center, quoted John Locke: "Each citizen gives up some rights in order to live in a civil society." He went on to state, "In those rare cases, society has the right to curb individual liberties to keep people safe."

I invite you to go back and study the lives and belief system of those who gave us our constitution. Ask yourself, as a reasonable person, if you really think they would have pledged their lives, their fortunes, their sacred honor to allow sexual predators to prey on their women and children. We have gotten away from basic common sense and the spirit of the constitution.

A person who would advocate the "rights" of a serial killer to be free to kill again over the rights of his human prey—wouldn't you call that person an extremist, even an anarchist, instead of a constitutionalist? If the law will not protect law-abiding citizens, it leads to a breakdown of society.

Another concern is the fear of mixing serial killers and sexual predators with those institutional mentally-ill patients. That's great! I don't want to mix them either!

Probably the most compelling concern is money. Having had twenty-one years in which to think, one of the things I have wondered about is how much in dollars and cents Don's killing rampage cost the citizens of Michigan. What was the total cost of the investigation into Martha's murder in dollars and cents?

- Expensive helicopter searches

- Massive foot searches

- Door-to-door searches

- Crime labs

- Police and prosecution hours

- Grand jury and court costs, and so on

Then multiply this by six—four murders, a rape, and two attempted murders.

I recently obtained some statistics from Senator Van Regenmorter. On the low end, one investigation can cost $72,000 per year. The median range is $173,000 and the high end is $1.2 million. Compare that to $30,000 a year to quarantine the killer. A quarantine is cost effective.

Make no mistake, the state will pay one way or another. When there is a murder, the state will spend whatever it takes to investigate. This does not take into account the pain and suffering to the family and community, plus the lost contribution of the victim's life.

In the future, could you look yourself in the mirror if your family member, neighbor, or constituent were murdered by a released killer? We are constantly reading about released killers who kill again.

Michigan's Leslie Allen Williams is an example of a violent predator who was released and subsequently killed again.

Don't delay to pass a bill, because this will happen again! Please. Give us a law. Hear me on this. This is not about one man. Unfortunately, there are others like Don Miller, but this is the face I know. This is the story I can tell, because I have lived it for twenty-one years. Miller's desire to continue to torture is evidenced by the fact that he located me from prison at my new home and sent me another of his distressing drawings. Again hear me—this is not about one man. If he were not here tomorrow, we would still need this law. Please pass a law.

Then a woman spoke on behalf of the Michigan Psychiatric Association. She opposed the legislation. When she concluded, Senator Van Regenmorter queried, is that "doctor?" To which she replied, "No, secretary for the association." Then the senator pointedly called, "*Doctor* Frank Ochberg" to the stand.

As the former director of mental health for the state of Michigan, Frank had initially had concerns about such legislation. However, his position had changed over time after he had taken the time to study the issue, exchange information with experts, and perform deep personal reflection. He was able to demolish the testimony of the spokesperson for the psychiatry association. In order to build consensus for new legislation, Frank knew he had to make lawmakers understand the rare type of individual who would fall under the scope of this new law. I would like to be able to include the text of his speech, but it was never written out. He speaks eloquently without notes. I have had the privilege many times of listening to Frank speak, and he has graciously shared his writings and reflections with me. Here I am paraphrasing his words to give a sense of the arguments he put forth to the Senate.

Frank stated that the FBI classifies these individuals as "organized serial killers." This term implies that "the perpetrator is personally organized, the killing is deliberate, the crime scene has 'orderly aspects,' and the episodes evolve in the direction of prolonged torture and greater skill in avoiding capture." Generally, organized serial killers are highly intelligent. They stalk, torture, mutilate, and murder. They are aware that their crimes are wrong, because they "are quite capable of changing their plans" to avoid capture. Frank acknowledged that among the psychiatric community, opinions are divided; some believe they "are evil but not ill, while others believe they are ill but not evil." Frank claimed they are both "mad and bad." Frank stated that psychiatry has long avoided the problem, because the field doesn't want to deal with this type of individual. Hence, they say it is the sole province of the criminal justice system. Frank stated it was time that psychiatry ceased avoiding the problem. He asserted a new classification in psychiatry needed to be added. Although these serial killers are cognizant of right and wrong, Frank asked, "Who could claim that someone who stalks, tortures, kills, and engages in necrophilia and cannibalism is normal?" Frank reflected, "Might that be beyond the public expectation of psychiatric care?"

These sadistic killers, he continued, have "never been successfully treated and released." As long as they have their freedom, they will kill again. Since there is no cure, the only treatment for such individuals is a denial of access to their prey.

According to Frank the costs for civil commitment would be minimal, since Michigan already had ample room in its budget. The Mental Health Authority of

Michigan had both the space and the staff at the Forensic Center in Ypsilanti to accommodate the small number of Michigan's serial killers. "The center," as he noted "currently handles far more difficult cases." Unlike psychotic patients, organized serial killers usually cause no problems in prison; therefore, they would typically become model patients in an environment lacking access to prey. "The Public Health Authority needs to step up and accept responsibility," Frank contended, "for housing these persons in a secure, non-punishing environment."

He argued that this is a sound public-health decision. There is long established precedent for the state's ability to quarantine persons with deadly diseases, such as the Ebola virus. In the same manner, he said, "the state may quarantine someone infected with compulsive lethal sadism."

Jeff capped off the presentation, employing the expertise of a seasoned prosecutor. He added compelling facts and legal arguments. Even so, Senator Virgil Smith expressed his concern that the bill would target black men, including him. Senator Van Regenmorter responded by saying, "Virgil, the bill could not possibly target you, for you are not a convicted killer. This bill targets only convicted serial killers about to be released from prison; almost 100% of these killers are white."

When I got home I decided to write to Senator Smith to thank him for considering Bill 647 and to let him know that I was sensitive to his concern that the bill would lead to abuse. I wanted him to know that I had a little understanding of what discrimination does. I told him of the first time that I had encountered it as a single mother. Six months after my husband left, the lease came up on the home in which we lived. During those six months, I had made the payments early, as I was so afraid of being without housing. However, when I tried to renew, they kept "forgetting" to send me the papers. They finally admitted it was because I was a single mother. I knew their action was illegal, but they were probably counting on the fact that I was in no position to fight it. Senator Smith never responded to my letter, so I am not certain whether it influenced his vote.

Later, when the committee vote was taken, the bill was approved and sent to the floor of the Senate for passage. This was unprecedented, because at the time the committee voted, its language had not been finalized. However, based on Van Regenmorter's reputation for quality legislation and the clear need for such a law, the other senators trusted him to get the words right by the time it reached the floor of the Senate for a vote. In the Senate, it was a bi-partisan effort. The senator from my district, Diane Byrum, a Democrat, was one of the early co-sponsors.

The TV camera crew was on the Senate floor and in the balcony the day the vote was taken. As I watched, one after another, senators stepped up to the mike and spoke as co-sponsors, citing the reasons they favored this legislation. Then, I sat anxiously as Senator Virgil Smith approached the mike. Knowing he had misgivings about the bill, I was not surprised when he re-stated his concerns; however, I was pleasantly shocked by his conclusion. His final statement was that this bill satisfied his objections and that he wanted "to congratulate the author because it was so well crafted" and narrow in scope that he was giving it his support. The bill was passed unanimously!

After the vote, I went back to Senator Van Regenmorter's office to thank his staff and rejoice with them. We knew that there was a hang-up in the House, so we talked about that. I was told it would be a good idea for me to walk over to the House and talk to some of its members in person. I found out that since the House was also in session, I could go down to the hallway outside its chamber to meet with representatives who came out to talk to lobbyists. One of the senator's staff showed me the way but told me I needed to do it alone. I asked, "How will I know the difference between the representatives and those who are there to lobby?" To get me started, she pointed to a man standing on the other side of the rotunda. I walked around to that area and waited until he had finished his conversation. Then I approached him, introduced myself, told him about the passage of the bill in the Senate, and asked for his backing. He seemed supportive of the bill, so you can imagine my excitement when I learned that he was the Speaker of the House.

I then started talking to the people who seemed to be just standing there, waiting. Many were lobbyists and expressed their willingness to help me by pointing out representatives. I began to ask the lobbyists more questions, and they were helpful, providing tips on how I should approach the representatives. Later that week, as I returned to the hallway outside of House chamber, I was told that I could select a representative I wanted to speak with and send in a note via the attendant at the door. That person would then come out to talk to me. I tried it, and it worked! The representative I had selected appeared, and I was able to make my appeal.

Frank was still convinced at that point that Mental Health Chair Laura Baird was an ally and actually trying to help us. He still believed that the only thing stopping her was the wording of the law, which was still unacceptable to those on her committee. He continued to spend a great deal of time working on acceptable language for the bill. By this time, I didn't share Frank's opinion about the reason the Mental Health Committee wasn't helping us bring the measure to the House floor for a vote.

I thought the interest that *48 Hours* had taken in the legislation might help us, so I stopped by Laura's office. When the House Mental Health Committee saw what had happened with the bill in the Senate, they did an about face and put forth their own version. As a result, the bill that had been sent over from the Senate would be tied up for an indeterminate amount of time.

My suspicions about Laura Baird's intentions were confirmed when she appeared at our next C-CAP meeting. Van Regenmorter's chief legislative assistant, John Lazet, had been working regularly with us for months. That day, *48 Hours* was also there to film the entire meeting. In front of television cameras, Laura Baird started demanding that John withdraw the legislation that had unanimously passed in the Senate in favor of the legislation that came out of her committee, even though her bill had not even reached the House floor. I sat there in disbelief. Everyone else was also stunned into silence as she continued to heap her demands on John. I listened, thinking that someone needed to come to John's aid. I finally found my voice and spoke up. In the first place, she should have known that as an aide, John had no right to speak for his senator without the senator's authorization. As a representative, she would never allow her own staff to speak for her without even consulting her. The Senate bill had passed unanimously, but John nonetheless could not speak for the entire Senate. John's behavior while under attack was exemplary. He remained calm and courteous amid the barrage.

Baird seemed to have a problem with Senator Van Regenmorter receiving credit for the bill simply because he had authored it, just as he had on other outstanding pieces of legislation. She tried to paint the senator as a man on an ego trip. Frank started to give an opinion, but Baird cut him short by saying, "It does not matter what you think!" What arrogance. Here she was, talking to her own constituents and telling them that none of the opinions in the room mattered except hers.

I wish that *48 Hours* had shown her tirade so that the voters could see what she was really like, but they did not. Today, this woman is a judge—a frightening thought, considering how autocratic and egotistical she can be. The truth is, the bill from Baird's committee would have been a disaster.

What are the differences between the two bills?

House Sexual Predator Bill 5247

House Sexual Predator Bill H5247 is loaded with language and provisions to make it as unattractive as possible to legislators. *H5247* creates more bureaucracy and is time consuming, inefficient, and deliberately costly. The provisions are as follows:

1. Department of Corrections creates a multidisciplinary team several months before the scheduled release of the serial killer.

2. This multidisciplinary team evaluates; if sufficient cause > refer to attorney general.*

3. Attorney general appoints a review committee.

4. Committee must have among its members a physician and one licensed psychologist.* Entire committee must be in unanimous agreement to > refer to court.

5. Court > turns to Center for Forensic Psychiatry.

6. Center for Forensic Psychiatry makes recommendations > to court.

7. Court proceeding.

Even if this bill were voted into law, the likelihood of a sexual predator ever reaching a court proceeding would be minimal. As a result, serial killers are released into the community. The reasons for this are as follows:

> * Step 2 creates more bureaucracy and is costly and unnecessary. The AG's office already has adequately trained staff capable of dealing with the evaluation of serial killers.
> * Step 4 creates additional bureaucracy that adds cost and allows unqualified persons to be part of the committee. (A surgeon or pediatrician is a physician but has no expertise in forensic psychiatry, and neither does a psychiatrist in family practice.) A unanimous decision prior to the individual standing before a court is unreasonable. Additionally, the Forensic Center does not need the recommendation of a committee to do its job of evaluation. Forensic Center staff are qualified to perform evaluations. It makes no sense for amateurs to be screening people for the professionals.

H5247 requires only one killing, meaning hundreds of people would be covered by this law. Legislators would likely view this as a costly law that would flood the system. The potential price tag could make this a very difficult bill for the House to pass. If somehow a person was civilly committed under this legislation, it provides for examination and evaluation at least once a year. It could be as much as every six months, meaning that every six months there would be a potential release date. This would be a continuing nightmare to victims. The frequent evaluations would also make the law cost prohibitive. This bill disregards the victims of sexual predators. It was designed to protect the rights of killers rather than the rights of citizens.

Senate Serial Killer Bill 649

Senate Serial Killer Bill 649 would have been the only one of its kind in the U.S. The provisions are as follows:

1. Department of Corrections notifies > attorney general.

2. Attorney general may if sufficient cause > refer it to judge.

3. Judge calls for > evaluation by Center for Forensic Psychiatry > When civil commitment is recommended >

4. Trial is conducted.

S649 requires two killings. This bill would be cost effective. It uses appropriate established channels and does not create new ones. An annual report would be required, but a new evaluation would be required only every three years. This bill protects the rights of victims while maintaining constitutional safe guards.

During the legislature's summer recess, Mark Blumer, a C-CAP member from the attorney general's office, told me about Jennifer Granholm, a prosecuting attorney in the Detroit area. This successful young attorney was being considered as a Democratic candidate for attorney general to replace the retiring Frank Kelly. Since this lawyer was a woman, we thought we might be able to persuade her to campaign on the passage of this bill. When I agreed that it was a great idea, Mark gave me her address. I wrote her a brief letter, in which I included a front-page story clipped from a Detroit newspaper. It provided some background, and since it was a front-page story ninety miles from the Lansing area, it demonstrated statewide interest.

My plan was to call her in three days, hoping her secretary would allow me to make an appointment to drive down to her office to meet with her. That proved unnecessary. I called and was connected directly to Ms. Granholm. Not only had she read the news article, she was already up to speed on the case! She promised, "If I am lucky enough to receive the nomination, I will be right there in Lansing fighting beside you!" She proved to be a lady of her word. It's perhaps no accident she went on to become not only attorney general but also Michigan's governor.

With the mental health chair blocking the chance to get the bill on the House calendar for a vote, Frank suggested we make an appointment to talk to the House speaker, Curtis Hertel. The speaker is the only person who can bring a bill to a vote if the chairperson refuses to report it out of committee. He was our only hope, yet bringing the bill to a vote would mean overruling a chairperson of his own party. This was the speaker's last year in office, and we were hoping he would leave this as a legacy to protect the women and children of Michigan. How naïve we still were.

Jennifer Granholm, now attorney general-elect for Michigan, squeezed in a half-hour meeting with the Speaker between others she had already scheduled. (However, she ended up staying much longer than half an hour.) I had expected the Speaker to meet with us privately, but instead he had invited our main opposition, Laura Baird, as well as Ted Wallace, chairman of the House Judicial Committee and also a member of the Mental Health Committee. They were already seated on one side of the table. Frank and I took our places on the opposite side. When Ms. Granholm arrived, she sat with Frank and me and argued vigorously on our behalf against the members of her own party.

At one point, Ted Wallace addressed me.

"Make no mistake, Sue, I have no love for Don Miller," he said. "In fact, if I ever encountered him, I would probably shoot him myself!"

"That's exactly what I am afraid of," I replied. "Some good man may become so fearful for his family that he will take the law into his own hands and ruin his life—and the lives of his family. That's why it's so important for the state to live up to its obligation to protect its citizens."

Wallace retorted, "Well, we would prosecute that man to the limit of the law."

"Ted, that makes no sense in view of what you just said you yourself would do," I responded. Today, Ted Wallace is also a judge.

The sad part is, we would have had enough votes in the House to pass this legislation overwhelmingly if the bill had gotten out of committee and onto the House floor. At the end of 1998, the bill died, so the second year we had to start all over in the Senate. Frank, Jeff, and I testified again. I was thrilled that Attorney General Granholm sent her personal representative, Tom Boyd, to speak on her behalf, stating, "We have studied this bill. The Supreme Court has ruled. It is constitutional. So what is the question?" Again, the bill passed overwhelmingly in the Senate, and again it never got to the floor of the House.

We were deeply discouraged, as we had believed legislation was the best hope. Instead, we found that stopping Donald Miller would depend on a shoelace.

Testifying before Senate Judicial Committee.

Michigan Victims Advocate of the Year Award, presented to Sue Young
by Senator Van Regenmorter in the Capital Rotunda.

14

Lives Hang by a Shoelace

Based on his conversation with Tom Robinson over the weapon in Miller's cell, Jeff Sauter began to take the idea of bringing charges against Don seriously. I remember feeling a surge of hope when he first started talking about it at our C-CAP meeting. I wondered if bringing suit was really feasible. We had few viable options. I thought back to my initial reaction at the parole hearing in 1995, when I heard that Don had been found in possession of a weapon. I had always considered it strange that the prison authority had revoked only two years of his "good time" for that. Finding a garrote sounded serious to me, and I wondered why they hadn't taken away the entire ten years. I had raised that question at the parole-board meeting, but I received no answer. I didn't realize that Jeff had not even heard about it.

Because the clock was ticking, every conceivable strategy was worth investigating. We had few alternatives, so Jeff set about exploring the possibilities. There was so little time left. In the spring of 1998, less than a year remained until Don Miller would be set loose to kill again. This would not be parole; it would be the official end of the thirty-to-fifty-year sentence! There would be no parole officers, and no supervision. His jail time would be complete. Once back home, he would likely realize that the area police would carefully monitor his movements (from a distance) during his first months of freedom. Of course, if he actually spotted the police surveillance, he could file charges of harassment. Miller would be clever enough to wait until the police attention waned, just as he had done after Martha's murder. It was, therefore, crucial to prevent those prison doors from opening.

In January, Stuart Dunnings III became Ingham County prosecutor. Jeff Sauter immediately invited Stuart to attend C-CAP's meetings. Stuart was appalled when he found out Miller was due to be released. Although Stuart had just come into office, and had a heavy caseload as the prosecutor for the Capitol City area, he nonetheless came. He could have easily assigned an assistant to attend in his place. However, his instincts told him that Miller's release would be a "homicide just waiting to happen." That opinion was confirmed when he listened to Richard Walters and Frank Ochberg.

Jeff recognized Stuart as an ally and talked to him about joining our cause. Since Don had committed crimes in Ingham and Eaton counties, there was the possibility of getting five years for each county. When the idea was presented at a C-CAP meeting, Stuart expressed his wholehearted willingness to commit himself to a two-county suit, pledging, "Jeff, I'll even carry your briefcase if that is what you need!" Stuart Dunnings meant exactly what he said.

At this point, it was not clear whether they could succeed in making a case, so the first step was to determine if a case could be put together. Captain Bob Dutcher of the Meridian Police Department, a C-CAP member and Jeff's good friend, was very willing to contribute his investigative skills. He and Jeff began a close collaboration. Had the prison weapon been destroyed? Who was the corrections officer who had found the implement and determined that it was a weapon? Could they find that person? Jim Koonce of Jeff's office was also a tireless investigator and helped us get answers to these questions.

We encountered obstacles immediately. First of all, the case would have to be tried in the jurisdiction where the offense had occurred. This meant the trial would take place in the northern Michigan town of Sault Sainte Marie, in Chippewa County. Therefore, the prosecutor in that area would need to be contacted. So, Jeff placed a call to Prosecutor Pat Shannon. Could Jeff persuade Pat to issue the necessary warrant to bring the case to trial? He would let Pat know that Eaton and Ingham counties would do all the work. He would assure him that they had the wholehearted dedication needed to do the job. Having stressed the urgency and commitment behind the request, Jeff acknowledged that this case was, at best, an extreme long shot. Ultimately, it would likely prove to be a futile effort. Knowing all of this, I felt it took great courage for Jeff to place the call. Having already invested so much time and hard work on what would likely be a losing proposition, Jeff and the team were willing to invest even more.

Pat vividly remembers Jeff's first call. Don Miller's actions had not reached the news in the northernmost regions of Michigan, so he didn't know anything about the case. However, Jeff had piqued Pat's interest. Still, Pat reserved judgment until he saw the state police reports. The initial call started Pat thinking about the events that had taken place in the late seventies. He began to connect what had happened in 1978, while he had been in the lower part of the state taking his bar exam, to what Jeff was now talking about. He realized that the murdered woman's body, discovered in a field near Lansing in 1978, was part of the case Jeff had called about. That's when Pat ordered up the state police reports.

Jeff's preparation for this case was tireless. As he stated, "For trial lawyers, there are difficult cases that make your job very stressful and then there are cases you cannot afford to lose. The pressure is on you so much. Lots of cases I have tried in Eaton County have been major ones, but there may also have been a lot of evidence. In fact, these cases might not have been that difficult to win because of the overwhelming evidence. Then there are those where we may not have as much evidence, but where the pressure is still there because they are so important that we cannot afford to lose them. This trial was one of the latter. We did not have overwhelming evidence, and it was very, very important that we do well."

Jeff and Stuart followed up the phone call by going to see Pat. "First, Jeff, and I were going to try the case," Stuart said. "We told Patrick, 'If you will just issue the warrant, Jeff and I will do the work.'"

Pat recalled, "I understood the importance of the case the more I spoke with Jeff and Stu." He added, "Remember, my county was a prison county, and officer safety was important to me. Weapons are not allowed. Miller possessed a weapon."

This was the beginning of long, exhausting days of hard work, as Jeff, Stuart, Bob, and Jim took to the road. Jeff already had a heavy caseload in Eaton County. Sometimes the trips involved Jeff and Stuart, sometimes Bob and Jeff went alone, and at other times all four men went. It is five hours one way to Sault Sainte Marie. Jeff recalled, "Anytime I wanted to go, at the drop of a hat, Bob Dutcher would say, 'Let's go!' There were times we left the first thing in the morning, attended an all-day hearing, and then returned that evening." Arraignment took place on Friday, July 25, 1997, but it took until the fall of 1998 to get to trial.

The authorities at the prison then gave us some bad news: the confiscated weapon no longer existed! It had been destroyed. The prosecution would therefore have to rely on testimony from prison guards who had seen it, if those guards could be located. Pictures had been taken of the item, but prison officials were able to find only two of the Polaroids.

Pat reflected, "We were always running into closed doors. The odds were against us." Jeff agreed as he thought about all the difficulties the prosecution had faced.

The first hurdle for the prosecution was the fact that the offense had been committed two years earlier. Jeff said, "Because the confiscated item no longer existed, the defense was able to suggest three major points:

1. The evidence was destroyed intentionally rather than accidentally, because it was Department of Corrections policy to do so.

2. It was an ordinary item sold in the prison store.

3. Don Miller had a number of valid uses for a long shoestring, including some kind of belt to tie up his coat."

Fortunately, Leo Schwesinger, the guard who'd found the implement, had been located. Since the weapon had been destroyed, there would be a lot riding on this man's testimony. What kind of witness would he make? Would the jury find him credible?

Despite all the problems, Pat began to believe the case could be made. However, it would require that the judge allow the prosecution to use a controversial provision known as 404B (the "prior bad acts" provision). Since we needed the jury to know that ligature strangulation was Don's method of choice in the murders he had committed, Jeff could think of no better person to speak about this issue than Lisa, who had come within seconds of dying at Don's hands. She could give irrefutable firsthand testimony that Don had used ligature strangulation on her. If additional testimony was needed, her brother, Randy, could also testify.

Stuart decided to use the Polaroid to make a replica of the confiscated device Don had made, using large buttons and seventy-two-inch bootlaces. He then made an appointment to see forensic expert Dr. Stephen Cohl in Grand Rapids, and he took the model with him. Stuart recalled, "I'll never forget the day I first met Dr. Cohl. I laid out the replica I had made. He just looked at it and stated with certainty, 'That's a garrote.'"

Just as the prosecution team began to feel they were making real progress, the judge ruled that the 404B provision could not be used, explaining, "It would be too prejudicial to the defense." This was an absolutely devastating blow. Pat believed that the case was winnable only if the jury understood Don's history. In light of the judge's decision, our team now had to decide whether the ruling was a lethal setback.

Stuart said, "We did a lot of soul searching."

Jeff told me later, "We just had to go for it—for you and Donna. If we were going to be shot down, we were going to go down in flames!"

Pat commented, "We were always running into closed doors, yet there was always a ray of light. We knew we had a daunting task, but we just decided to put on our seatbelts and go for it!"

At a C-CAP meeting, Jeff talked about appealing the judge's decision to the Court of Appeals. I remember thinking that questioning a judge's decision sounded risky, since afterward the case might be tried under that same judge. I asked Jeff about that. He assured me that it wouldn't create a problem with the judge, and I trusted Jeff's judgment. The appeal didn't work; the court let the judge's assessment stand.

Shaken but still resolute, the team continued with its preparations. Jeff thought that location could pose another obstacle for the prosecution with regards to jury selection. He knew the community was small and included families of prisoners. These were relatives who had moved to the area specifically to be near their incarcerated family members. Their sympathy could run in favor of the prisoner. The second concern about the location was that the jury pool could be prejudiced against Jeff and Stu for being outsiders from a "city" downstate.

In considering location, Pat said, "Look, this is my community. These are my people. I know the way they think. We will just present a 'straightforward case' and they will make the right decision. If you want me to, I will try the case and have you two appointed assistant prosecutors for Chippewa County."

Stuart described his feelings at that moment: "I recalled the book, *Anatomy of a Murder*, which was a case about a hotshot prosecutor from the 'big city of Lansing' going to a small northern Michigan town to try a case. All I could think about was how that 'big city' attorney had lost!"

This case was all about winning, not about status. Each of these men wanted to plan the best strategy for victory. It was always a total team effort. Here were three very powerful, extremely capable, and important men who never exhibited a trace of ego, only a tremendous dedication to accomplishing their mission. These men genuinely like and respect each other to this day. Each speaks with tremendous pride of the abilities of the other two.

After the judge denied any mention of Miller's past, they jointly analyzed each of their individual strengths in relation to the case. They decided that Pat would be the best one to try the case, while Stuart would handle the expert witnesses and Jeff would prepare to cross-examine Don in case they decided to put him on the stand in his own defense. Jeff would also handle the penalty phase.

After all the countless hours and the commitment it took to get this before a judge, none of us in C-CAP (except for the prosecutors) knew about the other enormous burden Jeff was facing. Some in the corrections department felt that they might be able to take away Don's "good time"—but only if he dropped the case. Jeff was told, "You know, if you lose this trial, we may not be able to yank his special good time, because we already took his good time back in 1994." In talking about this later, Jeff said, "In essence, they were saying, if you argue and lose this, he is going to get released in February 1999. I would be jeopardizing their opportunity to keep him locked up for ten more years. The implication was that it would be my fault."

I was fascinated by this strange line of argument against going to trial, considering the fact that at the last parole hearing, in 1997, all of us had been told that would be the final one. In February 1999, it would be out of their hands and there was nothing additional that could be done. On Friday, April 26, 1997, when the board denied Don's request for parole, the same message was reiterated the next day by *The Lansing State Journal* article. It quoted the spokesperson for the corrections department, Matt Davis, as saying, "Frankly, the position of the parole board is they don't want him out on the streets." In the next paragraph of the article, he added, "But even if the parole board still considers him a risk in two years, Miller will be released from prison when his sentence expires in February 1999." In short, in 1997, both the parole board and the correction department were saying the same thing. If, somehow, we had misunderstood, why didn't corrections contact Louise Knott, the writer of the article, and issue a retraction? One year later, Louise wrote an article with the headline, "Corrections Chief: early release unlikely for Miller." The article went on to state, "The corrections department has become frustrated because the media and a local organization (C-CAP) have been saying that Miller will be released next year. [Corrections' Chief] McGinnis said 135 prisoners since 1986 have not been given their special good time."

I didn't understand why they were frustrated with us, since they were the ones who had told us he would be released at that time. Additionally, the earlier article made it seem as though we were on the same side. We both wanted Miller kept away from the community. We had no quarrel with them. We were not saying the Department of Corrections was at fault. We never blamed them; we knew that they were just obeying the law. Why weren't they happy that citizens were getting involved and seeking a solution we both wanted? Now, Jeff was being told there was the possibility that Don's good time could be rescinded, but only if he dropped the case. This upped the stakes for Jeff.

Before the case could be brought to trial, a preliminary hearing and an arraignment before the district court, Judge Nicholas Lambros, had to take place. At the preliminary hearing, the challenge would be to survive the defense's motion to dismiss. As expected, defense counsel moved to have the pending proceedings dismissed. It argued the shakedown had occurred over two years earlier and that the defendant had been denied his right to due process and a speedy trial. The defense seized every opportunity it could to trivialize the contraband, referring to it in innocuous language. Instead of calling it as a seventy-two-inch bootlace, they called it a "shoestring." The defense was granted the right for Miller to appear in court wearing street clothing rather than prison garb. Additionally, the defense claimed the prosecution had not provided all of the items the defense had requested, including "the entire cell area."

Prosecutor Pat Shannon responded that he had turned over everything Don had as soon as he had obtained it. "I can't present to the court the entire contents of a prison cell," he said. "I've never been asked to do that before."

In ruling on the defense's request, the court stated, "I don't think this is an issue that the prosecutor has not complied with, as much as one he might not be able to comply with the specifics of." In light of that, he told Thomas Bengston that he could arrange to view a cell. He also said that he would reschedule the hearing and issue an order for the exact items the defense required—if those items, in fact, existed.

The various court procedures dragged on so long that by the time the actual trial date was set, Pat Shannon had already accepted a position as deputy superintendent of schools. Soon after beginning his new job, he found himself in the midst of contract negotiations. Nevertheless, without taking any vacation time, Pat took a leave from his new position to try the case. Later I asked Pat why he had done this. He responded, "That's easy—there was no decision to be made. Each of us felt that we were the last backstop here. It was my duty: once a prosecutor, always a prosecutor. It was the type of case you want to go out on as a prosecutor." Here was another example of the tremendous dedication that went into this trial. It is also another example of the incredible teamwork that united these men.

The team still did not know what kind of witness Corrections Officer Leo Schwesinger would make. "We were warned that we might have a problem," Jeff related. "Leo was a unique individual. Over time, I got to like him, however we were nervous. But, as the trial progressed, our respect for Leo as a witness grew. He told his story in a very credible, straightforward way. The defense couldn't shake his account or confuse him." Pat Shannon had Leo relate the events that led up to his discovery of Don's weapon. Leo was a rover at the time (a guard who wanders the prison yard when the inmates are there. He is not assigned to a particular unit but works where he is needed, providing lunch relief for the regular guards). Leo had conducted a shakedown of the prison cell occupied by "D. G. Miller" and the two other inmates who occupied his cell. As part of his job, Leo was required to do five random shakedowns a day. This was one of them.

By this time, the crew from *48 Hours* had arrived in the northern Michigan town of Sault Ste. Marie to cover the trial. First they interviewed Donna, Lisa, and Randy. Then they turned their attention to the prosecution team, virtually shadowing them. The crew had agreed to withhold airing information regarding any aspect of the trial until after the verdict was rendered. With this understanding, they were allowed to sit in on all discussions and strategy sessions.

In conversations between Jeff and me following the conclusion of the trial, I asked him about what the mood had been before the trial opened. "We did not have overwhelming evidence," he replied, "and it was very, very important that we did well. The pressure was compounded by having *48 Hours* watching every move, calling us in between court hearings, and sitting in on strategy sessions."

Bill Lagatuta was the *48 Hours* correspondent covering the trial. Just before it began, he asked Jeff one question: "Jeff, do you think you can prove beyond a reasonable doubt to a jury that this bootlace was a weapon? This guy has got this bootlace tied in a knot, and all you've got are two Polaroids." In asking that one question, he made our case seem not only ridiculous but hopeless as well. At this time, Jeff also remembered a statement from the judge. Because judges usually have heavy caseloads, they normally try to get the lawyers to settle without bringing the matter to trial. "During the pre-trial hearings," Jeff said, "the judge made some comments that seemed to trivialize our case, and that worried me."

In allowing the trial to go forward, the judge had said, "The photograph, I think, is clear, demonstrative proof that this item was found. The question is whether or not that's all that believable. And that is why I indicated that I think there's sufficient evidence, but I don't know how credible it's going to be as to prove it beyond reasonable doubt. Credible enough to get by me, but that doesn't say a lot for the credibility of the evidence under these proceedings."

These were certainly not reassuring words to Jeff, who stated, "At that point, we had not impressed him with the seriousness of our case." With these thoughts echoing in Jeff's head, the trial began.

Pat reassured us that we had gotten a really good judge. Over time, Jeff came to agree with Pat: "My respect for him kept growing by leaps and bounds. He controlled the courtroom without being nasty. He was very, very friendly. He was very courteous to all—respectful of the jury, court staff, and defendant. He was such a nice guy, but when it came time to rule on a legal issue, he was very, very sharp. He proved it time and time again."

In assessing the jury-selection process, Jeff recounted, "We had been warned that, since many residents of the area had moved there to be near family members who were imprisoned, there might be a predisposition to favor the inmate. However, as the jury selection proceeded, things began to change. In going over the events of the day on that first evening, we found that we were already feeling good. We could feel things going our way. The same thing occurred the second day. Every evening of the trial, the whole team, investigators and lawyers, evaluated our next moves. We paid a lot of attention to the ideas and opinions of our outstanding, dedicated investigators."

In his opening statement, the defense attorney ridiculed the prosecution's evidence. "Officer Leo Schwesinger did remove a shoestring of approximately seventy-two inches in length with two buttons on it," he said. "Two buttons were strung on shoelace and it was tied at the end in a knot approximately the size of a dime. That's the claimed dangerous weapon—a *shoestring* with two buttons strung on it."

He also noted, "Prosecution is required to demonstrate, to your satisfaction, that Mr. Miller was an inmate at the Kinross Correctional Facility. There is no question. We don't challenge that our client was an inmate at Kinross on November 4, 1994."

Following the opening statements, the prosecution called Corrections Officer Leo Schwesinger to the stand. Pat Shannon had Leo relate the events that unfolded on November 4, 1994. That day, Officer Schwesinger had been assigned to relieve Officer Jim Couling during his lunch break. Leo decided this would be a good time to conduct one of his required daily shakedowns. He explained to the court that a shakedown is, "where you go through all the property to look for contraband." In order to decide which cell to search, he consulted the master list of prisoners housed in unit B. As he looked down the list, he spotted a name he recognized, John Hudson, so he chose his cell. He did not continue looking down the list at the names of the other two occupants. When he arrived at the cell, Schwesinger recognized one of Hudson's cellmates as Donald Miller. He followed the standard procedure of sending the three men to the day room while he conducted his search. Leo began the shakedown with Hudson's area of control. This took only five to ten minutes, because Hudson "basically had nothing." Afterward, he shook down the second prisoner's area of control, and, finally, he started on Don's. As per his normal routine, he started with the bed. This was accomplished, "by stripping the bed, lifting the mattress, and checking the seams to make sure they [weren't] cut. Basically, the bed [was] taken apart." Next came the desk. Even the bulletin board was checked to make sure that it was tightly fastened to the wall so nothing could be hidden behind it. The search proceeded uneventfully, until he came to Miller's wall locker. If they own a footlocker, ordinarily prisoners keep them under their bunks. Miller's was inside his wall locker. "I thought that was rather strange, [the foot locker] being in the wall locker, and on top of that, it was padlocked. Most of the time, prisoners don't padlock their lockers while they are in their cells."

Leo went on to describe how he had taken out his master key and opened it. "When I lifted the tray, there was a small cardboard box that got my interest. When I opened it, it was covered with green velvet inside, and the velvet was pleated on the corners, very similar to how it would look in a casket—that's what it looked like to me. I pulled it out of the box to see what was underneath and to go through them contents. I found several small items, a cross, and a plastic package with an article rolled up in it."

Mr. Shannon: "What did you see once you opened it?"

Leo: "I found a heavy shoelace with two wooden handles attached and tied together with a large knot."

Shannon: "When you saw that, what went through your mind, Officer?"

Leo: "What went through my mind automatically was [that it was] a weapon that could be used to strangle someone."

Shannon: "Did you have any question in your mind when you saw that item?"

Leo: "No, I didn't."

Under Pat Shannon's questioning, Leo related how he had gotten on his radio and talked to his yard sergeant, Sandra Morningstar. She instructed him to take pictures. As soon as Officer Couling returned from his break, he began assisting Leo. When "about ten pictures" were taken, they were put in a packet along with the weapon and turned over to Sergeant Morningstar. She then sent it to the hearings division, along with the ticket.

During defense attorney Bengston's cross-examination, he tried to establish discrepancies in Leo's testimony. "In your report," he said to Leo, "you'd referred to the shoelace as a 'weapon,' but under examination you called it a garrote. Was there any reason for the change?"

Leo replied matter-of-factly, "A garrote is a weapon." As the defense continued to probe for any change in testimony, Leo was asked about other completely unrelated items, such as which items were found in the desk and which ones in the footlocker. Interspersed throughout this line of questioning were queries about the exact locations of individual items, such as, "Where was the box found, in the top tray or under it? Did clothing cover it? Where was the box placed in order to take pictures? Did you measure the exact length of the 'shoestring'? What was the size of the knot? Why didn't you measure the length of the weapon and the size of the knot that tied the ends together?" These questions failed to produce any inconsistencies in Leo's testimony. Leo proved to be an excellent witness. He clearly stated what he had done after discovering the weapon, without embellishment. The defense was not able to confuse him.

The defense counsel wanted the jurors to believe that Leo and other officers had unfairly targeted his client. The defense asked Leo if prison officers had targeted his client because they knew Don's release was approaching. When Leo said he hadn't, Bengston went on to ask if Leo, himself, had targeted Don. Leo replied that he didn't target *any* prisoners. Continuing to pursue that line of inquiry, he questioned him about a report that Bengston claimed Leo had written on Don the month prior to the cell search. Leo stated that the information was incorrect and that he had not written a report on Don. A later witness identified a different officer as having written the report.

Finally, the defense tried to prove that

1. Shoelaces were approved prison items, just as objects like TV cables and extension cords were.

2. Various items attached to shoelaces and worn around the neck were allowed; therefore, the shoelaces with the buttons attached were authorized. Leo kept repeating that the shoelace had been altered in a way that was *not* permitted. In a parting shot aimed at discrediting his testimony, Leo was asked if his nickname on the job was "Cowboy."

When the defense was finished, Prosecutor Shannon was eager to clear up any doubts the defense had raised concerning Leo's testimony. First, the prosecution needed the jury to be aware that Donald Gene Miller was not an innocent citizen who possessed a simple shoelace, as his court attire, a sport shirt and dress trousers seem to indicate. Although the judge would not allow Don's criminal record (which included rape, attempted murder by strangulation, and murder) to be mentioned, Shannon could ask about the types of prisoners housed at the Kinross facility. He asked if all of the prisoners housed there were convicted felons. On the basis that all the inmates were, in fact, convicted felons, Mr. Shannon asked what other potentially dangerous items Leo had seen in Kinross that were approved in their unaltered state.

Leo described how prisoners pulled thin pieces from heater vents then formed them into prison shanks (homemade knives). Razors taken from shavers were melted into either toothbrushes or pens to be used as slashing weapons. He had found ink pens with heavy needles melted into them to make "stickers."

Continuing with this line of questioning, Pat referred to other items—belts, socks, and locks. In the defense's cross-examination, Bengston had established that all three items were sold in the prison store, and Leo had acknowledged this was true. Shannon referred to this and then asked Leo if he had ever seen a belt made into a weapon and how this could be done.

Leo: "[A padlock is] attached to the end of the belt, locked on there, through the buckle, or sometimes…the buckle is looped back through the belt and then the lock is attached to that."

Shannon: "Each [item], though, is permissible to be possessed inside the prison; is that correct?"

Leo: "In their own form."

Shannon: "Have you ever seen a lock combined with anything else?"

Leo: "I have seen them in socks."

Shannon: "Do you wear work boots?"

Leo: "I wear a Western-style work boot."

Shannon: "Okay, could those commonly be referred to as cowboy boots?"

Leo: "Yes, they could."

Following Leo's testimony, Stuart Dunnings took over for the prosecution's examination of the people's witness, forensic pathologist Dr. Stephen Cohl. For Pat, the appearance of Dr. Cohl was one of the highlights of the trial. "His testimony was critical to prove beyond a reasonable doubt that the bootlace was a weapon or could be used as a weapon. We only needed to show that a bootlace 'could' be used as a weapon…Dr. Cohl supported this greatly." His vital testimony was made possible through assistance from the state police. Dr. Cohl's schedule did not permit him time to drive from Grand Rapids to the Sault and back again. The state police flew him to the Sault in their plane, and another state trooper picked him up at the airport and drove him to and from the courthouse. This is another example of the tremendous cooperation, manpower, and effort needed to bring this case before a jury.

Before introducing Dr. Cohl to the jury, the role of the forensic pathologist was identified. (A forensic pathologist is a physician who specializes in sudden, unexpected, and sometimes violent deaths.) The next task before Dunnings was to establish Dr. Cohl's credentials as an expert witness before the court.

Stuart stated that after graduating as an M.D. in general pathology, Stephen Cohl trained at Baylor College of Medicine in Houston, Texas, where he became an instructor in pathology. Afterward, he trained in forensic pathology at the

Institute of Forensic Science in Dallas, where he passed his exams in both general pathology and forensic pathology. Over the past sixteen years he had been employed at Spectrum Health Hospital in Grand Rapids, Michigan, where he was also the medical examiner for Allegan County and deputy medical examiner for Kent County. He had been called upon to assist law enforcement in homicide investigations and to testify as an expert witness in various counties in Michigan, as well as Indiana, Colorado, Texas, and Ohio. Specific testimony was brought out to show that Dr. Cohl was familiar with ligature strangulation. In his position, he had been called upon many times to determine whether or not certain instruments were consistent with the physical findings of ligature strangulation.

After the presentation, the judge ruled, "The court will qualify Dr. Cohl as an expert witness based on his knowledge and experience, skill, training, and education to assist the jury in understanding the evidence and the fact at issue in this case, which is ligature strangulation." Stuart found this widely respected man to be a willing and very capable witness. "His demeanor and entire court presence gave him an overall air of competence."

In order to demonstrate scientifically that the object in the photograph taken in Donald Miller's cell was a strangulation device, Dr. Cohl brought a replica of the device pictured. Here, Stuart wisely remembered a piece of advice that had been ingrained into him by his father, who was also a trial lawyer. His father had always told him, "Never demonstrate for the first time in court what you haven't tried out before you get to court, because, if you do, you will absolutely fall flat on your face in front of the jury!" Stuart heeded his father's warning. Jeff Sauter was used as a model to practice the exhibition Dr. Cohl would put on in court. Jeff had left his glasses on during this practice demonstration, and the device had caught on his glasses. If this had occurred in court, it would have distracted the jury. Consequently, when Jeff appeared as a model, he did not wear his glasses.

Using several different techniques, Dr. Cohl demonstrated on Jeff that the device could be used to strangle a victim. He explained how it worked as he demonstrated.

Cohl: "The handles basically enable one to grab it and get a grip, so that you don't have to rely just upon grabbing the loose ends with your hands."

Dunnings: "So would it be fair to say that the handles significantly increase the effectiveness of the weapon?"

Cohl: "Yes, I think that would be fair to say. I agree with that."

In the cross examination, Mr. Bengston hammered away at the proposition.

Bengston: "What is the big deal about having a shoelace with large buttons attached in a prisoner's cell? Now, with regard to whether or not an item could be used to inflict harm on another person, could your tie and my tie be so used?"

Cohl: "Absolutely."

Bengston: "My belt?"

Cohl: "Yes."

Bengston: "Shirt sleeve?"

Cohl: "Yes, a shirt sleeve could be used."

Bengston: "What if this article only had one button? What impact would that have on the opinion you've offered here this afternoon?"

Cohl: "Well, I think my overall opinion would stand. I think it could still be used as a ligature. I think it would be harder if there were just one button."

Bengston: "In summary, with or without handles on this item, either way, it can be used to strangle someone, is that right?"

Cohl: "Yes, sir."

The next people's witness, Sergeant Alfred McLean, was called to the stand. As the supervising officer of the Baker Unit, he corroborated the testimony of Leo Schwesinger. Al Mclean had been employed by the Department of Corrections for nearly fourteen years. It was his job to handle any serious incidents that arose, so when he was informed that Officer Schwesinger had found something he considered to be a dangerous contraband item, the sergeant went down to inspect the area.

The sergeant testified, "He showed me a device, which I considered to be a garrote made out of a shoestring, with two wooden handles on the end of it." The defense contended that Don had used the shoelace as a drawstring in his winter coat. Since the sergeant saw Prisoner Miller frequently, he was asked if he had ever seen Don using that item before. Sergeant Mclean stated that he had not.

The prosecution then called Arthur Tessmer, warden of the Kinross facility, as the next witness. The warden reinforced Leo's testimony by confirming that he had knowledge of the contraband found in inmate Miller's room and that he had done nothing to overrule the conclusion of the officers. The defense had argued that Don was authorized to possess shoelaces and buttons, so the warden was asked to refute the idea that anyone was authorized to possess the items in such an altered form. He also confirmed that it was routine to destroy contraband items after a period of time.

The defense had been successful in getting the court to allow Don to appear in regular clothing rather than prison garb and had blocked any reference to Miller's prior offenses. However, Shannon could get the warden to verify Leo's testimony that all inmates were convicted felons. He knew that he needed to get the jury to realize the seriousness of the charges. Prosecutor Shannon dictated a litany of serious crimes, at least one of which Don Miller had to have committed in order to be in that particular prison. On the list, Shannon included all of the crimes for which Donald Miller had been convicted.

Shannon: "And what types of felonies are represented within your prison population?"

Warden: "I would have to say virtually every felony that's on the state statutes."

Shannon: "Would that include child molesters?"

Warden: "Yes."

Shannon: "Killers and murderers?

Warden: "Yes."

Shannon: "Armed robbers?"

Warden: "Yes."

Shannon: "People who break into your homes?"

Warden: "Yes."

When Bengston began to cross examine Warden Tessmer, he wanted to know the extent of the warden's knowledge of Leo Schwesinger. He asked if the warden was aware of Leo's transfer from the facility. When he followed that question by asking if he had coordinated the transfer, it seemed the defense was going to try to slip in information about Leo's past performance in an effort to knock his credibility. At that point, Pat Shannon interrupted, "Excuse me, your Honor, I don't know if this is relevant, and this type of thing was already addressed prior. The Court found—"

Before he could finish, the judge broke in. "Would you approach the bench a moment, please?"

After the bench conference, the defense dropped that line of questioning. Again, the defense brought up a list of about a dozen common objects, including shoelaces and buttons, and asked the warden if they were authorized for sale at the prison store. Then he asked the warden, "Are you in a position to tell the jury the number of inmates in possession of a weapon which consisted of a shoelace and something strung onto it in 1994?" When the answer was "no," the defense continued, "Do you know if any were ever reported?"

The warden answered, "None that I recall."

Bengston then asked, "Did you make a determination in the fall of 1994 that corrections officers were profiling my client or targeting my client?"

The warden replied, "No, I did not."

In the redirect examination, Prosecutor Shannon was able to establish that indeed a report had been made against Miller. However, the report was made by Officer Peltier not Schwesinger on Oct 15, 1994.

After the warden's testimony, the prosecution rested its case. The next morning before the jury had been brought into the courtroom, Mr. Bengston made a motion for the court to consider a directed verdict, stating the people had failed to prove their case. I am especially grateful I was not present in the courtroom to hear it, because I am sure my heart would have stopped during this discussion. On this motion, the judge ruled as follows:

"In this case, there's been sufficient testimony offered by Dr. Cohl, Warden Tessmer, and obviously the corrections officers themselves who were involved in finding the implement in question here, that this was contraband in contravention of a statute. And certainly, the expert testified that this appeared to be a strangulation device, and he demonstrated its use.

"So in viewing that testimony, a jury could, in fact, reasonably find that the defendant is guilty of having a weapon or an implement to be used as a weapon or contravention of a statute. So the court will deny the motion to dismiss."

The jury was brought into the courtroom and the defense called their expert witness, David E. Balash.

Mr. Bengston spent much of his direct examination establishing Mr. Balash's credentials as a weapons expert. He told the court that after his first five years as a member of the Michigan State Police, Balash was assigned to the firearms, tool mark, bomb, and explosive unit, where he became a detective lieutenant in charge of firearms and identification in the Northville laboratory. He offered testimony that in his twenty-five years, he had been on as many as eighteen crime-scene locations in which strangulation was the cause of death. When Stuart Dunnings did his *voir dire* examination, he established that Mr. Balash had never been qualified as an expert to testify in ligature strangulation cases and had never attended any workshops or seminars on the subject. However, the court accepted him as an expert witness.

Under the examination of the defense, Mr. Balash testified that the element of surprise was essential in the use of a garrote. The purpose of a garrote is to quickly and efficiently strangle the victim. He contended that the length of the shoelace would ruin the element of surprise, the flat surface of the lace would make it an ineffective weapon, and the buttons would get in the way. He proceeded to demonstrate on Mr. Bengston.

The defense had made an issue about Dr. Cohl's model not being an exact replica. They maintained the model needed to reflect the exact length of the original. With that in mind, they decided to start with a new package of seventy-two-inch shoelaces and make "a more accurate replica in view of the jury." When they measured the first shoelace from the package they were met with a surprise—the lace measured sixty-nine inches rather than seventy-two. After pulling it tight to re-measure, it again came up three inches too short. Instead of "cutting their losses," the defense decided to measure the second lace in the package, which also differed from the desired length. It measured seventy-five inches. Obviously, they had not practiced their demonstration outside the courtroom.

According to Jeff, the prosecution team was now having a hard time to keep from laughing, particularly when Stuart said, "I will have to object if this is going to lead to some sort of definitive scientific-measurement kind of testimony." Stuart ended his objection with the statement, "If the shoe doesn't fit, don't try it on."

Undaunted, the defense said, "Let's try this once more, please." As they attempted another measurement, Bengston asked, "Do you have hold of the end? Maybe I don't know how to read a ruler." Then he questioned what the packet said. "Seventy-two. Now we have seventy-five." With that he moved on to estimating the length from the ruler laid beside the implement in the Polaroid. They sought to demonstrate that an unaltered shoelace would prove more effective than one altered by buttons and tied together at the ends.

In the cross-examination, prosecution referred to Balash's testimony, in which he had admitted it was possible for the device to be used as a weapon. Stuart asked Balash, "Why would you say, 'It does not appear to be a weapon'?"

During the previous evening, Jeff had had a spirited discussion regarding the cross-examination of the defense's expert witness. "We argued quite a bit on that. Stuart had called the defense's weapons expert, David E. Balash, on the phone, and he felt that Balash was not going to try to hurt us too much, that he was going to keep his opinion very narrow. Stu felt he could get the information that Pat would need to work with without attacking Mr. Balash. I, on the other hand, felt very strongly that this guy was going to try to stash us as soon as he got on the stand! Consequently, Stu would have to attack him and be aggressive. As I had predicted, Balash proceeded to stash us. Stuart tried to get him to come back to where he thought he would be, and he would not come. At that point, Stuart gave up on his tactics, turned to look at me, and said so softly that I don't think anyone else heard it, 'I am going to do this for you.' He then turned back and began the attack."

Stuart kept bringing him back to his admission that it was possible the lace could be used as a weapon, hammering him relentlessly on the point.

Dunnings: "Well, you said that one could, if one was inclined, absolutely use this to commit ligature strangulation?"

Balash: "That is correct, sir."

Dunnings: "Well, then, why is it not a weapon?"

Balash: "Screwdrivers and hammers have been used as instruments to kill people."

Dunnings: "Have you ever conducted any investigations in a prison?"

Balash: "I've been involved in two, but those were explosive in nature and not investigations, per se. So I would say no to that question, sir."

Dunnings: "Okay. Now, you realize that if you are in prison you only have a limited number of items available to you to make a ligature-strangulation device, if that's your desire. You understand that, right?"

Balash: "Right."

Dunnings: "If one is in prison and seeking to make a strangulation device, you sort of have to make do with what you have, don't you?"

Balash: "Right."

Dunnings: "Now, if I were to take this home with me tonight and perpetrate ligature strangulation and stand here tomorrow with, say, the same thing, would it be a weapon?"

Balash answered that if it had been identified as the item used to commit the crime, it could be called a weapon.

In re-cross, Dunnings restated Mr. Balash's assertion that "the altered shoelace was not the optimal item that you would use in ligature strangulation." Dunnings then asked, "Now, in your many years of criminal investigation, haven't you found occasions where criminals may have used less than optimal means to accomplish a crime?"

"Certainly," Balash replied.

"And isn't it, in point of fact, because criminals sometimes have personal preferences or a lack of knowledge that they attempt to achieve their criminal ends by less-than-the-most-effective means?"

Jeff commented that at the conclusion of Stu's examination, "David Balash seemed in a tremendous hurry to leave the courtroom."

Would Don now take the stand in his own defense? As he listened to the expert witnesses, Jeff was on edge waiting to find out. "Typically, lawyers call defendants last. Our prediction was that probably he would not, but I had to be ready," Jeff said. "We didn't know what kind of lawyer Bengston was, but what we did know about jury trials was that the defendant was the most important witness." Jeff's waiting came to an end when the defense rested its case without calling Miller to the stand.

In his closing statement, Pat Shannon reminded the jury that the prosecution's case was based on two things only. First, the prosecution had to have proven that on the date of the offense, Mr. Miller was incarcerated. Prison records and officer testimony had confirmed that.

The second fact the prosecution had to prove was that the prisoner had had an unauthorized implement in his control, a dangerous weapon that could have been used to cause serious injury. "Keep in mind, ladies and gentleman, we're talking about a law that applies inside a state prison, an area in which we have—based on testimony of the Warden—over 1200 convicted felons, people who have been convicted of murder, rape, and armed robbery. So we have to think of this case in terms of that community, a community in which your roommate is a convicted felon." Pat pointedly reminded the jury there were only 35 officers for 1200 inmates. He carefully reviewed the testimony of each officer and called attention to the fact that each had described the contraband as a "weapon."

Pat then talked about the compelling testimony of Dr. Cohl, adding that Cohl trained the FBI and Michigan State Police in ligature strangulation. He then contrasted these qualifications to those of the defendant's witness, Mr. Balash. He emphasized the fact that Dr. Cohl was a forensic scientist whose expertise was in ligature strangulation. Mr. Balash's area of expertise was firearms. He had never received training in strangulation and had worked on a very limited number of cases in which strangulation was involved. He had never worked inside a prison. He pointed out that Mr. Balash had admitted that the item in question could have in fact been used as a weapon. In that way, he showed that Mr. Balash's testimony was consistent with Dr. Cohl's.

Prosecutor Shannon stated, "In deciding beyond a reasonable doubt, a defense cannot be based upon a flimsy, fanciful defense. A mere possibility of innocence doesn't work here. Your decision must be based on the evidence….You are not looking for *any* doubt, but rather a *reasonable* doubt. In any important decision there is always going to be some doubt."

"In summary: Number one, was Donald Gene Miller legally incarcerated at the time he possessed the object in question? Yes, the records are clear, and this fact has not been challenged by the defense. Number two, did he have in his control an implement that could have been used to cause injury, and was it authorized? The evidence is clear that on November 4, 1994, Mr. Donald Gene Miller, an inmate, did in his locked footlocker—did in his area of control, identified by his own name, his own prison number—possess or have under his control a weapon or other implement that could have been used to assault, used as a weapon, or used to aid in an escape. And there was no legal justification for possessing this in prison.

"The case is clear. We ask that you find this man guilty beyond a reasonable doubt. Thank you."

Bengston began the defense's closing statement by saying that terms such as "reasonable doubt" were not for either the prosecution or the defense to define, but up to the judge to define. Then he asked the jurors not to spend any time on whether Miller was a prisoner November 4, 1994, or whether he had in his possession a shoelace with buttons attached. The issue here was whether or not it was a weapon or other implement, he said. Then Bengston initiated a review of the testimony, with the intent to discredit the witnesses for the people, beginning with Leo. Bengston revisited his own contention that Leo had targeted prisoners, looking over the master list and selecting John Hudson's room for the shakedown. Therefore, he claimed, this was a targeted shakedown rather than a random one. Then he asked the jurors, "How credible is this witness?" He implied that the nickname "Cowboy" was a mark against his character (never referring to the testimony that Leo wore Western-style boots on a daily basis). He insinuated that because Leo had been transferred without requesting it, he had done something wrong. He found it suspicious that Leo could not remember the name of the third prisoner in John Hudson's room.

He referred to the prison's policy guide, which had been introduced into evidence by the defense. In it, shoelaces and buttons were on the authorized list of prisoners' possessions. Up to this point, Don had shown little or no emotion. Now, uncharacteristically, as his defense attorney was speaking, Don listened intently, nodding his approval. Bengston pointed out that since the prison store sold shoelaces and buttons, shoelaces and buttons couldn't possibly be considered weapons or the prison store would be guilty of selling weapons. Don reacted to this statement with a self-satisfied smirk.

Then Bengston turned his attention to Dr. Cohl's testimony. He sought to discredit him as an expert witness by describing him as an advocate of the prosecution rather than an expert witness. In support of this, he referred to the claim that Dr. Cohl had made his initial judgment based on a description over the phone rather than a firsthand look at the photographs. He discounted the model Dr. Cohl made to demonstrate its use, saying the knot in the shoelace was not exactly the same kind that appeared in the photo.

He referred to warden's testimony that the shoelace had been destroyed on purpose, suggesting this was evidence that the higher prison officials did not consider it a dangerous weapon. He referred to this as "the most telling testimony."

In his rebuttal, Mr. Shannon directed the jurors' attention to the policy directive that listed shoelaces and buttons as authorized items. He then pointed them to a different page, which listed prohibited items. These items included sport coats, suit coats, and neckties. He pointed out that only clip-on bow ties were allowed because of the inherent danger of full-length ties.

"Everyone has come under attack by the defense, even me," he said. "I've been accused of contriving this particular matter." In Warden Tessmer's testimony, he had talked about the ninety-day appeal period in internal matters. "This is an external criminal matter that has been legally investigated by the state police." Detective Sergeant Robin Sexton of the Michigan State Police had conducted the investigation and signed the complaint. "He has attacked everyone. The corrections officers were attacked, and I was attacked. But I have not heard one piece of information authorizing Mr. Miller's possession of this item.

"The model is evidence. The judge has allowed this. This is a piece of evidence for your review. Let's not make fun of it…You cannot rely upon flimsy, fanciful defense. You can only base your decision upon the evidence that's presented. The mere possibility of innocence is not sufficient.

"Common sense rules. Look at this, look at the photographs, listen to the testimony, remember the testimony, and use your common sense. And remember, the only issue here is: did the defendant on that date possess or have under his control in his area of control a weapon or other implement that could have been used to assault a prisoner or another person or aid in escape? That's the operational issue in this particular matter, nothing else."

At the conclusion of the prosecutor's remarks, the court recessed for lunch.

Following lunch, the judge gave the jury final instructions: "Remember, you have taken an oath to return a true and just verdict based only on the evidence and my instructions on the law. You must not let any sympathy, bias, or prejudice influence your decision. You must think about all of the evidence and the testimony, and then decide what each piece of evidence means and how important you think it is. This includes whether you believe what each said. The defense does not have to prove his innocence, but the prosecution must prove their case beyond a reasonable doubt.

"A reasonable doubt is a fair, honest doubt growing out of the evidence or lack of evidence in this case. It is not merely an imaginary or possible doubt, but a doubt based upon reason and common sense. A reasonable doubt is just that, a doubt that is reasonable after a careful and considered examination of all of the facts and circumstances in this case."

The jury deliberated less than two and a half hours before reaching a verdict. CBS cameramen recorded every minute of the trial. Bill Lagatuta (the *48 Hours* reporter) was there at the beginning for pre-trial interviews but left town shortly after the opening of the trial. But he again walked through the courtroom door about ten seconds before the foreman read the verdict.

It was the verdict I had been praying for: "We, the jury, find him guilty."

Jeff later asked Lagatuta how he accounted for his fortuitous return. Bill's response was, "Just incredible good timing, I guess." He was now ready to do follow-up interviews.

Joy erupted from the prosecution team. Jeff reported, "There was lots of hugging! I just couldn't believe it. I remember I hugged Dutcher. I hugged Dunnings, of course. Donna came running up to hug us all! I think after the verdict, the sun was shining for Randy, too. I remember the look on Randy's face during the trial. He looked like he was still trying to be the tough younger brother. I think the prospect of Miller getting out put a dark cloud over his life. At least after the verdict he was smiling."

Mr. Bengston asked for the jurors to be polled individually. As each juror's name was called, the answer each time was "yes." Once the trial was over, the jurors, in conversation with the prosecution team and *48 Hours*, were told about Don's horrific criminal history. One jury member gasped incredulously. "He killed four people? I almost feel offended." Other jurors reacted with shock and anger that this information had been withheld from them. Some cried, while others said, "What if we had made the wrong decision?" I believe withholding that kind of information from a juror, is akin to trying a person for assault with a deadly weapon when he strikes someone on the street, and not telling the jury he is a professional boxer. (Outside of boxing rings, professional boxers' fists are considered lethal weapons).

After the trial, our next C-CAP meeting was a celebration honoring our "dream team." While we were rejoicing, I did not realize that Jeff's work was far from over. It never occurred to me that we might have gained only a couple of additional years. All that work would be worthwhile only if we could get a meaningful sentence. Jeff still had his work cut out for him, as he had to convince the judge just how dangerous Don Miller still was. Jeff did not take it for granted that the judge would give a stiff penalty. Consequently, in the brief that Jeff prepared for the judge, he "loaded it up" with all the facts about Don Miller that had been kept out of the trial. Jeff suggested that we, as victims of his crimes, also write letters to the judge. I wrote to Judge Lambros about Martha's death at Miller's hands, including what it is like to lose a daughter and how it had affected Kay, who had lost her only sister. Lisa also wrote a letter, which Jeff read at the sentencing.

The defense, of course, had the privilege of writing a sentencing brief. Bengston characterized Don's sexual assaults on his own sister as a "period of experimentation." Don's lawyer tried to sanitize everything that Don had done. He referred to his murders in such terms as "his difficulties" and "a difficult period of time."

On the day of the actual sentencing, Bengston asked the judge "not to focus on Don's past," since he had committed them "while he was mentally ill." He appealed to the judge "not to ignore the super job he has done in prison over the last twenty years, where he has tutored other inmates and not gotten into any trouble." He asked the court to consider a two-to-four-year sentence.

While Bengston was addressing the judge, Miller absent the smirk, sat with a mournful look on his face.

When Jeff addressed the court, it was with earnest intensity and passion. His voice rang with conviction when he asked for forty to sixty years. "He took their lives without mercy and left their bodies to decompose in remote fields," he continued. "I would like to read the court a letter from Lisa Gilbert.

"'Your Honor, we were two innocent teenagers enjoying our summer, when at fourteen I was assaulted, strangled, and left for dead. My brother was thirteen when Donald Miller stabbed, strangled, and left him for dead. My life has been a rollercoaster ride ever since. I don't want to live my life in fear.' She went on to state that she was still afraid of Miller, that if he ever got out he would find her and kill her."

Finally, Don himself appealed to the court. He told the court he was sorry and would undo the past if he could. Then he added, "I am trying to get my life together in a meaningful way. As a criminal-justice major, I would not keep a weapon in my cell."

Following Don's words, Judge Lambros' voice had an uncharacteristic edge to it as he pronounced sentence. Don's statement seemed to fill the judge with disdain as he spoke. "There is nothing in your history, Mr. Miller, that would lead this court to believe you are truly reformed and that the public has no more to fear from you. Indeed, this latest conviction compels the opposite conclusion." He then sentenced Miller to twenty to forty years.

Joy erupted on the faces of Donna and Randy as Don sat motionless except for the rapid blinking of his eyes. Sorrow registered on the countenance of his parents, as tears welled up in his mother's eyes.

Although Pat, Jeff, Stu, and all of us in C-CAP had been upset when the judge ruled that any prior act was inadmissible, Jeff now told us this would work to our advantage in any appeal Don might make. If the judge had allowed such information to be known to the jury, it could serve as grounds for a possible appeal. The Appeals Court might then agree that the knowledge of Don's history had resulted in a prejudiced jury. Now that was not an issue.

Nevertheless, Don did appeal (without the aid of his lawyer), charging "prosecutorial stalking." Jeff shook his head, saying he had never heard of such a thing. His appeal was denied. Still determined, Miller appealed to the Supreme Court of Michigan. That appeal was also denied.

Our retired forensic expert, Earl James, a member of "The Sons of the American Revolution," recommended that Jeff, Stu, Pat, and Frank be awarded their annual medal. Ordinarily, this honor is given to only one person in law enforcement each year. However, the award was given to all three prosecutors. Frank Ochberg was given the award as well, for his outstanding work helping the prosecutors; it was the first time someone outside the law-enforcement community had received the honor. Michigan Victims' Alliance hosted the event. Pat came down from Sault Sainte Marie, and all of us celebrated again. State Senator Bill Van Regenmorter joined us and presented a framed "Senate Declaration of Honor" to each of our thirty-one C-CAP members. It declared,

> Let it be known, that it is a privilege to recognize the valuable services provided by the Committee for Community Awareness and Protection (C-CAP) on behalf of the people of the state of Michigan, a community collaboration of criminal-justice professionals, victims, victims advocates, and concerned citizens.

It went on to recognize the work we had done to keep Michigan safer by keeping Miller behind bars, as well as C-CAP's conference and work toward legislation. It was dated May 4, 1999, and signed by William Van Regenmorter, chair, Senate Judicial Committee, and John Engler, governor of the State of Michigan.

People keep asking even today, what Don's original thirty-to fifty-year sentence meant. I have repeatedly asked the same question. As far as I can tell, after all the years of dealing with this issue, the fifty years *meant absolutely nothing*. What transpired was the good time was deducted from the thirty years and in 1997, nineteen years after he had first been jailed, he was scheduled for release (*not parole—release*). Because two years were deducted by the warden for the weapons offense, the release date was moved to February 1999.

Despite our joy in our moment of victory, the issue is still not settled. His twenty-year sentence, we are told, means that Don will again be eligible for parole in 2018. Even so, he will be only sixty-three that year, still physically able to indulge in his fantasy, ligature strangulation. I don't want to leave this issue unresolved, a legacy with which my daughter, Kay, will have to contend. We still need to establish legislation that will protect our citizens instead of laws that work against the will of the people.

We were fortunate to have good judges at the crucial times in our quest to end Don's murderous career. However, today I cringe, because I know there are judges on the bench who would free sadistic predators like Don. They would free them even in cases where there was a total absence of doubt. Too often, truth takes a backseat to technicalities and precedence in our laws and courts. Smear campaigns are often mounted against the victims. The release of violent criminals is routinely based on prison capacity rather than the danger posed to society. Wouldn't it make more sense to free non-violent offenders first if prisons are so overcrowded? Read any current newspaper and you will find examples of multiple murderers coming up for parole on their "life sentences" in a few short years. Remember the words of Edmund Burke: "The only thing necessary for the triumph of evil is for good men to do nothing."

Jeffrey Sauter, Sue Young, William Van Regenmorter.

Jeffrey Sauter, Donna Irish, Jay Kohl, Frank Ochberg.

Dream Team:
Pat Shannon, Stuart Dunnings III, Jeff Sauter.

Peter Houk, Sue Young, Emily Brodeur.

15

Our Hope

"Her Compassion: Virtue or Flaw?" was *The Lansing State Journal* headline for a story written by John Schneider on December 3, 1978, the one-year anniversary of Martha's disappearance. This article about Martha gave her story a Shakespearean flavor. (Her interest in Shakespeare was well known and dated back to early elementary school, when her class put on a performance of *Macbeth*. She would have found it fascinating to have her life compared to an Elizabethan character.) This headline alluded to the theme in classic tragedies in which the virtue of the hero or heroine was carried to excess and transformed into a tragic, and usually fatal, flaw. The implication is that Martha's compassion and care for "those who did not fit in" somehow contributed to her death. I do not disagree. Because of her kindheartedness and sympathetic nature, she placed herself in the presence of the wrong person at the wrong time. However, this does not make Martha wrong, nor does it mean her loving kindness was a flaw. (I don't think John really thought so, either.)

The world needs more compassion, not less. In fact, to be connected to the source of unselfish Love is the only hope of the world. In the presence of evil, nothing else can overcome it. Only Love is stronger than hate, for God is Love. Education certainly cannot eradicate evil; we have only to look to men like Osama Bin Laden, one of the latest in a line of educated but evil men. A couple of generations ago, when Nazi Germany was committing its atrocities, it was one of the best educated nations on the face of the earth. Many of history's villains came from the wealthy and privileged, while others were bred in poverty and oppression. Eliminating poverty does not eradicate evil, for a lack of money and possessions does not create the evil in the heart and mind. Evil springs from self-absorption and a lack of regard for anything or anyone that does not advance one's own interests. It is self-interest raised to the last degree—the absence of Love—the absence of God.

No, Martha's empathy for others was not wrong. I am proud of her for it, and I would not have wanted her to become anything less, even to save her life. The fault lies in the heart of the person who took advantage of her trust.

Another trait that came to define Martha in her short life was her steadfastness to stand against that which she considered wrong. I remember a family member who, concerned for Martha's safety, unsuccessfully counseled her to "appear" to go along if ever she were in a life-threatening situation. I am not suggesting that Martha had to be reckless, to put her life in jeopardy by remaining a friend to Don. What I am saying is that she did so—and I allowed her to do so—simply because we did not recognize the face of evil.

What did our world lose when it was robbed of Martha's unique talents and abilities? What would she have been? What dreams would she have fulfilled? I can't help but wonder. She had so many interests. At one point, she wanted to become a doctor. She was interested in helping deaf children; perhaps she would have become their teacher. One of her dreams was to use her skill with language on the world stage in the U.S. Diplomatic Corps; would she have one day been named an ambassador? Most likely, she would have become a wife and mother. Possibly, with her passion for justice and the rights of others, together with her command of language, she would have become an attorney, a judge, a congress-woman, or a senator. Instead, she might have chosen writing or journalism.

One thing we know is that she wanted her life to make a difference. In a prayer Martha wrote, she said,

> Lord, please help me to forget myself and think of others. Please strengthen me to be of some use…I know, Lord, that Your Power makes the difference. If you can transform a mustard seed into a great tree, harboring many birds, then You can transform a little human named Martha Young, who only has a small grain of faith, into a power for Your Glory!

Martha had a special gift for inspiring others. In once again going through her papers for this chapter, I found two letters. They made me realized she did not limit her praise, appreciation, and encouragement to her peer group and her friends; she reached out to those in leadership roles. I discovered that on August 2, 1976, in the last few months of her life, she had written Durwood Fleming, the president of Southwestern University, where she had spent her first two years of college. It must have been quite a letter, judging from the reply she received. In the second and third paragraphs, Fleming wrote,

My, how your letter delighted and heartened me! It was so meaningful and impressive that I read a portion of it in an address I made to the resident assistants during Orientation Week. While we fully understand your rationale for transferring to Michigan State University, it does not diminish our regret that you could not return and be with us at Southwestern.

Your encouragement, confidence, and faith in Southwestern, including those of us who have responsibilities for directing its life, are sources of inspiration to us. That you would take the time to express yourself so well, out of such concern and feeling, goes a long way in helping us to keep the grand morale and the steady stride.

If the school doesn't treat you right, you just tell them that you know of a small university in the heart of Texas that will receive you gladly anytime and do everything possible to help you fulfill your dreams.

The second letter, ironically, was a two-page handwritten letter from Dr. Hardy, the minister of the church we were attending when Martha vanished. It was a very warm letter written to Martha in the last days of her life. It came in response to an encouraging note she had sent to him. Dr Hardy's daughter, Lana, came to Martha's memorial service with a mutual friend, Linda. Because she had read in the local newspaper that Martha's service was to be a private one and she knew of the strained relationship we had with her father, she approached me prior to the service to ask, "Is it all right if we stay for Martha's memorial?"

"Yes, of course it is," I said. "You were Martha's friends." I appreciated their coming, and I believed Kay did also. Kay felt close to Linda, because she was the older sister of one of Kay's friends. It took courage for Lana to come and risk the possibility that she might not be welcome. Neither of us mentioned her father, and he never contacted me after we left his church, even after Martha's body was discovered.

Martha was forgiving. I am sure if she could have talked to me about what Don had done to her, she would have said, "Mother, he just didn't understand." My assumption is based on the words of yet another letter, one Martha wrote to God. In it, she asked Him, "Help me to be loving, in spite of spiteful people. Help me to love these people more, because they most need it. That is certainly true, Lord; the person who is least lovable most needs it. Oh, Lord, help me forget myself and minister to those people.

"The most important thing is to help people know that God loves them. And that's what I know is most important…to let all those starving for love find it in your Love." She went on to ask, "Let your Love show through me even though I am but a darkly stained glass."

Although Martha was a forgiving person, she believed that one's actions do bring consequences. She would have approved of our ongoing struggle to see to it that Don never had the opportunity to kill again. Certainly, she would have championed the rights of women to be free of violence. I know that Martha's solution, which is the transformation of the human heart, is ultimately the best solution. In the meantime, laws do matter.

As I stated in the beginning, one person can make a difference. I want this book not only to inspire you but to fill you with outrage—to inspire you so that you will realize that you do make a difference, and to fill you with outrage so that you will act. Indeed, I want you to care enough to be informed about the judges you vote into the courts, and to encourage your representatives and senators to enact legislation to quarantine killers rather than have them released into society.

One final note: Martha's fondest hope for you as you put down this book would have been that you allow this marvelous God to flood your life with His love for you, so that you will experience His life-giving joy. In the words of Dr. Williams, "Let the Lord God, who swallows up death, forever wipe away tears from our faces. Then let us rejoice in God's salvation."

"In this riveting reflection of a parent's worst nightmare, Sue Young has given voice to victims everywhere. Much more than a gripping story, this extraordinary book inspires faith and action."

—Wm Van Regenmorter, Chair, Criminal Justice Committee of the
Michigan House
Former Chair, Senate Judicial Committee

◆　　　◆　　　◆

"Sue Young takes the reader on a riveting emotional odyssey that starts with the murder of her older daughter and ends with a community effort to find justice. Writing in the first person, Ms. Young describes how her strong religious convictions, and those of her daughter, gave her the strength to survive a parent's worst nightmare and to join others in protecting the public from a serial killer. Every parent should read this book. I highly recommend it to anyone interested in the criminal justice system and how it treats victims."

—Stephen Lacy, Professor
Michigan State University School of Journalism

◆　　　◆　　　◆

"A 'must read' for every parent who is interested in the safety of their own daughters. A compelling true story told, as nobody else could, by the mother who lived through the terror of every parent's nightmare—the disappearance and murder of her precious daughter. Sue is dedicated to sharing facts and information in the hope that they will help others to prevent such a tragedy from happening within their own families."

—Idell Moffett, President, PBS STARS
Professional Member
National Speakers Association

◆   ◆   ◆

"Sue Young is a woman who has walked 'through the valley of the shadow of death.' This is a must-read story of faith, pain, loss, persistence, and justice. Ultimately, it is a powerful present-day description of God's sustaining grace even when life seems to be at its darkest. On the other side of the valley, you will find a woman who is modeling and experiencing God's peace and joy."

—Brad Mitchell, Senior Pastor
Trinity Church, Lansing, Michigan

◆   ◆   ◆

"This is a must-read book for everyone. This book brought out many emotions in me: tears of sorrow for Martha and her family, anger that there are people out there like Don Miller, respect for our law enforcement for all they do, and healthy fear for my own safety. I highly recommend this book."

—Mary L. Cane, National Sales Director
Mary Kay Cosmetics, Inc.

◆   ◆   ◆

"In 1971, Sue Young was honored as the first independent Mary Kay Sales Director in Michigan—a pioneer and leader! She went on to expand those leadership skills with a courageous determined pioneering spirit. This foundation helped her to face the daunting task of experiencing and chronicling this horrific story. Choosing not to accept victim status, she aggressively pursued truth and justice.

The reader is taken along a full range of emotions and education from naïve to acutely aware, as Sue transparently shares her thought processes of events as they unfold. It is sobering, empowering, and filled with valuable life skills, especially for women and parents.

*She consistently seeks God's leading and courage to act and make this tragedy yield change **that counts for good.***"

—Gwen Sherman,
Independent National Sales Director Emeritus
Mary Kay, Inc.

◆   ◆   ◆

"*Lethal Friendship proves my belief that the most powerful creature on earth is a mother. And when that mother is empowered with faith in prayer and an unflinching trust in God, her power knows no bounds. I found Sue's book to be heart wrenching, heart warming, inspiring and eye opening. All who read these pages will find a renewed faith in God, strengthened by family bonds as well as the need to become a more enlightened, concerned, and involved citizen.*"

—Danton R. Thomson,
Internationally Renowned Makeup Artist, Author, and Motivational
Speaker

978-0-595-34422-2
0-595-34422-4